Smart on Crime

The Struggle to Build a Better American Penal System

Smart on Crime

The Struggle to Build a Better American Penal System

Garrick L. Percival

CRC Press
Taylor & Francis Group
Boca Raton London New York

CRC Press is an imprint of the
Taylor & Francis Group, an **informa** business

CRC Press
Taylor & Francis Group
6000 Broken Sound Parkway NW, Suite 300
Boca Raton, FL 33487-2742

First issued in paperback 2020

© 2016 by Taylor & Francis Group, LLC
CRC Press is an imprint of Taylor & Francis Group, an Informa business

No claim to original U.S. Government works

ISBN-13: 978-1-4987-0313-0 (hbk)
ISBN-13: 978-0-367-59875-4 (pbk)

Library of Congress Cataloging-in-Publication Data

Percival, Garrick L., author.
 Smart on crime : the struggle to build a better American penal system / Garrick L. Percival.
  pages cm
 Includes bibliographical references and index.
 ISBN 978-1-4987-0313-0 (hardcover : alk. paper) 1. Corrections--United States. 2. Prisons--United States. 3. Criminal justice, Administration of--United States. I. Title.

HV9471.P42 2015
364.60973--dc23   2015026067

Visit the Taylor & Francis Web site at
http://www.taylorandfrancis.com

and the CRC Press Web site at
http://www.crcpress.com

For Mary, Ethan, and Andrew. Let the future be bright.

Contents

Preface xi
Acknowledgments xiii

SECTION I   Rise of the Smart on Crime Movement

Chapter 1   Smart on Crime Politics 3

    Introduction 3
        Washington, DC..3
        Ohio 4
        California 4
    Crime Politics in the American Political System..................10
    Coalition Politics and Reform in the Criminal Justice
        Subsystem...13
    Rise of the Smart on Crime Coalition....................................17
    Explaining the Emergence of the Smart on Crime Coalition ...22
    Policy Learning 22
    Bringing Policy Back into the Picture 26
    When Is Reform *Really* Reform? 28

Chapter 2   Collapse of the Rehabilitative Model and Rise
    of the Tough on Crime Coalition.................................... 31

    Calm before the Storm...32
    The Storm: The Rehabilitative Model Gets Blown Away......35
    Politicalization of Rehabilitation Research............................ 42
    Sagging Support for Rehabilitation on the Left 49
    Building an Institutional Legacy...52
    Tough on Crime Coalition 55

Chapter 3   Crisis and Opportunity in the American Penal System... 59

    To the Victors Go the Spoils.. 60
    Problems on the Ground: Consequences
        of the Tough on Crime Regime................................... 64

The Penal System and Inequality...67
Diminishing Marginal Returns of Mass Incarceration........ 68
Conditions Facilitating the Search for Alternatives
    and Policy Learning..69
Economic Crisis..69
The Contemporary Prison System Is a Different Beast........71
Examining Changes in Public Attitudes on Crime
    and Punishment...72
Fear of Crime..72
Saliency of Crime..74

SECTION II   The Smart on Crime
Movement in National Politics

Chapter 4 Prisoner Reentry and the Politics of the Second
              Chance Act 81

Pressure from the Bottom Up 82
Conceptualizing Prisoner Reentry...83
Ohio Plan... 86
Developments in Corrections Policy Research......................89
Conservatives Begin the Push for Prisoner Reentry............93
Introduction of the SCA 97
Prison Fellowship Ministries...98
Fight to Protect Inmates' Religious Freedom....................... 99
Framing the Meaning of the SCA...103
Correctional Associations 105
Second Chance Advocacy in the Senate 108
    Sam Brownback...109
Political Progress in the House 112
Roadblocks in the Senate..113
Closing the Deal..115

Chapter 5 Fair Sentencing Act of 2010... 119

Policy Context..119
Challenging the Unique Dangers of Crack Cocaine.......... 122
Proposals for Change 126
Legal Challenges to the Federal Sentencing Process...........127

New Proposals for Crack Sentencing Reform......................130
Mobilizing Support for Crack Sentencing Reform.............132

SECTION III   The Smart on Crime
Movement in the United States

Chapter 6   Texas... 147

Introduction to the Problem Environment..........................147
Bringing an Engineer's Perspective to the Texas Penal
        System...150
Emergence of New Organized Groups 152
Justice Reinvestment 157
Broad-Based Smart on Crime Coalition 159
Texas Penal System and the Shifting Dimensions
        of Political Debate..160
Appendix 166

Chapter 7   Ohio.. 171

Diffusion of Smart on Crime Policy Ideas...........................171
Ohio Seeks Technical Assistance 175
Policy Learning among Conservatives in Ohio 177

Chapter 8   California.. 185

Shifting Political Environment...188
Return of the Structural Injunction 196
Prison Realignment in California...197

Chapter 9   Evaluating the Smart on Crime Movement.................. 209

De-Incarceration and Crime... 209
Is the Glass Half Full or Half Empty?.................................212

References... 227

Index... 243

Preface

This book is the product of a long intellectual journey. I became engrossed in criminal justice issues while writing my doctoral dissertation at the University of California, Riverside, in 2004 and 2005. My dissertation examined the politics and implementation of California's Substance Abuse and Crime Prevention Act—Proposition 36—which diverted nonviolent drug offenders from the state's prison system. The original idea behind Proposition 36 was the right one; the problem was in the program's flawed design. It mostly succumbed to California's multiple budget crises during the Schwarzenegger years.

Yet Proposition 36, adopted in 2000, served as one of the earliest signs that voters were willing to begin turning back the worse aspects of the tough on crime era. I know now, however, that I failed then to sufficiently grasp the terrible injustices the criminal justice system waged on minorities, the poor, and the most marginalized Americans in the name of fighting crime and drugs.

Bruce Western's *Punishment and Inequality in America* and Loïc Wacquant's 2001 "Deadly Symbiosis" article in *Punishment and Society*, I credit with helping me begin to better understand how the growing tentacles of America's justice system became a merciless tool for black subjugation. But curiously, the *political* story they and others told seemed mostly absent from political science circles. The politics of the modern penal system involves so many issues and forces political scientists putatively care about—race, class, inequality, organizational power, and institutional constraints. Why were so few in my discipline paying attention?

Yet even as researchers from other academic disciplines became focused on "mass incarceration" and the worst aspects of the tough on crime regime, I also began to ask myself whether we were missing something. As I completed my graduate studies and prepared for my first teaching assignment at the University of Minnesota, Duluth, in 2005, I began reading about a growing movement to help released prisoners return successfully to their communities. "Prisoner reentry" seemed innovative; it seemed different. Were we, as a community of scholars, overlooking meaningful criminal justice reform unfolding beneath our collective noses?

The *meaning* of social movements and social change varies across time and space. The messiness of the here and now can, with a bit of distance, mark clear points of departure. With the passing of time, I became more convinced than ever that my initial thought—that something different *was* brewing out there—was correct. After securing a generous Grant-in-Aid of Research, Artistry, and Scholarship from the University of Minnesota in 2009, I conducted field research to see for myself. Prison officials, lawmakers, researchers, and reform advocates—people directly working on the problem—what did they think? Did they see change? If so, why? Even if practitioners (and indeed many lawmakers) failed to grasp the "big picture"—even if they and I did not speak the same professional language, I was convinced talking with people "on the ground" was a worthwhile pursuit.

Much of what I learned from this work is found in different parts of the book. I am indebted to the more than two dozen people who took time out of their busy schedules to speak with me in person about what they knew and saw. Some of them are explicitly mentioned in the chapters ahead, but I use many of their experiences and insights to inform the book's broader narrative. Of course, any misreading or misjudgment of my interviewees' perceptions, beliefs, or positions is my fault alone.

Over time, I grew frustrated with the pace of my writing. I confronted a puzzle that, for me at least, not only had too many pieces but acted as if someone routinely reorganized the pieces I left on the table. How does one make sense of a penal reform movement that in many ways is just getting started and one that involves a complex web of activities and decisions made by actors at all levels of our government? Peace of mind finally came with the recognition that the political story I tell is an ongoing one. There will be much more to say and do after the last word of this book.

Acknowledgments

I was the beneficiary of so many people's support and encouragement. My wife, Mary, and I met in graduate school at San Diego State University (SDSU) in 1998. Since then we've been on a life journey filled with tremendous joy and our share of heartache along the way. She is without doubt my favorite political scientist. If not for her continued interest in the book and encouraging me to work longer and harder, even if it meant time away from "us," I would have never finished. I just hope the final product befits the costs. My son Ethan is my greatest source of pride. At home, I often wrote at the kitchen table. This offered a place close enough to hear the sounds of family while my mind focused on the screen in front of me. Ethan proved an inspiration when I often watched him, seated next to me at the table, pound away on an old family laptop, writing his own "books." My parents, Thornton and Elaine Percival, and my brother, Todd, have offered me strength and stability. They've always taken an interest in my pursuits. Whatever successes I've had are a testament to their love and guidance. My stepson Andrew is now well on his way to adulthood. Only a bright future awaits. It's with great pride that I've watched him grow.

I would like to extend thanks to my colleagues in the Department of Political Science at San Jose State University (SJSU). I moved to the department in the middle of writing this book, and I cannot think of a more inspiring and nurturing place to work. Larry Gerston took a special interest in the project, taking time out of his hectic schedule to read several chapters. Charles Andrain, not of SJSU but my alma mater SDSU, is my longtime mentor and friend. Charles read chapters and offered invaluable feedback. I owe tremendous credit to Max Neiman, my advisor at the University of California, Riverside, who piqued my interest in criminal justice policy. I thank Max for his continued friendship and interest in my career. I am also indebted to California State Senator Jim Beall and his staff, who invited me on fact-finding and policy-related trips inside a number of California's prison facilities. For far too long, too many of California's elected officials simply gave up caring about the men and women serving long sentences inside California's overstuffed prisons. But for my money, there is no stronger advocate for building a more humane and just California prison system than Senator Beall. Several half-baked chapters were presented at the American Political Science Association meeting in Seattle and State Politics and Policy conferences at Dartmouth College and Rice University. I thank all the panelists and conference participants who offered constructive feedback that helped improve the manuscript. Finally, I would like to express my thanks to my editor, Lara Zoble, at Taylor & Francis. She believed in the project and brought it to print in such a professional and timely manner. Again, any errors in the final product are mine alone.

Section I

Rise of the Smart on Crime Movement

1

Smart on Crime Politics

INTRODUCTION

Washington, DC

"I was wrong. I repent!" So declared Mark Earley, one of the most successful evangelical Christian politicians to emerge out of the Virginia Commonwealth in recent years (Suellentrop 2006). He spoke these words at a 2006 gathering of the Congressional Black Caucus in reference to his record on crime while serving in the Virginia legislature. Virginia, like many other states over the years, adopted nearly all the hallmarks of the tough on crime era. It enacted three-strikes-and-you're-out laws, eliminated parole, and lowered the age for trying juveniles as adults. Earley saw himself as one of the toughest lawmakers in the bunch. "I was elected to the Virginia legislature and served 10 years ... and quite frankly, spent most of my time in the legislature working on how to put more people in jail and keeping them there longer. I'm 52 years old," he said, "and for the first 48 years of my life, I didn't think much about prisoners. And when I did, it went something like, I'm glad I'm not one, and I'm glad they are where they are. And I really pretty much had the view that prisoners were at the end of the line. That if you were in prison, you had no hope, you'd made a mess of your life, and it was better for me that you were there, because my family could be safe" (Suellentrop 2006, pp. 47–48).

Of course critics of the policies he helped enact would say Earley's repentance came too little too late. The damage was done, and he is not making laws anymore to make things right. But what is important is that he was speaking in his role as director of the policy arm of the Prison Fellowship Ministries, an evangelical organization that has become a major part of a remarkable and much larger fight evangelicals and conservatives have waged in the name of reforming the nation's penal system.

Ohio

In 2011, after signing HB 86, Ohio Republican Governor John Kasich remarked, "This kind of reform legislation sat idle for 25 years, maybe. Nobody wanted to touch it … it will result in the saving of many, many lives" (Fields 2011). One could be excused for accusing the governor of hyperbole. After all, politicians are guilty of it all the time. Yet, in this case, Kasich was on the level. The governor, despite fierce opposition from the state's prosecutors association, had just signed a sweeping set of criminal justice reforms not seen in that state in a generation. The reform package in HB 86 gave judges in Ohio newfound discretion to send a variety of nonviolent felons to community halfway house facilities and treatment instead of prison. It increased offenders' earned credit off their sentences after they completed education courses or drug treatment while incarcerated. It equalized penalties between crack and powdered cocaine, and allowed the release of nonviolent offenders who have served 80 percent of prison term of one year or more (Wyler 2011). All hold the promise of reducing the size of the state's prison population and making the system far more just.

California

In Orange County, California, Marvin Thomas decided to turn his life around. After being released from jail, Thomas wanted to earn his high school diploma and enter the job market. Thomas enrolled in Orange County's Center for Opportunity, Reentry, and Education (or CORE), a joint program run by the county's probation and education departments. To enroll, students have to commit to at least 30 days, 8 a.m.–2:30 p.m., Monday through Friday. Once there, participants tackle math, reading, and life skills. Upon nearing completion of his program Thomas told the Orange County Register that he looked forward to studying automotive or motorcycle technology at the college level (Emery and Hernandez 2012). CORE's programming has been viewed positively enough that it is serving as a model for future day reporting centers in the county.

While perhaps unremarkable at first glance, what makes Thomas's personal story important from a public policy perspective is that he is one of thousands of felons affected by California's historic prison realignment plan adopted in 2011 after the federal courts ordered California to reduce its overflowing prison population.

California's Prison Realignment (or commonly referenced as AB 109 after the assembly bill that authorized it) produced major changes to the state's criminal sentencing and, perhaps most important, how postprison supervision is carried out. Statutorily defined "nonviolent, nonserious, and nonsex offenders" are now being incarcerated in county jails or other types of community supervision (such as house arrest) instead of state prison. Released prisoners who had previously been placed on parole and supervised by state parole agents are now placed on "postrelease community supervision," which is under the control of county probation departments.

Realignment is reallocating thousands of low-risk felons from state prison to county jails or some other alternative form of community supervision. The plan gives all counties control to implement a host of data-driven or evidence-based practices designed to more effectively fight crime and stop repeat offending. These strategies combine a mix of new risk assessment tools, probation practices that impose swift and certain sanctions for offenders, and the use of drug treatment and social service programs that reduce recidivism.

There are many challenges and uncertainties surrounding realignment, but both supporters and critics agree that it represents the end of mass incarceration as the Golden State has practiced it.

While separated by time and geographic distance, these brief vignettes all represent important components of a slowly building, but no less important, "smart on crime" movement in America. The movement, as we will see ahead, is dramatically changing criminal justice politics and policy for the better.

For the past generation, the U.S. penal system has been dominated by a "tough on crime" governance that fought crime using policy instruments overwhelmingly focused on punitiveness and custodial control. The politics of crime made a dramatic turn in the 1960s when, for a variety of reasons, the issue became defined in emotionally and morally laden terms: crime, criminals, drugs and drug users all became understood as clear-cut matters of good versus evil. As the politics shifted, the U.S. prison population swelled dramatically beginning in the mid 1970s—a period that began a trend toward mass incarceration that today has ensnared a record number of Americans, a disproportionate number of whom are racial minorities and the urban poor. By 2006 the U.S. incarceration rate reached about 750 per 100,000 population, a distinction that placed the country in the unenviable position of the world's incarceration leader. For black men, the rate was 3,000 per 100,000. For poor uneducated black men, conditions are even bleaker. Those without a high school degree have nearly a 70 percent chance of going to prison in their lifetime (Western 2006).

Paradoxically, despite all the punishment handed down, the United States still suffers from crime rates that are too high. Violent crime rates have steadily declined since the 1990s—a fact that can be attributed at least in part to the increase in incarceration—yet still remain five times higher than other industrialized economies in the world (Kleiman 2013). Crime, or fear of crime, is still too much a part of people's everyday lives, especially for those living in poor neighborhoods of color. People in these neighborhoods, it turns out, bear the twin tragedies of being at greater risk of victimization as well as seeing more and more of their young men carted off to prison. In short, the penal system is terribly broken.

This book seeks to demonstrate that the most punitive era in American history reached its apex in the 1990s and to explain how and why the trend has begun to reverse itself in recent years. As noted above, it emphasizes the rise in the 2000s of a "smart on crime" movement in U.S. politics and policy making. The term "smart on crime" is certainly not original. Elected officials, criminal justice practitioners, and journalists now commonly use the term (Harris and Hamilton 2009). It symbolizes the ongoing shift in thinking about crime and penal policy that is at the center of this book. At its core, "smart on crime" is a movement about constructing a penal system more *rational* and *humane*. In this case, the concept of *rational* means governments adopting smarter (empirically based) alternatives that are more effective at reducing crime rather than simply locking up more people. They are also demonstrably less expensive. And by *humane*, it is a movement for a penal system that puts far fewer people behind bars and does a lot less harm on the lives of individual offenders, their families, and communities.

The two tenets of the smart on crime movement share a common bond in that they both require far less use of prison and place fewer people behind bars, many of whom should never have been (or should never go) there in the first place. Reform occurs in new statutes, regulations, practices, and legal decisions that reduce criminal penalties for drug use, divert offenders away from prison, and place them into community corrections programs. Marked new investments emerge in prisoner rehabilitation and human capital development. New probation and parole practices impose swift and certain (but not severe) sanctions that cut recidivism and reduce crime.

Remarkably, reform now arises in states long considered to be those "toughest" on crime as well as vertically in the federalism system where national-level actors and institutions in both their political discourse and action led the cheers for get-tough politics and policy. In addition to Ohio and California mentioned earlier, policy makers in Texas, a state with one of the highest imprisonment rates in the nation, recently made new investments in drug treatment, adopted a variety of alternative sentencing statutes designed to divert nonviolent offenders from prison, and revamped its probation and parole systems. These states are not alone. A report by the National Conference of State Legislatures found that in 2009, there were twenty-eight major correctional policy revisions adopted across the United States (Lawrence 2013). That number has continued to grow since then, reaching forty-one in 2012 (Porter 2013).

Change is evident in federal policy making as well. Congress adopted the Fair Sentencing Act in 2010 that reduced a mandatory minimum drug sentence. In so doing the Act limited the reach of one of the country's most draconian drug policies and reversed a punitive trend of the past forty years. Congress has also taken steps to incentivize prisoner reentry efforts in the states, most notably with the adoption of the Second Chance Act in 2008, a bill that has authorized a new federal infrastructure to disseminate best (rehabilitation)-practices research while targeting new funding for prisoner rehabilitation and successful reentry.

In the executive branch, President Obama's Office of Drug Control Policy has quietly, but no less importantly, eliminated the "war on drugs" rhetoric. Federal law enforcement budgets, which serve as better indicators of policy priorities, show real signs of change. In its first three years, the Obama administration spent more on drug prevention and treatment than on domestic law enforcement and incarceration (the 2011 fiscal year, $10.4 billion was spent on prevention and treatment, and $9.2 billion for domestic drug enforcement and incarceration) (Office of National Drug Control Policy 2011). Federal funding for drug courts increased, and the number of drug courts grew by nearly 400 between 2009 and 2012 to a number that now totals more than 2,700 (Office of National Drug Control Policy 2012). The Justice Department is working to scale up "smart probation" strategies showing evidence of effectiveness by funding research studies and start-up grants (Office of National Drug Control Policy 2011). Perhaps most overlooked are dramatic changes coming from legislation that superficially has nothing to do with criminal justice policy. The Affordable Care Act, the biggest piece of social legislation since the advent of Medicare and Medicaid, requires health insurance companies to cover substance abuse disorders in the same manner as other chronic diseases. This requirement raises the prospect of intervening before an individual's drug use becomes a crime issue, but also encourages offenders who need substance abuse treatment to get more assistance as they are released back to their communities.*

In the federal judiciary, the Supreme Court has ruled in recent years against severe prison overcrowding, sentences of life imprisonment without parole for juvenile offenders (imprisoned for nonhomicidal offenses), and death sentences for capital crimes committed by juveniles and the severely mentally impaired—all hallmarks of the get-tough era. According to rulings, all these practices violate the Constitution's Eighth Amendment protections against cruel and unusual punishment.

As a result of these changes the rate of incarceration in America has recently declined. After increasing every year since the mid-1970s, the U.S. incarceration rate and the number of people under custodial supervision (i.e., those on probation and parole) have now declined for five straight years. After the U.S. Supreme Court mandated California to reduce its prison population, inmate numbers declined nearly 18 percent. Nine other states, including Hawaii, Michigan, New York, and South Carolina, have all experienced a prison population decline of at least 10 percent over the past five years ("States Cut Both Crime and Imprisonment" 2013).

The smart on crime movement seeks to reshape criminal justice policy. Taking readers on a journey through the American federalist system in the 2000s, *Smart on Crime* explains the forces and processes that have propelled criminal justice reform onto the governing agenda.† A key motivating question is this: How has this unlikely set of penal policy reversals managed to reach governing agendas when too many policy makers for the past generation have largely rejected less punitive alternatives because of a pervasive fear of being labeled "soft on crime"? The puzzle becomes all the more intriguing when one considers that few people (except for professional criminals) view crime as legitimate behavior. Crime produces deleterious effects; no one is *for* criminals in the way they might be *for* guns

---

* This is important because more than a third of those arrested in the United States are under the influence of alcohol or an illegal drug (or both). Many of those incarcerated have a diagnosable substance use disorder. See Humphreys (2012b).
† For reasons of readability and style, I use criminal justice reform, penal reform, and prison reform interchangeably.

in a debate about the meaning of the Second Amendment, or pro-choice in relation to the abortion issue. Moreover, many groups who directly gain from reform, African Americans and the poor, have little influence in the power centers of criminal justice politics and policy making (Miller 2008).

Many recent journalistic accounts of reform offer a short-run economic explanation. Deep state budget deficits caused by the Great Recession force states to take drastic austerity measures. State and local governments have shed over 3 percent of their public workforce since 2009, 265,000 jobs in 2011 alone (Shierholz 2014). The move to cut correctional expenditures can be understood through this broader lens of state and local governments trying to reduce budgetary deficits in difficult economic times.

Economic calamity in the states, the most commonly offered culprit, indeed forms an important part of the story. But an economics story alone is too disconnected from political institutions that debate and decide criminal justice policy. It fails to sufficiently answer the question of why policy makers are taking significant steps toward reform *now,* yet when the country faced a variety of economic recessions in the past, no reductions in the inmate population occurred (U.S. Bureau of Labor Statistics 2012). In fact, in many recession years over the tough on crime period, the inmate population increased unabatedly, seemingly irrespective of what it cost in dollars or lives. The economic lens overlooks critical processes associated with agenda setting and policy change.

The central explanation reflects the argument that a meaningful shift in the nature of group conflict on crime arose in the 2000s; this change has formed a new "smart on crime" coalition that allied political actors from the left, center, and most counterintuitively the conservative right of American politics. The book contends that significant opportunities for reform are opening and policy is changing because the smart on crime coalition has successfully organized across multiple criminal justice policy-making institutions within the federalist system. At the same time the scope and dimensionality of the crime policy debate has broadened.

With the emergence of the smart on crime coalition, policy makers are asking far different questions: Are extremely punitive sanctions effective? Is the imprisonment of more people, for more types of activities, worth the financial and human cost? How can empirical analysis and evidence-based, "smartly" designed policies improve public safety but also give offenders a second chance? Whereas policies that once diverted offenders from prison or invested in human capital were largely understood as "coddling criminals," lawmakers increasingly understand smart alternatives as good public policy. Politicians have begun moving past the soft on crime label, allowing them to approach issues of criminal justice reform from a position of electoral strength rather than weakness.

CRIME POLITICS IN THE AMERICAN POLITICAL SYSTEM

To explain crime politics, we must recognize the importance and complexity of criminal justice policy-making institutions. Political scientists have long recognized that political institutions—the formal rules and structures of government—have major consequences for policy makers, organized interest groups, and citizens alike by encouraging certain choices and strategies while discouraging others (Donovan et al. 2010).

Indeed, when we consider scholarship about the rise of the prison boom, numerous persuasive accounts have stressed changes in national politics, namely, how conservative presidents and members of Congress blocked civil rights advances and used crime and drugs as symbolically potent racial wedge issues that heightened whites' (particularly southern whites) support for punishment (Alexander 2010; Tonry 1995; Wacquant 2002; Weaver 2007). However, these compelling accounts that have made generalizations about the "American" criminal justice system pay too little attention to American federalism and ignore the fact that the bulk of criminal justice activities are concentrated at the subnational level (Lynch 2011). The president certainly has some control over law enforcement efforts because he has authority over agencies like the Federal Bureau of Investigation, the Drug Enforcement Administration, and Bureau of Alcohol, Tobacco, Firearms, and Explosives. But these agencies and the federal prison population account for only a small fraction of the entire criminal justice apparatus. Examining policy at the subnational level, where almost all activity takes place, one finds more variation. Political scientists have documented that even in the tough on crime era, which has seen the prison population explode, there remains significant variation among the states (Nicholson-Crotty 2004). Texas, California, Florida, and Georgia, for example, all practiced tough on crime politics with earnestness. Minnesota or Washington, however, have faced a growing prison population but not to the same degree.

Accounts that paint big generalizations using a lens of national crime politics or viewing at the subnational level are incomplete. Both perspectives have meaningful lessons when trying to explain the rise of the smart on crime movement.

These perspectives force us to acknowledge that the contemporary criminal justice system has several moving parts. The United States, in effect, has fifty-one different criminal justice systems. Each of the fifty states, where the bulk of activity takes place, have their own criminal statutes, judicial systems, police forces, prosecutors, and correctional guards. The federal system serves as an overlayer to the state systems (Lynch 2011, p. 676). With this kind of institutional diversity, previous research tells us that context matters—state politics and institutions, for example, influence the propensity of states to punish (Barker 2009). Yet we also know that with the growing tentacles of the federal government in all matters of public policy during the twentieth century, including criminal justice policy, the once clear divisions between state and federal responsibilities have become blurred. This complexity makes the actions and activities of the national and state governments on crime highly interdependent.

How can we best understand the forces behind criminal justice reform? First, although the bulk of criminal justice activity takes place at the state (and local) level, not all systems have equal importance. Not all governing institutions within the federalist system are equally tough on crime and need equal reform. Minnesota, for example, a state with an imprisonment rate of 184 per 100,000 persons, does not typically top experts' lists of correctional systems in need of major reform. Minnesota hardly runs a perfect correctional system; its officials are trying to find ways to reduce the size of their relatively low prison population. Yet policy makers there have taken effective strategies to produce a comparatively rational criminal justice system.

Smart on Crime focuses more interest in examining and understanding reform efforts in Texas, with an imprisonment rate of 684 per 100,000 persons (U.S. Department of Justice 2012) than in Minnesota, Maine (incarceration rate = 146), or Vermont (incarceration rate = 263) (U.S. Department of Justice 2012). Why? Understanding reform in jurisdictions and institutions that have enacted some the toughest policies on crime brings a greater share of substantive and analytical benefits. As shown in Figure 1.1, because of their size and their get-tough politics, just a handful of states—Texas, California, Florida, Georgia, Michigan, and New York—housed 39 percent of the nation's prisoners in 2006 (U.S. Department of Justice 2007). Just two states—California and Texas—held 20 percent of U.S. prisoners (U.S. Department of Justice 2007).

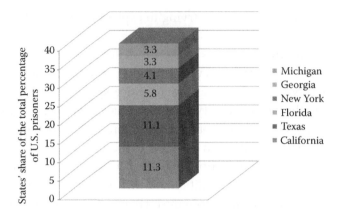

FIGURE 1.1

Six states imprisoned nearly 40 percent of U.S. prisoners. (From U.S. Department of Justice, Office of Justice Programs, Bureau of Justice Statistics, "Prison and Jail Inmates at Midyear 2006," 2007. Available at http://www.bjs.gov/content/pub/pdf/pjim06.pdf.)

Substantively, finding ways to successfully reduce the prison population in some of the toughest states will have a disproportionate impact on reducing the overall size of the U.S. prison population. Analytically, understanding the organizational, political, and institutional forces behind successful reform efforts in some of the most punitive settings may produce significant positive feedback effects throughout the federalist system.

Even though the substantive focus highlights reform in some of the "hardest" cases, the book's theoretical investigation behind the mechanisms driving change looks more broadly on the political contestation that reflects an ongoing struggle conducted over time within and across multiple institutions and contexts in the broader federalist system. State governments, in search for innovative solutions to problems, consider other states for possible answers (Karch 2007a). Actions in Minnesota, or Washington, or any other state, can inform policy makers in a state like Texas or California. The opposite relationship holds true.

Problems at the state and local levels bubble up to influence the federal agenda when state-level actors lobby Washington to help solve state problems and spread innovative policy solutions. Although the federal prison system, as Keith Humphreys notes, is only marginally bigger than the state of California's, activity at the federal level can have an outsized influence on what happens in the states (Humphreys 2012a). Research shows clear evidence that the topics debated in Washington can quickly influence the dimensions of political debate in state legislative houses (Karch

2006). Moreover, federal money funneled to the states via the grant-in-aid process or federal judicial rulings can diffuse policy change down to the subnational level. State and local governments, by controlling many of the levers of implementation, can shape the delivery and eventual outcomes of top–down policy. It is a very fluid system.

COALITION POLITICS AND REFORM IN THE CRIMINAL JUSTICE SUBSYSTEM

Policy making in the contemporary federalist system is complex and interdependent. Criminal justice policy is no exception. The reform movement is best understood as unfolding within a criminal justice policy subsystem (Sabatier and Jenkins-Smith 1988). The idea of a policy subsystem, most strongly advanced by Paul Sabatier and Hank Jenkins-Smith, is particularly applicable to the criminal justice policy realm (Sabatier and Jenkins-Smith 1988). Why? This perspective recognizes that understanding policy change in the multilayered federalist system does not require examining the behavior of one government, organization, or program, but rather multiple programs, regulations, and rulings initiated and operating at different levels of government, many times simultaneously.

A policy subsystem involves the interaction of a whole host of actors from different institutions and organizations at the national, state, and local levels of the federalist system that actively shape policy outcomes in a policy area. Sabatier and Jenkins-Smith show that within a policy subsystem, political actors tend to aggregate into distinct advocacy coalitions. Typically anywhere between two and four different coalitions competitively struggle to influence government decisions to achieve a set of policy objectives over time. Advocacy coalitions are composed of organized interest groups, think tanks, agency officials, lawmakers from multiple levels of government, applied and basic researchers, and even journalists, who share a nontrivial degree of coordinated activity over time (Sabatier and Jenkins-Smith 1988, p. 17). A coalition will share deep normative views such as beliefs about the size and role of government (say, along the traditional left/right ideological scale). But a coalition will also share what Sabatier and Jenkins-Smith call "secondary" policy beliefs about the seriousness of a policy problem, the principal causes of a problem, the level of government best suited to address it, and the policy instruments used. Secondary policy beliefs within a coalition can differ somewhat depending on the locational context of its members, but they form the glue that binds a coalition (Sabatier and Jenkins-Smith 1988, pp. 25–30).

Advocacy coalitions mobilize resources instrumentally. They disseminate policy research, ideas, and evaluations of implemented policy and programs (Kingdon 1995). They work to frame problems on terms favorable to their policy objectives. In a multi-institutional federalist system, they "venue shop"—that is, they look to sell their preferred policies in institutions where actors will be most receptive to their arguments or at least open to persuasion.

Not all coalitions have equal access to resources. A coalition with greater resources can gain agenda access in multiple venues of government simultaneously, giving it a disproportionate influence on the definition of social problem, the dimensions of political debate that capture the most attention, and the policy instruments deemed most viable. Political scientist E.E. Schattschneider observed years ago that the mere mobilization of interests was a form of bias in that it favored some types of problem definitions and solutions more than others (Schattschneider 1960). In their pioneering work on agenda setting and policy change, Bryan Jones and Frank Baumgartner showed empirically how issue frames or the "image" of a policy that comes to dominate an issue, in many cases for a prolonged period, helps generate enduring winners and losers in politics and policy making (Baumgartner and Jones 1993; Jones and Baumgartner 2005). Within complex multidimensional issues, actors within political institutions or organizations will attach greater importance to the status quo understanding of an issue—an incomplete understanding rather than comprehensive. Rarely do actors conduct a full-scale review of the underlying issues in their decision-making processes.

To fully understand crime politics and policy in the tough on crime era, as Lisa Miller shows in her influential book *Perils of Federalism*, the interaction between organized interests, issue framing, and the U.S. institutional structure helped secure the rise of mass incarceration in America (Miller 2008, p. 7). Miller shows convincing evidence that the "federalization" of crime—the simultaneous making of crime policy at all three levels of government—has shaped the very nature of group conflict on crime, political argumentation surrounding the issue, and alternative solutions.

Specifically, Miller argues that while growth in the federal and state bureaucracies in the twentieth century expanded opportunities for claim making, federalism's institutional arrangement actually marginalizes groups that lack the organizational capacity to simultaneously compete for attention at the state and national levels of government (Miller 2008, pp. 7–11). At the local level where elected officials are closest to the crime problem and barriers to participation are generally lower, a hodgepodge of complex and pragmatic (but mainly disorganized) arguments on crime comes from numerous community and neighborhood-based organizations, ex-offenders, and parent groups. But these resource-starved and less organized groups typically cannot mobilize beyond their immediate communities.

At the state and national level where sentencing laws are actually decided, elected officials are relatively isolated from the complexities of the crime problem. Hence officials face a different set of constituent pressures on the issue relative to their local counterparts who, given their close proximity to the problem, cannot afford to ignore the issue and its complexity. State and national institutions, then, create incentives that narrow citizens' concerns about crime into dimensions that fall into focused and manageable conflicts. In short, the propensity of actors across institutions to receive particular arguments about crime reveals an asymmetric relationship.

This structurally induced combination of forces produces a systematic bias in the "interest group environment across levels of government," which, for Miller, proves an important political advantage for what would effectively become the "law-and-order" coalition (Miller 2008, p. 7). The law-and-order coalition was originally energized by increasing crime rates in the 1960s when conservative politicians used crime and urban riots as racially charged wedge issues to appeal to white southern voters (Beckett and Sasson 2000; Weaver 2007). Over time a whole network formed of actors both inside and outside of government. This list included conservative presidents, entrepreneurial members of Congress, leading conservative intellectuals, single-issue groups, and crime control bureaucracies and organizations (e.g., narcotics officers, corrections officers, prosecutors, judges, probation and parole agents, and private prison corporations).

The original intellectual centerpiece of the coalition believed in a volitional theory of crime—one that saw crime as an individual choice perpetrated by immoral wrongdoers and drug users. From this view, crime increased in the 1960s because "crime paid." With criminal justice policy focused on rehabilitating offenders through much of the middle part of the twentieth century, volitional theorists perceived too few costs and not enough penalties for bad behavior. This perception led to policy prescriptions calling for tougher criminal sanctions and greater use of the prison to incapacitate known offenders, deter new ones, and expand a generalized moral outrage against criminals and drug users.

As Miller contends, this coalition, whose ideological and material interests (in the form of higher criminal justice budgets, staff, prestige) intersected around the simple idea of punishing offenders, had large resources and organized and operated across multiple venues in the federalist system. Along with the greater receptivity of actors within these institutions to their arguments, this mobilization of resources more effectively narrowed the range of problem definitions and policy solutions about crime at the state and national levels than in many cities where more disparate, disorganized, and poorer groups tried to influence local governments. Miller states

> At the state and national levels, the presence of criminal justice agencies and a few single-issue citizen groups creates a policy environment in which punishing offenders becomes the focal point of policy objectives … in this context, where police, prosecutors, and narrow single issue citizen groups stake out claims for resources, offenders are central to the problem definitions and solutions … The resultant policy process reinforces existing problem definitions and policy frames into which existing groups can easily fit their claims. State and national political institutions are particularly responsive to pressure groups that frame policy solutions in ways that are consistent with existing programmatic efforts, and the professionalized nature of contemporary policy advocates makes it possible for highly resourced groups to feed into existing policy programs. (Miller 2008, p. 10)

For Miller, punishment and mass incarceration occur in a federalist system that overwhelmingly focuses the crime debate on punishment through its influence on what groups have access to state and national policy making venues over time and the receptivity of actors within those institutions to the law-and-order coalition's policy solutions.

A key theme of this book, and one that Miller and many others certainly recognize, concentrates on the ongoing contest in politics and policy making. *Smart on Crime* contends that the story does not end there. Miller's analysis, like much of the research on the politics of punishment, covers that crucial period through the 1980s and 1990s, but fails to capture critical changes in the nature of group conflict and the politics of crime over the ensuing decade. In fact, Miller's analysis of congressional agenda access ends in 2002. Her analysis of state-level agenda access takes us up to 2004 but only in the state of Pennsylvania. During her period of study she notes, "One of surprising (sic) findings of the research reported in this study is the relative absence of groups at any level of government that advocate alternatives to incarceration in an effort to alter the law-and-order, punishment frame of other policy venues" (Miller 2008, p. 172).

RISE OF THE SMART ON CRIME COALITION

Slowly over that next decade, numerous members of the law-and-order coalition—or what I refer to as the tough on crime coalition—depicted so forcefully in Miller's work and the work of many others, have formed a key conservative block of a new smart on crime coalition. This has opened up new dimensions in the crime policy debate and found receptive audiences for prison alternatives in multiple venues within the federalist system. The coalition includes a growing number of prominent leading ideological conservative opinion leaders—a group that has long championed and defended the get-tough approach to crime and drugs. At the national level this list includes George W. Bush; Congressman (and then Senator) Rob Portman of Ohio; Chris Cannon, Republican House member from Utah; Republican Congressman Randy Forbes of Virginia; former House Speaker and leading 2012 Republican presidential candidate Newt Gingrich; and U.S. Senator Sam Brownback [R-KS], now Governor of Kansas. At the state level this emerging coalition includes Republican Governors Rick Perry of Texas, John Kasich of Ohio, and former California Governor Arnold Schwarzenegger. The list comprises leading chairmen of legislative committees such as Jerry Madden, Republican and chairman of the Corrections Committee in the Texas House of Representatives. Although these officials support less punitive crime policies, votes on most legislative reform packages have passed by such large majorities that change has certainly spread to the rank-and-file lawmakers.

The story not only documents leading figures on the conservative side, but also how the conservative block of the smart on crime coalition now includes the entry of conservative groups and organizations whose core interests now align with criminal justice reform. Organizations associated with the evangelical wing of the conservative movement play a key role. The Prison Fellowship Ministries is the most prominent; however, others, such as the Washington, DC–based Family Research Council, actively support reform. The coalition also includes members of law enforcement—those very groups and officials that Miller and others show to be instrumental in shaping the criminal debate around punishment. Law enforcement agents still hold significant agenda access, and indeed some members of the old guard, mainly prosecutors, continue to talk tough and raise public fears. In many cases law enforcement agents, particularly those coming into the profession after the mid-1990s, now sing a different tune. State-level secretaries of corrections, prison guards, probation officers, and parole officials increasingly advocate "evidence-based" practices that work more efficiently and effectively.

In addition to these figures, new organizations, like the recently formed "Right on Crime," a nationally organized reform campaign and offshoot of the Texas Public Policy Foundation, are joining the cause. In other cases, long-standing power players in conservative politics have begun mobilizing around criminal justice reform after years of advocating for punitive policy responses or just simply ignoring the issue. Grover Norquist's anti-tax crusading Americans for Tax Reform, a big-time powerbroker in conservative politics since the early 1990s, falls into the latter category but now backs reform. Leading conservative think tanks that routinely formed the genesis of conservative lawmakers' policy stances are also playing a part. The CATO Institute and the Heritage Foundation, two of the most prominent Washington, DC–based organizations, have since the mid-1970s backed punitive criminal sanctions, but now advocate "smart" sentencing reforms. The American Legislative Exchange Council (ALEC), an organization of conservative state lawmakers that pushed controversial "stand-your-ground laws" and prison privatization bills in state houses throughout the country in the 1990s, advocates reform.

Two primary dimensions solidify the smart on crime coalition in its effort to alter the penal policy debate. In the first "government run amok" dimension, pragmatic, instrumental, and utilitarian views of prison based on cost–benefit calculations play a critical role. Conservatives are thinking differently about the *effectiveness* and *efficiency* of the prison. Questions about policy effectiveness ask if a policy (or set of policies) achieves a desired outcome. Has a greater reliance on and greater use of the prison improved public safety? The efficiency of a policy considers the financial costs versus the benefits of a program. The key question here is whether a policy delivers a desired outcome at the lowest possible cost to society?

For fiscal conservatives and law enforcement organizations, both of whom closely align ideologically, the answer is increasingly "no." Elected fiscal conservatives who have spent the better part of three decades trying to shrink the social safety net are coming to see the prison, with its criminogenic effects, high rates of recidivism, and, most important, burgeoning effect on state budgets, as another symbol of government waste and largess. Fiscal conservatives now perceive prison reform as closely adhering to their core beliefs in limited and efficient government. For law enforcement officials, self-interest also assumes importance but for different reasons. At the front lines, probation officers struggle with larger caseloads. Prison guards, concerned for their own safety, resent increasingly overcrowded prison conditions. Prison wardens and top administrators have become frustrated by the inefficiencies of prisoner "churn"—the constant cycling of prisoners in and out of the system. In short, mass incarceration has made it more difficult to cope with the realities of their daily work life.

The second dimension involves a "prisoners are people" assumption that changes the moral dimension of crime. Moral, spiritual, and expressive features of policy affirm ultimate ends about the cultural values of justice. Actions expressing morally right values become ends in themselves, not just a means to avoid costs and increase benefits, whether these involve personal security, more money, or higher social status. For many conservatives, particularly those who believe in the authoritative power of government policy to elicit first principles, punitive criminal sanctions expressed moral outrage against vicious criminals and immoral drug users. The government should uphold good values against bad behavior; criminals and drug offenders who break the social contract should be punished severely. This dominant moral frame emerged with the conservative movement in the early 1980s.

However, as we will examine later in the book, a group synonymous with America's culture wars—evangelical Christians—is leading the moral change. Chuck Colson founded the Prison Fellowship Ministries in the late 1970s after serving a stint in federal prison after the Watergate Scandal. Colson along with Pat Nolan, himself a former California Assembly leader who served time in federal prison, have helped lead the Prison Fellowship Ministries and its policy arm, the Justice Fellowship, into a national conservative force for prison reform.

The strength of the Prison Fellowship Ministries' political network, along with the personal experiences of the men who have led it, has profoundly affected the conservative members of the smart on crime coalition. Their work has altered the debate in large part by engendering a more nuanced understanding of criminal offenders among conservative opinion leaders. It starts with a renewed emphasis on the idea that prisoners share a common human dignity inherent in all people. It extends to the idea that those who have paid their debt to society by serving their sentence should have real opportunities for a second chance at a better life. Debt and salvation—long associated with Christian faith—lends support, for example, to prisoner "reentry" and prisoner rehabilitation efforts. This same nuanced view of offenders also separates violent from nonviolent offenders. This conceptual distinction has important implications for concerns about fairness in criminal sentencing, namely the principle that penalties imposed should be proportionate to the crime committed. Is it morally justified to incarcerate an individual, many for a prolonged time, for a nonviolent criminal offense? For a growing number of conservatives, issuing long prison sentences to nonviolent offenders makes little economic sense; also more powerfully over the long run, it represents a moral injustice.

Because a growing number of conservatives now understand the prison in profoundly different ways, evangelical organizations like the Prison Fellowship Ministries play a vital policy role. The Prison Fellowship Ministries and the work of evangelical senators like Sam Brownback talked about the prison in a new way before many fiscal conservatives paid any attention. Research in political science demonstrates that the relative ideological positioning of an actor can send strong signals about the legitimacy of particular policy arguments and the effectiveness of alternative solutions in uncertain informational environments (Grossback et al. 2004; Lupia 1994). As foot soldiers in Republican-framed discourses, the Prison Fellowship's and evangelical leaders' messaging on prisons was automatically treated with greater seriousness by Republicans than if the same arguments came from the Congressional Black Caucus. The messenger matters; evangelical organizations made and continue to make significant political inroads with the old guard in conservative Republican politics.

Increasing concern over the ineffectiveness, inefficiency, and morality of the prison boom is now moving members of the tough on crime coalition closer to the preferred dimensions of the left-leaning but long-marginalized progressive coalition; the latter forms the "other half" of the larger smart on crime coalition.

A progressive coalition has had a prolonged presence in the criminal justice policy debate. Traditionally the coalition had comprised probation officers, prison wardens, social workers, mental health professionals, education specialists, liberal legislators, public health agencies, and criminological researchers. As David Garland documents, it was a coalition that had a pro-found effect on penal policy through the 1950s and 1960s (Garland 2001). To understand the philosophical and policy beliefs of this once influential coalition, Chapter 2 will document how the progressive coalition under-stood crime as a product of complex social forces—poverty, dislocation, and addiction. Progressives mainly viewed addiction from a medical and pub-lic health perspective. Only the worse offenders were suited for prison. The progressive coalition promoted professionalized administrative agencies of the state armed with a cadre of experts who, following the most modern and objective social scientific research, could lessen inmates' deepest patholo-gies (Simon 2007). Prison officials, it was believed, should offer individu-alized treatment. Institutional arrangements gave expert decision makers the authority to offer scientifically oriented treatment regimens, develop informed release programs, and advise sentencing decisions. Judgments on social–psychological behavior, antisocial behavior, and sentencing reflected decisions on technical merit and sound empirical research.

But as crime became widely politicized in the 1960s, and as the tough on crime movement gathered steam in the mid-1970s, the progressive coali-tion lost members and both political and policy battles. In the fight for supremacy, the tough on crime coalition not only attacked rehabilitation supporters for their "soft on crime" positions, but also challenged the sci-entific validity of the entire rehabilitation model. Many elected officials on the political left, some of the biggest champions of rehabilitation, began to disassociate themselves from the progressive coalition out of political fear of being caught on the "wrong side of the issue."

Even as the left-leaning coalition weakened, especially in those contexts where the tough on crime regime held its firmest grip, it never fully disap-peared. The discussions ahead will document how in the 1980s and 1990s, progressive members conducted best-practices research. They continued to organize, recruit new members, and learn lessons from mistakes made in that critical juncture during the mid-1970s. These lessons have impor-tant implications for how progressive coalition members began framing the issue in the 2000s. This process not only moved the debate to dimen-sions that more closely matched progressives' policy goals but also devel-oped a broad bipartisan appeal.

So a shift on the political right has captured the headlines. But this change may not have happened, or least not happened when it did, if the long-term organization and strategic decisions of members of the progres-sive coalition had not retained some policy influence.

EXPLAINING THE EMERGENCE
OF THE SMART ON CRIME COALITION

Changes in advocacy coalitions and their belief structures do not emerge out of thin air. Instead of just describing the composition of the smart on crime coalition and the shifting nature of political debate, *Smart on Crime* goes further to explain the reasons behind it. The story told is about policy learning—the strategic work of members in the losing coalition to reshape the dimensions of debate through policy analysis rather than just coercive power. The get-tough policy, changing public opinion, lower crime rates, and economic crisis, when combined with institutional constraints of state governments, give the *inefficiency, ineffectiveness,* and *moral failings* of mass incarceration far greater attention and receptivity among members of the law-and-order coalition than at any time during Miller's period of study.

POLICY LEARNING

In political systems of dispersed power, rarely do political actors reach a majority-supported position through repressive power alone. Rather they must convince others about the benefits of their position against other alternatives (Riker 1964). Actors within advocacy coalitions, whether part of a "winning" coalition or a "losing" one, constantly search for information. For actors in the winning coalition who benefit from the current policy arrangement, searching for information helps strengthen their current policy position or make policy adjustments to realize their goals more efficiently. But for members of the losing coalition, gathering and disseminating information via research reports, public speeches, and conferences and seminars can help shift the "locus of attack" or alter elite level discourse and the dimensions of political debate (Baumgartner and Jones 1993; Schattschneider 1960; Weaver 2007). By highlighting the severity of a problem, the causes behind it, or proposing new alternatives for action, losing coalition members move the debate in directions more favorable to their interests.

Beneficiaries from the current arrangement will resist such challenges by attacking the quality of their opposition's analysis, the validity of their data concerning the severity of the problem, their causal assumptions, and the workability of their policy alternatives. Raw political power may carry the day against a growing body of superior evidence. But in a democracy, this engenders great risk, most notably the loss of credibility (Esterling 2004). Over time because of their opponents' activities, the gradual accumulation of evidence can become impossible to ignore.

Some pundits assume partisans and organized interests groups hold rigid policy beliefs and positions that never change. Yet when viewing coalitions within a policy subsystem over a decade or more, evidence reveals many aspects of a coalition's belief system that change. Such changes lead to what Sabatier and Jenkins-Smith call "policy learning" (Sabatier and Jenkins-Smith 1988). Policy learning involves "relatively enduring alterations of thought or behavioral intensions that result from experience and which are concerned with the attainment or revision of the precepts of the belief system of individuals or of collectives" (Sabatier and Jenkins-Smith 1988, p. 19). For Sabatier and Jenkins-Smith, learning is instrumental. Members of a coalition aim to better understand the world to achieve their policy preferences or improve the effectiveness of policy. This dynamic process can involve changing perspectives about the severity of a problem, its causal mechanisms, or the effectiveness of alternative policies. Policy learning can unfold within and across coalitions. But by no means does learning always occur. When it does happen, it does not emerge overnight. Research in diverse policy areas indicates that change in a coalition's beliefs depends on the rate of turnover in personnel, the persuasiveness of the evidence, and the compatibility of the information with existing beliefs. Given the power of inertia behind coalition members' worldviews, if learning does occur, the group will first resist the new information before diffusing through members of the group.

For the progressive coalition, mobilizing efforts behind criminal justice reform involved two broad but interrelated efforts: it accumulated a robust set of empirically based evidence showing the consequences of an overly punitive policy regime, and it framed the issue along more favorable dimensions within this new informational environment. Although lacking tight coordination, prominent academics, organized interest groups, think tanks, and public agencies slowly started (especially in the 1990s) to collect and disseminate evidence of a failing penal system, with its high recidivism rate, its inability to deter crime sufficiently, and its devastating impact on blacks, Latinos, and the poor.

Chapter 3 will document how the growing number of arrests, longer prison terms, and high rates of parole revocations associated with the tough on crime movement meant that, over time, more people fell under custodial supervision. When more people went in prison, more came out. By the end of the 1990s thousands of prisoners returned to their communities each year when they were released on parole or finished their sentence. Especially correctional officers on the front lines had to deal with offender populations who were less educated, sicklier, and more prone to substance abuse problems than the general population (Petersilia 2003). The spike in prisoners meant that states not only had more people to feed, clothe, and house, but also needed to control a population with numerous complex social disorders extremely costly to monitor and handle. For prisoners returning home, many suffered from addiction or mental health problems and had few marketable job skills. They faced a mountain of civil punishments, such as ineligibility for food stamps and public housing. Many returned to prison after committing technical violations or new crimes.

For members of the progressive coalition, empirical data showing the large number of prisoners recidivating offered a small but important window of opportunity to begin reframing the issue. But progressive members refrained from retreating to the same battle-worn tactics of the 1970s. In the late 1990s top officials in President Clinton's Justice Department recognized the political constraints surrounding rehabilitation since it had fallen out of favor nearly three decades earlier. By the early 2000s, the prisoner "reentry" movement arose to build on past information as well as contemporary events and challenges.

The eventual success of these efforts resulted from broader structural forces both past and present. By the end of the 1990s, the financial costs of the get-tough approach loomed. With many states' prison populations swelling, corrections spending took an ever-larger slice out of states' general fund budgets. Yet unlike Medicaid, another area that saw states' spending spike, the federal government does not reimburse corrections costs. Given public safety's traditional status as a "state issue," state officials had to finance increased corrections expenditures.

This truth became more evident when state revenues declined significantly—first with the 2001–2003 recession and then even further with the Great Recession of 2007–2009, a period that witnessed state tax revenues shrink at a rate unlike anything seen since the Great Depression. Chapter 3 reminds us how the structure of state institutions shapes the politics of reform, in this case by constraining the budget choices policy makers had before them. Unlike the federal government, most state constitutions prohibit states from running large budget deficits when outlays do not match revenues. States must balance their budgets through a mix of tax increases or spending cuts when deficits emerge. Theoretically at least, states in tough economic times could choose to maintain an even level of prison spending or even increase it to meet demand. But in lean times when the whole budgetary pie is smaller, that policy option reduces programs and services much more popular with the voting public—namely health care, education, and transportation spending. Boxed in by stringent budget rules and the difficult politics of cutting popular programs and services, policy makers sought ways to lower corrections spending during the early 2000s.

Exogenous shocks to the political system, like an economic crisis, can quicken the pace of policy change by altering coalitions' resources. For members of a losing coalition, economic crises like those witnessed in two different points in the aughts can provide opportunities to propose new interpretations of an event, to "change the intensities of interest" in a problem, and to help gain great receptivity to their message (Weaver 2007, p. 236). The economic crisis, the runaway corrections budgets, and institutions that constrain budgetary choices dramatically changed the equation Miller set forth. Most elected officials in state and national government no longer viewed the crime problem as far removed from their lives. More groups than the law-and-order coalition mobilized followers; the debate no longer focused mainly on punishment. Crime, or more specifically the consequences of the punitive tools chosen to deal with crime, posed, and continue to pose, a salient problem confronting national and state lawmakers. Of course, crime represents a less salient issue for national and state officials than it does for local officials who must deal on a daily basis with neighborhood safety, gang violence, and questions about policing strategies and law enforcement budgets. But skyrocketing corrections spending, overcrowded prisons, and high recidivism rates concern today's state and national policy makers.

Members of the progressive coalition now have a more receptive audience for prison alternatives. Members of the old tough on crime coalition have joined the chorus and have begun singing a different tune—a sign of policy learning. For fiscal conservatives, cutting correctional discretionary expenditures helps balance the state budget. For correctional officials, a burgeoning prison system filled beyond capacity motivates the search for alternatives. For evangelicals and values-based conservatives, mass imprisonment has a devastating effect on individuals, families, and communities. The failure of many returning offenders to get a real second chance and an opportunity for redemption highlights a series of moral injustices.

BRINGING POLICY BACK INTO THE PICTURE

Political coalitions do not just happen. Interest groups, lawmakers, think tanks, and bureaucratic officials that make up advocacy coalitions come together to shape policy. Policy is the prize—it forms the central basis for contestation in our politics (Hacker and Pierson 2011, p. 3). And thus by placing priority on policy in the analysis, this book explains how the smart on crime coalition has emerged, how and why policy research matters, how and why policy learning has unfolded across coalitions, and the strategic arguments and decisions made by important actors along the way.

Chapters 4 and 5 document the emergence of the smart on crime coalition in national-level politics and policy making. Chapter 4 places emphasis on the rise of the prisoner reentry movement on the governing agenda, a process that culminated with the passage of the historic Second Chance Act in 2008. Perhaps more so than any policy area, investigating the politics of prisoner reentry illustrates the fluid nature of policy change in the criminal justice policy subsystem. The issue of prisoner reentry reached the agenda of the Justice Department, Congress, and eventually the White House, largely because of the strain felt at the subnational level where overstretched correctional officials began their search for a new way of doing things. Through examining the debate around the Second Chance Act, we can see more clearly the important role that policy research about "what works" played in moving the debate forward. The religious right became active in national crime politics, propelled new moral arguments around the issue of reentry, and members of the coalition on both the political left and right came on board.

Chapter 5 examines how the smart on crime coalition secured the most sweeping piece of federal criminal sentencing reform in forty years via the Fair Sentencing Act, which significantly reduced the country's horrific 100-to-1 crack/powder cocaine disparity. Changes to federal drug laws proved even harder than expanding services for prisoner reentry. The Second Chance Act addressed increasing recidivism rates and problems at the back end of the criminal justice system. Any benefits offered to offenders came after an offender had served time. Changes to drug sentencing forced lawmakers to reduce criminal penalties at the front end of the criminal justice system. At least at the federal level, policy makers had no examples to follow.

Tracing this policy fight, we will again document the importance of policy research, this time involving new evidence clearly repudiating mistaken beliefs in the 1980s that crack cocaine was more far more addictive and dangerous than the powder form of the drug. The U.S. Sentencing Commission, along with progressive sentencing reform organizations, persistently mobilized efforts to expose the devastating effects of mandatory minimums. Building on their past policy success, Prison Fellowship activists fought the ineffectiveness, inefficiency, and the irreparable damage stringent crack sentences had on the black community. The Prison Fellowship Ministries helped mobilize other religious-based organizations such as the National Association of Evangelicals, the United Methodist Church, and fiscally conservative organizations like Americans for Tax Reform. This new coalition weakened the influence of antinarcotics agents and prosecutors who lost credibility and sought to limit their losses.

Chapters 6 through 8 examine the rise of the smart on crime movement at the state level using case studies of successful (but ongoing) reform efforts in three states—Texas, Ohio, and California. While these represent just three of the fifty states, they include some of the most "difficult cases." Each of their past performances epitomizes the very essence of the tough on crime era in both their politics and policy.

The extent, timing, and path to reform in each state depend on the relative strength of the smart on crime coalition, which derives its influence from a state's political and institutional context. Texas experienced its first major burst of reform in the 2006–2007 period. As we will see, reforms there served as a political bellwether that resonated with policy makers well outside its borders. After several false starts, Ohio's major reform package was adopted in 2011. In each of these cases, prison alternatives reached the state's governing agenda with the emergence of a strong smart on crime coalition as measured in its bipartisan character and institutional breadth. Conservative lawmakers, aided by the emergence of new highly resourced organizations like the Counsel of State Government's Justice Center and Pew's Public Safety Performance Project, mobilized in multiple jurisdictions. This mobilization effort sold "smart" reforms as good public policy that protected public safety, spent fewer dollars, and held the promise of ruining fewer lives. California, however, had a very different experience in adopting its historic "prison realignment" plan in 2011. Reform in the Golden State came after political attention had shifted to dimensions favorable to reform (and four years after Texas passed its first major reform package) but managed to get through the California legislature only after a historic "structural injunction" of the U.S. federal courts.

WHEN IS REFORM *REALLY* REFORM?

This book is intended to engage a variety of audiences both inside and outside the academy. Still, while the book seeks to put the best-case forward about what is happening in contemporary criminal justice politics, many will not share such an optimistic outlook on things. And thus the final chapter attempts to begin to answer an important question: When does reform constitute *real* reform? This is a logical question to ask because over the past two decades, a considerable body of work has been published, in what might be best classified as the "politics of penology," that shows us how bad things are. Certainly Lisa Miller's *The Perils of Federalism* is one that is engaged with most closely here; however, there are many others— Michael Tonry's *Malign Neglect*, Katherine Beckett's *Making Crime Pay*, Marc Mauer's *Race to Incarcerate*, David Garland's *Culture of Control*, Marie Gottschalk's *Prison and the Gallows*, Jonathan Simon's *Governing through Crime*, Bruce Western's *Punishment and Inequality in America*, Loïc Wacquant's *Punishing the Poor*, William Stuntz's *The Collapse of American Criminal Justice*, and Robert Ferguson's *Inferno* are just examples (Beckett 1997; Gottschalk 2006; Mauer 1996; Miller 2008; Simon 2007; Stuntz 2011; Tonry 1995; Wacquant 2009; Western 2006). Michelle Alexander's *The New Jim Crow*, which argues that the prison system and the modern war on drugs are new tools in a long lineage of racial subjugation, has left perhaps the biggest imprint on public discourse on the topic. After an initial printing of only 3,000 books by the New Press, *The New Jim Crow* has now sold over 175,000 copies (Schuessler 2012).

Although commonly overlooked as important voices in policy making, these talented researchers both inside and outside the academy are important actors in this struggle, precisely because they have shown us the tragedy of criminal justice programs. Collectively their work has helped move the debate even if at times their work has undoubtedly seemed to some like background noise amidst the hysteria of the tough on crime era. We cannot understand the politics behind the reform movement in the 2000s—and the political barriers it still faces—without understanding past developments. The remarkable and unlikely story behind the smart on crime movement in America has occurred within the context of the past forty years that researchers have aptly documented. This scholarly research also offers clues about future prospects of criminal justice policy that build on past and present experiences.

Chapter 9 joins a dialogue with this larger body of literature, which raises direct or implied questions that come from "sympathetic critics" of reform. These scholars, some of whom have written the major works listed above, want to end mass incarceration and return U.S. penal policy to conditions around 1965, just before the prison boom began. They argue that policies associated with the smart on crime movement merely reflect tinkering at the margins, given the scope and size of the problem (Alexander 2010). Critics appear frustrated by the limited scope of policy change. I certainly recognize the constraints and limitations of the smart on crime movement as it currently stands. The coalition's focus, for example, on reducing sentences for nonviolent drug offenders, mostly overlooks the ratcheting up of penalties for violent crimes—a major source behind the increase in the custodial population. Critics rightfully ask: How are we to seriously curtail the prison population if violent criminal sentences are not sufficiently addressed?

Michelle Alexander argues that to overcome nearly four decades of mass incarceration and the debilitating impact of the punitive regime on racial minorities and the poor, what the United States really needs is a new civil rights movement (Alexander 2010). Similarly, Michael Tonry, a prominent legal scholar, makes the case that for real reform to unfold, Americans should perceive mass incarceration not as a financially costly exercise but a deep moral stain on our society. More people must share the belief that locking millions of people in cages for longer and longer periods represents a moral injustice. The question becomes, what effect will the smart on crime movement have on future conditions?

Possible answers to these questions will close the book. For now, we must remember that the prison boom did not naturally transpire or emerge as a by-product of governments responding in some organic way to ever-increasing crime rates. Instead political forces built and shaped prison growth. In an ironic twist, these political forces provide optimism. When political actors construct policies, they can also create newer, more just programs.

2

Collapse of the Rehabilitative Model and Rise of the Tough on Crime Coalition

Telling any story of policy change, whether it is penal reform, health care, education, or any other policy, requires context. What forces drove the get-tough policy approach? Under this policy, what groups experienced the most benefits while others faced major losses? How did we get to a point where enough people in positions of power began a movement to change? Only when we begin to answer questions like these can we begin to comprehend the hurdles the smart on crime movement has overcome, the constraints that were in place, and the opportunities that enabled success.

During the past fifteen to twenty years, knowledge has grown about what transformed the American criminal justice system in the 1970s and 1980s to conditions that differ from the earlier period. This chapter will rely on this superb body of scholarship, much of it coming from sociologists, criminologists, legal scholars, and a few political scientists. I analyze several interdependent themes that will guide the analysis of the reform movement at the center of this book.

This chapter stresses the dynamic nature of political coalitions in corrections and criminal justice from about the 1950s period to the 1990s, paying special attention to the rise of the tough on crime coalition that brought together conservative lawmakers, members of the law enforcement bureaucracy, evangelicals, and later, a good number of Democrats into a powerful force. I highlight the shifting nature of how political elites and much of the public understood crime and criminals, and how this structured policy was designed over time. How did political elites from presidents, to members of Congress, state leaders, and academic experts talk about crime? How did they want people to understand the issue, and what the country should do about the problem? The chapter will also uncover an often hidden role that policy research plays in the policy process, illustrating how research combined with an already shifting political environment added fuel to the tough on crime coalition and punitive policy choices that would define an era.

Politics and policy contestation illustrate an ongoing, dynamic process. The policies that came out of the era dominated by a get-tough coalition developed into a set of monumental policy challenges by the late 1990s. The story of reform now under way in the twenty-first century depicts shifting coalitions, the reframing of the issue, and policy research pointing in new directions. These trends laid the groundwork for the smart on crime reform movement and secured conditions more favorable to less punitive policies.

CALM BEFORE THE STORM

If an astute observer could somehow hop in a time machine and view the U.S. correctional system of the 1950s and early 1960s, some things would remain the same—cement walls, bars, and prison guards—and all the typical features of the physical prison space. But the system itself and values that guided it would be almost unrecognizable to the contemporary eye. Correctional practices of that era represented modes of reasoning and values and ideals popular in the New Deal. The New Deal initiated a profound era that witnessed the expansion of social insurance, secured a more active role for government, and saw public professionals as caretakers of human well-being (Simon 2007). The New Deal marked a transformation, a different ideology from that of the nineteenth century when trust in limited government and free market forces reigned in both politics and legal reasoning. For those born into wealth, lax regulations, along with the continued fostering of elite social and economic network ties, almost guaranteed the maintenance of a privileged status. Those with ambition, an eye for innovation, and a bit of luck could soon move up the socioeconomic ladder. But the poor, disabled, sick, and unlucky confronted a life extraordinarily cruel, made only worse by the Great Depression. After the end of World War II, however, states and regions of the country most influenced by New Deal values witnessed new broad-based investments in public education and several new social welfare agencies and services.

Resembling the broader New Deal philosophy, correctional institutions and penal practices of this era comprised what sociologist David Garland calls "penal welfarism" (Garland 2001, pp. 27–29). Penal welfarism's central axiom affirmed a fundamental belief in prisoner rehabilitation based on two core ideas. First, penal welfarism promoted the idea that the state, with its professionalized administrative agencies and armed with a cadre of experts following the most modern and objective social scientific research, could handle inmates' deep individual pathologies (Simon 2007). Criminological knowledge and expertise served as reliable guides to rehabilitation (Garland 2001, pp. 34–35). Institutional arrangements gave expert decision makers the authority to offer scientifically oriented treatment regimens to specific clients who needed individualized treatment. Social workers, psychologists, psychiatrists, and education specialists were all star players in the process. They classified inmates, consulted prisoners and families in helping prepare offenders for release, developed informed release programs, and informed sentencing decisions. Second, policymakers gave these experts wide discretion to do their work and insulated them from politics and broader public debate. Their judgments on social–psychological behavior, antisocial behavior, and sentencing stemmed from technical decisions based on sound empirical research. These experts were not expected to eliminate moral vices.

The focus on rehabilitation and on individuals largely derived from broader beliefs about what caused criminality in the first place. Causal attributions placed emphasis on structural or so-called root causes of crime. Professionals and practitioners in this era understood criminal deviancy as a structural problem—a social pathology inflicting individuals. Larger societal forces such as poverty, social disorganization, deprivation, coercion, and alienation caused this infliction (Currie 1985; Scheingold 1984). Criminal offenders, especially young offenders from impoverished neighborhoods, were considered both offenders and clients in need of treatment. As crime became intricately linked to impoverished social contexts, the correctional system, with its emphasis on individual rehabilitation, became a state-making institution and played a crucial role in public provision and human well-being during the immediate postwar years (Garland 2001, pp. 34–35; Simon 2007, pp. 22–23).

The degree to which this broad philosophy took hold among key supporters depended on structural–cultural context, both within different locales and institutions. Social workers, probation officers, reformatory supervisors, and criminological and sociological researchers formed the core coalition in support of the rehabilitation and social service provision approach to crime and criminal offenders (Garland 2001, p. 27). Conservatives, it is fair to say, talked more than those on the left about personal responsibility; however, even they acknowledged the importance of social and psychological conditions and circumstances and the need for correctional treatment.

The national party platforms on crime and punishment exhibited wide sections of agreement with respect to adherence to the rehabilitative model and the need to find the root causes of crime. Even as late as 1968, the Republican National Platform, for example, despite its leading candidate's tougher talk on crime, advocated for more research and rehabilitation. Specifically, the platform that year called for "increased research into the causes and prevention of crime, juvenile delinquency, and drug addiction" and "a new approach to the problem of chronic offenders, including adequate staffing of the corrections system and improvement in the rehabilitative techniques" (Johnson 1978, p. 751). More of the same was found four years later in 1972 when the platform read, "we have given the rehabilitation of criminal offenders more constructive, top-level attention than it has received at any time in the nation's history" (Johnson 1978, p. 869). The 1968 Democratic platform pledged a "vigorous and sustained campaign against lawlessness in all its forms—organized crime, white collar crime, rioting, and other violations of rights and liberties of others." The campaign would be furthered, the platform read, "by attacking the root causes of crime and disorder" (Democratic Party Platform of 1968). In 1972 the Democratic Party again said the "problems of crime and drug abuse cannot be isolated from the social and economic conditions that give rise to them." Drug addiction was a "public health problem" that should emphasize the "rehabilitation of addicts" (Democratic Party Platform of 1972). As David Garland notes, "The penal welfare framework, the rehabilitative ideal was not just one element among others. Rather it was the hegemonic, organizing principle, the intellectual framework and value system that bound together the whole structure and made sense of it for practitioners" (Garland 2001, p. 35).

The focus on rehabilitation largely influenced the widespread use of an indeterminate sentencing structure at the time. Judges and parole boards had a near monopoly on deciding the sentences of criminal offenders and their release into the community. In the indeterminate model, a legislature (a state legislature or national Congress) set maximum penalties as defined in the criminal code.* From there, however, a judge had the authority to sentence a convicted offender to probation or to prison. In the latter case, a judge would typically prescribe a maximum sentence and a parole board decided later when a prisoner was released. Each offender's needs differed. The time required to rehabilitate an offender was unpredictable. How could a judge estimate how long it would take to rehabilitate at the time of disposition? Rather, parole officers with expertise could best determine when an offender became ready for release (Allen 1981). Prisoners could serve the maximum sentence, but as long as a prisoner showed good behavior, posed no danger to other prisoners or staff, and participated in drug or alcohol rehabilitation courses, eligibility for parole typically came after serving a third of the maximum sentence (Blumstein and Beck 2005, pp. 50–79; Tonry 1996). Every state and the federal government used an indeterminate sentencing structure in 1970, exemplifying the widespread adherence to the rehabilitation ideal (Tonry 1996, p. 6).

The cadre of practitioners who believed in the model and the shared values of both major political parties contributed to minimal reliance on the prison. The toughest prisoners still went to prison, but prison officials at this time hardly viewed it as the best way to achieve rehabilitation. Widespread adherence to this broader philosophy produced a constant and stable rate of imprisonment during the middle decades of the twentieth century.

THE STORM: THE REHABILITATIVE MODEL GETS BLOWN AWAY

If the correctional system produced a "model prisoner" in the 1950s and early 1960s, an example to the rest of the democratic world, one could be forgiven for overlooking the significance of societal changes that set the stage for dramatic upheaval. Crime inched upward in the 1950s; however, by the 1960s, crime spiked dramatically. In 1962 the U.S. homicide rate was 4.5 per 100,000 persons; however, by 1964 it had jumped to 5.6 per 100,000. By 1972 the rate increased to 9.4. Robberies nearly tripled from 1959 to 1968 (Wilson 1975a, pp. 5–6).

---

* Some jurisdictions imposed minimum penalties but these were typically short sentences of one to two years.

Before 1960 the federal government had little involvement in crime and law enforcement (Calder 1993). Except for issues of treason, espionage, counterfeiting, mail fraud, and immigration issues, the federal government had no jurisdiction over law enforcement. State governments held broad authority to protect public health and safety under the U.S. Constitution. Local police forces and state court systems controlled nearly all crime-fighting efforts. As crime rates increased in the 1960s, however, the crime issue jumped onto the national agenda and into presidential politics.*

About this time fractures developed between the two major political parties on crime. Interparty divisions proved pivotal to growth in a broad-based tough on crime coalition, first led by conservative Republicans and later joined by self-interested law enforcement officials. A Democrat, however, controlled the executive branch. President Johnson introduced a crime agenda in his first two years that mimicked long-held rehabilitation ideals. Johnson focused squarely on the structural causes of crime and argued that his "War on Poverty" also served as a cure for crime (Beckett 1997). Yet even as crime rates grew, the Supreme Court, operating in the so-called rights era, ruled in cases that expanded the rights of criminal defendants (*Gideon v. Wainright*), and limited the admissibility of obtained evidence (*Mapp v. Ohio*) and confessions in court (*Mapp v. Miranda*). A court filled with liberal judges decided these cases. They reflected growing leftist concerns about abusive state power, arbitrariness, and inequalities across race, class, and gender in the criminal justice system. The political right became chiefly concerned about remedies to judicial leniency, "soft" sentences, and the expansion of prisoner rights under the Warren Court (Murakawa 2008).

In the 1960s conservatives began modifying their political rhetoric on crime, if not yet policy. In the midst of civil rights advances, conservatives used race and racial animosity as a potent wedge issue (Alexander 2010; Tonry 1995; Wacquant 2002; Weaver 2007). Vesla Weaver argues rising crime rates and talk of "law and order" provided conservatives a crucial vehicle to oppose advances of the civil rights movement (Weaver 2007). In the very early 1960s, when overt racial hostility did not carry quite the same risks it would just a few years later, southern segregationists framed

---

* This is not to say that the federal government did not have any involvement in law enforcement before the 1960s. Marie Gottschalk, in *The Prison and the Gallows*, provides several examples of the federal government crime control; namely dealing with prostitution, immigrant crime, airline highjackings, and prohibition. These efforts were more limited in nature compared with the broad and sustained effort beginning in the 1960s.

civil rights protests, freedom rides, and sit-ins as punishable criminal acts rather than acts of political protest. When those arguments failed to gain sufficient traction, Senator Strom Thurmond, the staunch anti–civil rights crusader from South Carolina, warned that "forced" racial mixing would have violent consequences. His southern Democratic colleague Senator John McClellan (AR), in a debate over the Civil Rights Act in 1964 said, "Serious crime will greatly increase rather than diminish following the passage of this measure" (Murakawa 2006).

Another more prolonged strategy was to attack the Supreme Court and the larger federal judiciary for inciting violence, first through the court's desegregation rulings (most notably *Brown v. Board of Education*), and then through its lenient decisions that widened the rights of criminal defendants.* As Naomi Murakawa explains, southern conservatives caustic complaints about "judges wrongly empowering black civil rights" in the immediate years after *Brown* easily transferred during the mid-1960s to the argument "judges wrongly empower (black) criminal rights" (Murakawa 2006, p. 486). The same basic principles applied. The political attacks became more potent as events on the ground started to unravel. Harlem and Rochester race riots that same year gave civil rights opponents a focusing event to enlist the additional argument that social unrest in the North occurred because of overly generous social policies backed by big northern city liberals. According to conservatives, by opening their cities to blacks fleeing the South, northern urban politicians caused lawlessness and crime. The racist story claimed northern cities were essentially reaping what they were sowing.

If the 1961 through 1964 period was a testing ground for using crime as a tool to oppose civil rights advances, Barry Goldwater, the conservative Republican from Arizona running against Lyndon Johnson in the 1964 presidential election, became the first candidate to seriously inject law-and-order politics into a national presidential campaign (Beckett and

---

* Between 1957 and 1966 the Warren Court dramatically expanded the rights of prisoners and criminal suspects, many of whom were poor and black. In *Trop v. Dulles* the court held that "cruel and unusual punishment" (found in the Eighth Amendment) is determined by the "evolving standards of decency that mark the progress of a maturing society." In *Robinson v. California* the court ruled that imprisonment for drug addiction was indeed "cruel and unusual" because addiction required treatment rather than incarceration. In *Gideon v. Wainright* the court ruled poor defendants charged with a felony had a constitutional right to counsel. *Escobedo v. Illinois* held that police must inform criminal suspects of their right to remain silent when questioned by law enforcement. *Miranda v. Arizona* reaffirmed this right (see Murakawa [2006], for a more detailed discussion of the Supreme Court's role in expanding procedural rights of criminal defendants).

Sasson 2000, p. 48). Although crushed by an astounding 434 Electoral College votes—a margin of defeat unheard of in the closely divided electorate of the modern presidential era—Goldwater presented a political road map on how to "get tough" on lawbreakers. By equating crime, riots, and violence with race using language that sought to maximize fear, Goldwater strove to drive a wedge in the American electorate.

Richard Nixon and Ronald Reagan later used the racial road map. Marc Mauer argues Goldwater blurred the boundary between political dissent of the civil rights process and conventional crime in political discourse; it all fell under "crime in the streets" (Mauer 1996). Goldwater's rhetoric put imminent pressure on Johnson to do something about crime. President Johnson, however, still supported policies focused on prevention, rehabilitation, and the "root causes" of crime. In 1965 he signed an executive order establishing the Commission on Law and Enforcement and Administration of Justice, which aimed to investigate the complex social conditions that contributed to increasing crime.

In March of that year, Johnson made a major speech before Congress on crime—the first of its kind—where he formulated a legislative crime agenda that by year's end saw the adoption of the Law Enforcement Assistant Act. The legislation sought to help states modernize their law enforcement operations. It helped set the wheels in motion for a much stronger federal government presence in law enforcement (Weaver 2007, p. 246). Following urban riots in Watts, Detroit, and Washington, DC (the latter following the assassination of Martin Luther King, Jr.), as well as the growing protests over the waging of the Vietnam War, the crime issue received extensive attention in the 1968 campaign. Long considered the front-runner in the 1968 election given his vice presidential stint under Eisenhower and a narrow defeat to Kennedy in the 1960 election, Nixon called the crime rate a "national disgrace" and promised that if elected he would restore "freedom from fear" ("Nixon Assails Rate of Crime in the Capital" 1968). Nixon gave no less than seventeen speeches on crime during the campaign, asking voters to reject the lawlessness of civil rights activists and embrace "order" (Alexander 2010, p. 46). Taking cues from his Republican colleagues, Nixon lambasted the Warren Court for permissive criminal procedural rulings that were "hamstringing the peace forces in our society and strengthening the criminal forces" (Markham 1972). In a fundraising speech, Nixon accused the court of giving a "green light" to the "criminal elements in this country" ("Nixon Links Court to Rise in Crime" 1968).

Nixon's tough discourse became part of a much larger project known as the Southern Strategy. Subsequent to the adoption of the Civil and Voting Rights Acts, the Republicans' idea (primarily advanced by Nixon's campaign advisor, Richard Dent) sought to build a "permanent Republican majority" by pealing off southern, white, working-class voters closely aligned with the Democratic Party on pure economic issues. Because many white southern voters opposed the Democratic Party's policies for desegregation, school busing and affirmative action, they might switch parties (Beckett 1997). Lower and working class whites in the South confronted a disproportionate share of the social and economic burdens of racial integration (Edsall and Edsall 1992). They competed with blacks, who were now on ostensibly equal terms for job and educational opportunities.

The Southern Strategy stressed racial animosities in political discourse. This racist strategy, however, faced new political hurdles. Political candidates could no longer explicitly use race as a justification for exclusion, subordination, and discrimination. They had to craft more subtle racial appeals. As one Nixon advisor said about Nixon's racial strategy in the 1968 campaign, "He emphasized that you have to face the fact that the whole problem is really the blacks. The key is to devise a system that recognizes this while not appearing to" (Alexander 2010, p. 43). In the South, discussion about "states rights" and spending cuts became coded language for policies designed to maintain white privilege and social position. The issue of crime served the same function.

Nixon's two main conservative challengers that year, California Governor Ronald Reagan and segregationist George Wallace, the former Alabama governor who ran as a third-party candidate, both helped push the crime rhetoric in an even more punitive direction. Wallace said, "The same Supreme Court that ordered integration and encouraged civil rights legislation" was now "bending over backwards to help criminals" (Beckett and Sasson 2000, p. 32). Reagan also excoriated the "permissive attitudes" found in the courts, homes, and schools. But Reagan also decried the structural theory of criminal activity, placing blame squarely on the individual. In remarks to a Republican platform committee in Miami Beach that summer, Reagan said that it was "too simple to trace all crime to poverty or color." "We must reject the idea that every time a law is broken society is guilty rather than the lawbreaker. It is time to restore the American precept that each individual is accountable for his actions" ("Nixon and Reagan Ask War on Crime" 1968). While trying to protect his right flank, Nixon left the door open for a balanced approach. "A militant national crusade to protect society from criminals," he said, "does not preclude a continuing national crusade to eliminate the social conditions from which so many of today's criminals have emerged and tomorrow's criminals are sure to emerge. The two go hand in hand" ("Nixon and Reagan Ask War on Crime" 1968).

As the victorious Nixon settled into his first term, he faced two big problems. First, despite all the tough talk, crime continued to increase. As president, Nixon could do little to solve the crime problem given the structural constraints of federal power over criminal justice matters. Second, growing concern about heroin-addicted servicemen in Vietnam opened a window into a much larger domestic drug problem. Yet the domestic drug problem, ironically, provided a political opportunity. Because drug trafficking dealt with interstate commerce, the federal government had greater regulatory power. Increasing federal drug enforcement efforts and tying drugs to crime effectively killed two birds with one stone.

Drugs and drug addiction rose to the top of Nixon's first-term agenda. Administration officials began making links between the drug trade and street crime, claiming that, despite flawed empirical evidence, drug addicts committed the bulk of crime to pay for their addictions (Beckett and Sasson 2000). In a highly publicized 1971 speech, Nixon claimed drug addiction had "assumed dimensions of a national emergency" and was "public enemy number one." "For those who traffic in drugs and for those who, for example, make hundreds of thousands of dollars—and sometimes millions of dollars—and thereby destroy the lives of young people throughout this country, there should be no sympathy whatever and no limit insofar as the criminal penalty is concerned" (Schmidt 1971).

Nevertheless, a disconnect separated Nixon's rhetoric from his actual policies. Although he continued to expound the drugs/crime nexus, his press secretary, Ronald Zeigler, said Nixon's remarks only meant drug pushers would be prosecuted to the fullest extent under *current* (emphasis added) law—a far cry from the more severe punishments Reagan's war on drugs imposed a decade later. Nixon had fairly strong prohibitionist tendencies (Courtwright 2004). But like every other president, he was constrained by institutions. He had to placate a house of representatives full of liberal members brought in with the landslide 1964 election. Nixon's drug addiction legislative package introduced in 1971 called for an additional $155 million for enforcement and rehabilitation efforts ("President Orders Wider Drug Fight; Asks for $155 Million" 1971). With his unwillingness or inability to expand supply side enforcement, Nixon's war on drugs paired drug enforcement with treatment measures.

Nixon's signing of the Controlled Substances Act (CSA) in 1970 illustrates his hybrid approach. The CSA solidified the federal government's role in drug law enforcement (Courtwright 2004; Lynch 2012). It reconciled a hodgepodge of federal drug laws by creating a "scheduling table" that assigned a prohibitive weight to substances as a function of their medical value, harmfulness to health, and their addictive qualities (Lynch 2012, p. 176). Rather than being overly punitive, the law provided for a variety of rehabilitative and health-based approaches, and gave more money and authority to the Department of Health, Education and Welfare (HEW) to establish community mental health centers and public health service hospitals (Courtwright 2004). It actually eliminated some federal mandatory minimum sentences originally set under the Narcotics Control Act of 1956 and reduced maximum penalties for drug possession crimes (McLaughlin 1973). The CSA also had some important elements on the enforcement side. It introduced a provision for "no-knock" search warrants. It increased funding to pay for 300 new drug enforcement officials in the Bureau of Narcotics and Dangerous Drugs (the precursor to the Drug Enforcement Agency), and dramatically expanded that agency's power to regulate new drugs (especially relative to public health agencies like HEW). Its scheduling table platform established a conduit by which new substances could be easily added in its prohibition framework. By 1977 regulators had scheduled thirty-five additional drugs and rescheduled eight others (mostly amphetamines and barbiturates) to the more restrictive schedule II (Courtwright 2004, p. 12).

At this point in the story the rehabilitation model still maintained its supremacy, a lingering by-product of the dominant coalition made up of liberals, conservatives, and a whole cadre of practitioners who supported rehabilitation and the indeterminate sentencing structure. But this dominant coalition that built the rehabilitation model showed serious strain. Most notably the two parties' respective beliefs about the principal causes of the crime problem began to diverge. Democrats still pushed root causes. Leading conservatives, especially presidential candidates who mixed crime, race, and drugs, chose the law and order–individual–responsibility route and tougher responses to criminal offenders. Yet in terms of policy, because of constraints imposed by decentralized institutions and divided government, conservatives offered more noise than a radical policy departure. One area of agreement between the parties involved the federal government's expanded role in combating crime and drugs. Johnson advanced the Law Enforcement Assistant Act. Nixon supported the CSA. These acts advanced the "federalization" of crime, as Lisa Miller calls it, and they affected the strength and effectiveness of the tough on crime coalition once the punitive era took hold.

The focus solely on national-level politics misses other mechanisms at play. To enlarge our understanding of why the advocacy coalition framework proves useful requires us to look at actors and forces within the subsystem often regarded as tangential to the policy-making process.

This next section investigates the often-arcane world of policy analysis and policy research, where ideas unfold in academic journals and some of the most influential elite media sources. Researchers launched a powerful "volitional" theory of criminal activity that attacked rehabilitation science and the whole indeterminate sentencing model.

POLITICALIZATION OF REHABILITATION RESEARCH

By the mid-1970s the intellectual foundations for the highly successful, ideologically-fueled conservative attack on rehabilitation and indeterminate sentencing came from inside the academy, most prominently from James Q. Wilson. Few single academicians have made such a profound impact on thinking about a subject, especially a scholar writing in the social sciences, yet Wilson influenced thinking on almost every aspect of American criminal justice policy (Petersilia 2012). Wilson epitomized a public intellectual. After earning his PhD in political science from the University of Chicago, he published his first major book, *Varieties of Police Behavior*, in 1967. The publication led to his appointment on President Lyndon Johnson's Commission on Crime and Administration of Justice that same year.

When the Commission issued its report, "The Challenge of Crime in a Free Society," it included over 200 policy prescriptions. Many focused on reducing prison sentences, funding prison diversion programs, and eliminating the root causes of crime. Although just as concerned about increasing crime rates as everybody else, Wilson rejected the report's main recommendations. Wilson believed the government lacked the capability to tackle the root causes of crime. He argued there was no empirical evidence that suggested tackling poverty and racism through greater social service provision had any significant impact on reducing criminal activity.

Wilson's 1975 best-selling book, *Thinking About Crime*, profoundly affected the long-term trajectory of criminal justice policy in America because it helped shape and solidify the framework of how conservative politicians understood crime. The book served as a powerful conceptual tool to bludgeon supporters of rehabilitation and the larger indeterminate sentencing structure in favor of more uniform but much more punitive sentences.

Wilson's central thesis strengthened a volitional theory of criminal justice. Wilson, along with prominent University of Chicago economist Gary Becker, understood criminal activity as a conscious individual choice (Becker 1968). The relative risks and rewards of crime shaped individuals' rational calculations that supposedly weighed the costs and benefits of a criminal act. If the benefits of a crime outweighed the costs, committing a criminal act exemplified a rational decision. Crime was increasing because the risk of getting caught, convicted, and punished was too low. In short, crime paid. Punishments needed to be tougher so they would deter criminal choices by increasing the costs of criminal behavior. For criminal justice officials, this view called for a more generalized use of longer (more punitive) and fixed-term (certain) sentences that meant greater severity for more serious crimes and for repeat offenders.

Wilson recognized the limits of utilitarian reasoning. In a lengthy excerpt from *Thinking About Crime* published in the *New York Times Magazine* in 1975, Wilson stated, "Some persons will commit crimes whatever the risks; indeed, for some, the greater the risk, the greater the thrill—while others—the alcoholic wife beater, for example—are only dimly aware that there are any risks" (Wilson 1975b, p. 45). Because some individuals remain impervious to changes in the risk of criminal behavior, Wilson wanted tougher sentences to extend beyond pragmatic instruments of criminal deterrence. Criminal punishments had to send a message about right behavior and right values: punishment must express the idea that crime is a moral evil.* Wilson noted, "The most serious offenses are crimes not simply because society finds them inconvenient, but because it regards them with moral horror. To steal, to rape, to rob, to assault—these acts are destructive of the very possibility of society and affronts to the humanity of their victims" (see footnote).

---

* Wilson in fact published similar arguments in other widely read publications including the *Atlantic Monthly, Washington Post, Commentary,* and *The Public Interest.* Publishing arguments in these outlets no doubt raised the impact that *Thinking About Crime* had on public discourse.

Retributive punishment stigmatized criminal behavior and those who conduct criminal acts. To do otherwise—to destigmatize crime—Wilson concluded, "would be to lift the weight of moral judgment and to make crime simply a particular occupation or avocation which society has chosen to reward less (or perhaps more!) than other pursuits. If there is no stigma attached to an activity, then society has no business making it a crime" (see footnote on p. 43).

Wilson presented what Stuart Scheingold called a "moral individualism" criminology (Scheingold 1998). Tougher, more certain criminal sanctions served a dual purpose. On one hand, they acted as an effective deterrent by raising the costs in the calculus of crime. On the other hand, they expressed moral values that symbolized moral indignation against criminal behavior. The purpose of the criminal justice system, Wilson wrote in that same essay, "is not to expose would-be criminals to a lottery in which they would either win or lose, but to expose them in addition and more importantly to the solemn condemnation of the community should they yield to temptation" (Wilson 1975b, p. 45). Yet Wilson also recognized a close interdependence of the pragmatic and ethical aspects of punishment. "It is my experience that parents do not instruct their children to be law abiding merely by pointing to the risks of being caught, but by explaining that these acts are wrong whether or not one is caught" (Wilson 1975b, p. 45). Instilling the right values and stigmatizing crime would produce an additional cost in the crime calculus. He would write later that internalized prohibition against offending behavior might be strong enough to prevent criminal acts even when there is no risk of being caught and punished (Wilson and Herrnstein 1985).

Mark Kleiman argues that a "reasonable" case could have been made for more prisons in the early 1970s if we consider the ratio of the incarceration to the crime rate—or what he calls a "punitive index"—essentially a calculation of the average punishment (or average number of days incarcerated) for various offense types during a given period of time (Kleiman 2009). Through statistical analysis, Kleiman found that the punitiveness index dropped by 68 percent from 1962 through 1974, reaching its low point that year, before quadrupling over the next three decades. The likelihood of getting punished with a stint in prison for, say, burglary, fell to its lowest point in 1974 before heading upward dramatically over the next three decades. "In the intervening three decades," Kleiman notes, "we have built prisons, and built prisons, and then built still more prisons, until some of us who supported expanding prison capacity from its low 1970s levels have started to feel like the Sorcerer's Apprentice, vainly looking for the 'off' switch on a mechanism gone completely out of control" (Kleiman 2009, p. 14).

Around the same time the volitional framework gained greater support from elite researchers, an equally powerful line of attack started against prisoner rehabilitation. In this gestalt appeared Robert Martinson's endlessly cited article in *The Public Interest*, an influential magazine published by another leading conservative thinker, Irving Kristol (Martinson 1974*). The title of the essay was, "What Works? Questions and Answers in Prison Reform." Martinson participated in a survey of evaluations of American prison rehabilitative programs. Joining two other researchers, Doug Lipton and Judith Wilks, the three reviewed over 231 studies (published between 1945 and 1967) on different types of offender improvement measures, including adjustment to prison life, vocational success, educational achievement, personality and attitude change, and recidivism. Their research ended in 1970. A 736-page report, "The Effectiveness of Correctional Treatment," appeared in 1975 (Lipton et al. 1975). Martinson wrote *The Public Interest* essay, however, without the consent of his coauthors (Lipton 1998). The compendium dealt only with the effects of rehabilitation treatment on recidivism. According to Martinson, recidivism represented the "phenomenon which reflects most directly how well our present treatment programs are performing the task of rehabilitation" (Martinson 1974, p. 24). The studies reviewed varied widely in both their method and the groups studied, making it more difficult to draw conclusions. Martinson intimated the difficulties of the job: "The groups that are studied, for instance, are exceedingly disparate, so that it is hard to tell what 'works' for one kind of offender also works for others" (Martinson 1974, p. 24). Despite these challenges Martinson concluded with the now famous line, "with few isolated exceptions, the rehabilitative efforts that have been reported so far have had no appreciable effort on recidivism" (Martinson 1974, p. 25). Not long after, the common refrain was that "nothing works" in prisoner rehabilitation programming.

Several scholars have reiterated the huge effect of Martinson's report. Writing just after the report was published, Stuart Adams argued the work

---

* Interestingly, this is the same publication James Q. Wilson would use the following year to promote selective incapacitation and fixed sentencing.

had "shaken the community of criminal justice to its root" with many now "briskly urging that punishment and incapacitation should be given much higher priority among criminal justice goals" (Adams 1976, pp. 75–91). According to Ted Palmer, "Rarely if ever did a research article have as powerful and immediate impact on corrections … Within a year, the view that essentially no approach reduces recidivism was widely accepted" (Palmer 1992).

Francis Cullen suggests Martinson could have made more technical arguments about his findings or called for more research to help improve implementation of interventions (Cullen 2005). Rather than doing that, he included much broader, more sweeping claims, noting "a more radical flaw in our present strategies—that education at its best, or that psychotherapy at its best, cannot overcome, or even appreciably reduce, the powerful tendency for offenders to continue in criminal behavior" (Martinson 1974, p. 49). His most grandiose public positions came on CBS News' *60 Minutes* program in 1975 in a story titled "It Doesn't Work." When asked by newsman Mike Wallace about his research, Martinson claimed rehabilitation and treatment had "no fundamental effect on recidivism," cited parole as an "almost Machiavellian attempt" by offenders to secure release from prison, and that psychological programs were a good way to pass time but otherwise had "no effect" (Cullen 2005, p. 8).

Martinson was hardly the first to claim rehabilitative projects have limited success—other scholars reached similar conclusions years before (Bailey 1966; Berleman and Steinburn 1969; Cressey 1958; Kirby 1954; Wooton 1959). Martinson's report did not actually claim "nothing works." Few people seemed to have actually read the full 1975 report. Following its publication, some leading scholars commented that it was perhaps the most frequently quoted ("Nothing Works!") but least read articles in the history of rehabilitation literature (Cousineau and Plecas 1982; Gendreau and Ross 1987).

One of the first scholars to point out some of the nuances within the report shortly after publication was Ted Palmer, a psychologist who had worked in the corrections field as a researcher for the California Youth Authority. Actively involved with evaluative studies of intervention programs for the Authority, Palmer found much of Martinson's conclusions to lack empirical validity (Cullen 2005). In his own research, Palmer found several interventions that showed signs of rehabilitation success (Palmer 1978). Referring to Martinson's report, Palmer found that among the cited studies, thirty-nine of them—or 48 percent of the total—specified "positive or partly positive results" (Palmer 1978, p. xxi). A number of programs actually reduced recidivism for a sizable portion of the offender population. Instead of evaluating treatment effectiveness only across modalities as Martinson had done, Palmer argued analysts should categorize offenders by their individual characteristics, treatment settings, or the training level of treatment providers. This would make it possible to understand what works not for offenders as a whole, but what treatment works for specific types of offenders facing specific conditions.

Palmer represented just one of several scholars dismayed with Martinson's research. Francis Cullen and Karen Gilbert said Martinson failed to sufficiently qualify his conclusions (Cullen and Gilbert 1982). Others pointed out that the programs evaluated lacked sufficient funding to achieve desired outcomes or that researchers' judgments of "failure" reflected a bias. Others argued that the criminogenic effects of prison life (where the bulk of rehabilitation services were offered) superseded any benefits that accrued with rehabilitation (Vito and Allen 1981). *The Effectiveness of Correctional Treatment*, the larger research project from which Martinson drew his conclusions, took a more guarded view of rehabilitation. It noted, "The field of corrections has not *as of yet* found satisfactory ways to reduce recidivism by significant amounts," suggesting researchers still pinned hope on rehabilitation while they made efforts to collect better data and improve diagnostic tools (Sarre 2001).

Finally, even Martinson himself appeared to recant much of what he said in that original *Public Interest* article. The first sign of a capitulation came when Martinson reaffirmed the value of probation as a rehabilitative tool in a 1977 article he published with Judy Wilks (Martinson and Wilks 1977). The complete reversal arrived in the *Hofstra Law Review* just a year before his death. He noted, "... contrary to my previous position, some treatment programs *do* have an appreciable effect on recidivism. Some programs are indeed beneficial; of equal or greater significance, some programs are harmful (emphasis in the original)" (Martinson 1979). Martinson wrote further, "The most interesting general conclusion is that no treatment program now used in criminal justice is inherently either substantially helpful or harmful. The critical fact seems to be the *conditions* under which the program is delivered. ..." (Martinson 1979, p. 254). By the late 1970s, then, Martinson held a more sanguine view on rehabilitation. Although evidence revealed numerous programs secured effective results, their success depended on specific conditions.

Policy analysis rarely gets used just to seek "truth" (Sabatier and Jenkins-Smith 1988). Political actors first develop a policy position and then they use analysis in an "advocacy" fashion to justify their position. Clearly, Martinson advocated an agenda. How did Martinson's research shift the political and policy debate over such a short period? Policy makers' attention shifted from the argument that "rehabilitation works" to "nothing works" within about a two-year period from 1974 to 1975.

Sabatier and Jenkins-Smith contend that strong empirical evidence accumulated over a prolonged time can, under some conditions, alter the dimensions of political debate, forcing policy makers to reexamine their positions. Yet Martinson's research indicated no significant shift (objectively speaking) in the underlying science of rehabilitation, nor did it reveal novel findings. Even if his research showed definitive evidence of the ineffectiveness of rehabilitation programming, any effect on the political system would usually take years to emerge because actors resist evidence conflicting with their policy position.

From Bryan Jones and Frank Baumgartner's work, we know that a variety of messages come into the political system; not only what those messages say matters but also their importance given by political actors (Jones and Baumgartner 2005). The facts surrounding an issue or problem scarcely have to shift in any objective sense for attention to focus on other arguments or dimensions of an issue. When politicizing science for the purpose of promoting policy change, politicians need only to get enough people to believe that facts have changed, or encourage more attention to different facts more favorable to advocates' cause. That change can happen regardless of how accurately an "objective" measure portrays this new "reality."

The "nothing works" mantra had such a sweeping effect within conservative circles because it matched a fundamentally different worldview about criminal offenders and the causes of crime. Francis Cullen and Paul Gendreau note, "Martinson's study assumed such a lasting significance not on the basis of its empirical merits but because it gave scientific legitimacy to existing deeply felt sentiments" (Cullen and Gendreau 1989, p. 30). Placed within the larger context of increasing crime rates and racial anxiety, an ideology formed around beliefs in the uselessness of attacking root causes. From the conservative perspective, rehabilitation meant too soft treatment of moral wrongdoers who made an individual choice to commit crime. If nothing worked, then tough penalties, longer punishments, and the death penalty became much easier for the conservative movement to sell (Sarre 2001).

Sympathetic members of the public agreed with the conservative out-look on crime. This August 1976 letter published in the *New York Times* from a distraught mother, Maxine Cutler (whose sons were both crime victims—one a homicide victim), attacked the rehabilitative model, dis-credited the root causes of crime, rejected the humanity of criminal offenders, and called for tougher sentencing in one fell swoop.

> I write in protest against the permissiveness of the law, the courts, the politicians, social scientists, judges, psychiatrists and psychologists who have allowed our cities to become jungles ... Let [them] stand personally responsible for the hell let loose in our streets. Let citizens have the right to sue those responsible for wrong decisions concerning a homicidal crimi-nal, under age or not. The myth of rehabilitation has supported endless exercises in futility ... Economic deprivation, social, political, and cultural alienation have meaning only in regard to the very young, who have not yet committed a crime. Once they have tasted blood, like the animals they are, the hoodlums are beyond human considerations. Let us isolate them for long prison terms at hard labor and turn our attention, effort and finances to making our country safe for the majority. (Cutler 1976)

The progressive side of the rehabilitative coalition, composed of lib-eral academics, social service providers, probation officers, and liberal Democrats felt deflation, even anger. The process resembled how a group of voters overly enthusiastic for a politician during a campaign experi-ence a big letdown once the messiness (and inevitable compromise) of gov-ernance begins. Despite the best efforts of Palmer, Cullen, and others to oppose the claim that nothing worked, by the mid-1970s few politicians defended the rehabilitative ideal. The promise of rehabilitation and the state's capacity to change offenders, so fervently supported by so many liberals for so long, lost its luster. Correctional practices that seemed good in theory led to problems in practice.

SAGGING SUPPORT FOR REHABILITATION ON THE LEFT

For many on the progressive side of the coalition, rehabilitation became a euphemism for vengeful punishment and racism (Allen 1981). By the mid-1970s liberals had witnessed beatings suffered by civil rights workers, the shootings at Kent State, the Attica prison riot, the mismanagement and resulting carnage in the Vietnam War, and the Watergate scandal. Within the academy Martinson's attack fit nicely within an ascendancy of critical criminology and labeling theories that saw the rehabilitative ideal as an agent of state control—and thus tapped into a groundswell of concern about arbitrary treatment and state abuse of power over marginalized populations. Cullen notes, "For criminologists, being against rehabilitation—rejecting it as a case of good intentions corrupted for sinister purposes—became part of the discipline's professional ideology, an established, unassailable truth that required no further verification. Scholars spent little time studying how to make interventions more effective and won enthusiasm for showing that treatment programs did not work or, even better, 'widened the net of state social control'" (Cullen 2005, p. 8).

In 1971, a depressing report titled "Struggle for Justice," published by the leftist Working Party of the American Friends of Service Committee, concentrated on class and race-based discrimination (Garland 2001, p. 55). It highlighted the perceived arbitrary, coercive, and destructive powers of the carceral state. Attacking the correctional system's ability to punish (mainly through imprisonment) blacks, the poor, and other cultural minorities, the report claimed that individualized treatment and rehabilitation justified the punitive actions. Treatment without prisoners' consent, the report noted, left prisoners (e.g., disproportionately racial minorities) open to abuse from professionalized correctional staff given wide discretion to enact coercive sanctions. "Prisoners will no longer submit," the report noted, "to whatever is being done to them in the name of 'rehabilitation' and 'treatment'" (Garland 2001, p. 55). Concern about abuse and unequal treatment that resulted from the broad set of discretionary powers of state officials led to a growing chorus on the left for a "justice model" of corrections. A call to end the unfettered powers enjoyed by state officials, the justice model opposed the indeterminate sentencing system (Cullen and Gendreau 1989). The most persuasive cases against rehabilitation and the indeterminate model came by the early 1970s from inside judicial circles.

The most salient critique occurred in a 1972 book, *Criminal Sentences: Law without Order*, written by U.S. District Judge Marvin Frankel (1972). Drawing on his fifteen years of experience as a federal judge, Frankel laid out his case that unrestrained judges working within the indeterminate sentencing system produced unfair and biased sentencing outcomes. The system offered few standards that determined what sentences federal judges should set. It produced wide disparities in the sentences imposed on similar defendants for similar types of crimes. When Frankel wrote his 1972 book, strong evidence revealed racial and gender bias in criminal sentencing decisions (Tonry 1996). Frankel called for a "Commission on Sentencing" that would instill broader oversight and more detailed rules over judges by offering "presumptive sentencing" guidelines tying the severity of punishment to the seriousness of the crime. Frankel advanced the original "just desserts" model; his recommendations sought sentences that treated like cases alike. By the end of the 1970s Minnesota and Pennsylvania established sentencing commissions, as did several other states.

By the 1980s, crime became a pawn within a much larger debate about the size and scope of the welfare state and about big symbolic and moral questions related to the meaning of contemporary citizenship in the neo-liberal era that blossomed during the Reagan presidency (Soss et al. 2009). Criminal deviancy meshed intrinsically with broader-based conservative attacks on the welfare state. Proclaimed chiefly by Ronald Reagan at the national level, concepts like individualism, responsibility, and self-discipline all became synonymous with "good citizenship" (Soss et al. 2009). As Francis Cullen notes, conservatives came to believe "rehabilitation was infected with the worst aspects of the social welfare state: the willingness to give human services to a population that was undeserving and would only learn from this generosity that waywardness is rewarded" (Cullen 2005, pp. 6–7). Criminals and drug users, those who chose not to "play by the rules," failed to exemplify the kind of self-control expected of good citizens.

Ronald Reagan advanced this individualistic theory of deviancy beginning in the 1960s but later brought it all the way to the White House. In a 1984 speech to the Annual Convention of the National Sheriffs' Association, Reagan argued, "Choosing a career in crime is not the result of an unhappy childhood or a misunderstood adolescence; it is the result of a conscious willful choice made by some who consider themselves above the law, who seek to exploit the hard work of their … fellow citizens" (Nicholson-Crotty and Meier 2005, p. 239).

Reagan's moralistic rhetoric on crime, and his effort to bifurcate good and evil forces in American politics, reflected beliefs in the Protestant fundamentalism movement and the rise of Religious Right. Groups like the Moral Majority, the Religious Roundtable, the National Association of Evangelicals, and later the Christian Coalition became a major intellectual and mobilizing force in Republican Party politics during the 1980s (Green 2007).

Protestant fundamentalists view morality in clear categorical terms (Nagata 2001). Unlike other religious groups, conservative Protestants make fewer distinctions about degrees of wrongful behavior (Curry 1996). They perceive any crime as a sin and assume God punishes sinners. Hence fundamentalists seek to punish criminal acts, not for reasons of deterrence but out of retribution. As Kenneth Wald and Allison Calhoun-Brown explain, Protestant fundamentalists' belief in an image of a "cold and authoritative" God extends support for the government's role in securing order (Tonry 2011a; Wald and Calhoun-Brown 2007). Indeed, survey research validates this belief. Protestant fundamentalists who view God as a dispassionate figure who dispenses justice hold more punitive attitudes toward criminal offenders (Unnever et al. 2008, pp. 45–96).

Led by individuals like Jerry Falwell and Cal Thomas of the Moral Majority, the Religious Right assumed crime resulted from moral chaos— an inevitable consequence of an erosion of a Christian consensus in America. If individuals chose a right relationship with God, behaved in ways that pleased Him, and held fast to His commandments, they would be less likely to become involved in criminal behavior (Day and Laufer 1987). Pat Robertson, another leading figure of the Religious Right, continued the moral crusade against criminals and many others into the late 1980s. "I have no intention of giving the streets of America to the radical homosexuals, the criminals, and the drug dealers" Robertson said in November 1987, as he kicked off his campaign for president that year (Dionne 1987).

By the 1990s conservative scholars like John DiIulio espoused a new fear-invoking charge. DiIulio, a former student of James Q. Wilson, helped pen a book titled *Body Count*, where the authors warned Americans of a new generation of "superpredators," "the youngest, biggest, and baddest generation any society has ever known." The predators exemplified a wave of "radically impulsive, brutally remorseless youngsters" motivated by a "moral poverty" and committed to a "nothing else matters" lifestyle except one of "sex, drugs, and money" (Bennett et al. 1996). Singling out lawbreakers—criminals and drug addicts—for punishment came with low risks and high rewards when people saw punishment as a severe sanction that immoral citizens deserved.

BUILDING AN INSTITUTIONAL LEGACY

The story not only tells us about presidents changing their rhetoric but narrates the effect their actions and that of other leading figures had on the institutionalization of get-tough politics and policy. How did these policies shape the evolving coalition within the subsystem? A spike in attention to issues and shifts in the dimensions of political debate can leave institutional legacies that affect ongoing politics around an issue. As attention to an issue increases and then recedes, the institutions built on the original response to the problem continue to shape the policy process long after the original problem that created the institution left the front pages of newspapers.

As Lisa Miller carefully documents, once crime rose on the national agenda in the 1960s, it never really disappeared. Some particular aspect of crime always replaced the one that faded. In the 1960s Congress focused on urban riots, police, and prisons. In the 1970s and 1980s came an interest in drugs. By the 1980s and 1990s the topic of drugs took up almost a third of Congressional hearings on crime-related matters. Over a 15-year period between 1985 and 2000, drug topics comprised about one-third of all congressional hearings on the topic of crime. From 1987 through 1990 drugs comprised nearly half of all hearings on the issue. Miller shows persuasively that this spike, along with attention focused on volitional theories of crime and get-tough policy, bolstered the political power of the "law-and-order" coalition—a network of criminal justice agencies and single-issue groups at the federal, state, and local levels (Miller 2008, p. 56).

First, law enforcement agencies saw their budgets increase substantially. Immediately following World War II, federal spending on justice administration, including spending on all law enforcement, courts, and corrections costs, as well as aid to state and local law enforcement, was less than one-fourth of 1 percent. By the turn of the twenty-first century that number had increased to about $38 billion, or about 2 percent of the entire federal budget (Miller 2008, p. 51). At the federal level, the Federal Bureau of Investigation, the Department of Justice, and a whole host of other criminal justice institutions including the Drug Enforcement Agency and the Bureau of Alcohol, Tobacco, and Firearms, while not created during the 1950s and 1960s, nonetheless saw both their budgets and their power over the congressional agenda grow substantially during this time.

Second, criminal justice agencies had a near monopoly on how the issue was defined. In the second half of the twentieth century, as crime became a major topic of debate, witnesses from criminal justice agencies represented more than one-third of witnesses and appeared at four out of every five congressional crime hearings. Between 1981 and 2002, criminal justice agencies supplied more than two of every five witnesses and appeared in 85 percent of all hearings. As Miller finds, "This represents a plurality of witnesses across crime hearings, and no other type of witness comes close to this dominating presence" (Miller 2008, p. 64).

Law enforcement officials also expanded their presence. Law enforcement witnesses more than doubled over the time of Miller's study. "Prosecutors, law enforcement officers, corrections and probations officers, judges and other criminal justice personnel are not simply routine participants in the policy process," Miller notes, "they form the backbone of national crime policy making Members of Congress, then, are exposed to a bulwark of strong, sustained, and routine witnesses representing the concerns, perspectives, and interests of criminal justice agencies" (Miller 2008, p. 66).

Citizen groups also became better organized. But the organizational firepower did not come from professional associations representing the interests of minorities or organizations representing education, medical, or social-services interests. By the 1990s Miller finds groups representing minorities' interests, for example, constituted only 1.5 percent of all witnesses (Miller 2008, p. 68). Single-issue groups with a large presence in the political process were on both sides of the gun debate. Victims-rights groups such as Women Against Rape, the National Center for Victims of Crime, and Citizens against Physical and Sexual Abuse mobilized pressure against policy makers.

These organizations revealed several trends. The governing agenda became nearly monopolized by actors that amid increasing crime rates, the spread of volition theories of criminal behavior, and the downfall of the rehabilitative model in scientific research, brought a shared law-and-order platform overwhelmingly individualistic, offender focused, and punishment orientated (Miller 2008, p. 80). Arrests, prosecutions, and incapacitation measured their goal achievements. With their high degree of organization, deep resources, and perception among Congress of their superior levels of expertise, these organizations and actors deterred other groups from joining the policy debate. As a result, the process became less about solving social problems and more about trying to get Congress to attend to their particular instrumental needs. It produced "a symbiotic environment in which the groups already at the table can generate problem definitions and policy solutions in ways that reinforce their organizational missions" (Miller 2008, p. 71).

TOUGH ON CRIME COALITION

The dominant actors in the tough on crime coalition included conservatives in Congress, the White House, and in many state legislatures—the latter of which often followed the lead from trends in national political discourse. Prominent groups also included evangelicals, police officers, sheriffs, drug enforcement personnel, corrections officers, probation and parole agents in state and federal agencies, as well as powerful prosecutor organizations. All organized around the idea that morally deficient individuals made rational choices. Policy instruments centered on deterrence and incapacitation.

Previous work on agenda setting shows that when one party or coalition develops a monopoly on understanding an issue to the point that the opposition sees the dominant perspective as a liability, the disadvantaged side will take a position nearer the rivals to avoid blame, even when its new position falls outside its original "zone of acceptable outcomes" (Weaver 2007, p. 236). As Michael Tonry notes, "When issues are defined in polar terms of morality and immorality, or responsibility or irresponsibility, few elected officials are prepared to be found on the wrong pole" (Tonry 2004, p. 41).

This strategy explains the significant rightward shift many Democrats took on crime in the late 1980s and early 1990s. Presidential candidate Bill Clinton assumed this stance; numerous Democratic governors, including Gray Davis of California, and Democratic members of state legislatures also adopted similar positions. Crime is a sensationalist issue. One horrific event that captures the attention of the media can too often shape misperceptions of the overall crime problem. In political debate "objective reality" becomes less important than perceptions that drive policy choices. Bill Clinton saw firsthand what the soft on crime label could do to stall a political career. He blamed his failed 1980 reelection bid for the Arkansas governorship in part on his Republican opponent's ability to paint him as "soft on crime" after a released prisoner (convicted for first-degree murder) under Clinton's watch killed again. Moreover, Clinton witnessed the severe damage the infamous "Willie Horton" ad inflicted on Michael Dukakis, the 1988 Democratic nominee for president. Clinton took lessons from those years and painted himself as a "New Democrat" who would be tough on crime and "end welfare as we know it."

Most leading presidential aspirants adopt a tone and political strategy that go beyond themselves to affect their entire political party. Clinton wanted to lead the path forward for the entire Democratic Party. If Democrats wanted to win the presidency, close contests for governor, and mayoral elections, they needed to take the crime issue away from Republicans by essentially neutralizing it. Clinton believed that a "tough on crime" strategy would secure Democratic victories.

Figure 2.1 presents a summary outline of the membership, belief structure, and policy goals associated with the dominant criminal justice coalition of each broadly defined era.

By the early to mid-1970s, members of the progressive coalition that dominated policy making in the middle part of the century started to lose influence as conservative opinion leaders gained more credibility. Law enforcement agents and organizations, including correctional officers, prison administrators, and probation and parole officers increased their support for more punitive measures. Liberal-leaning criminologists and sociologists became disenchanted with the perceived failures of the rehabilitative model and saw too many opportunities for abuses of state power under indeterminate sentencing. Over time, increasingly active victims' rights organizations and private prison firms joined the struggle to punish violent offenders. Prosecutors gained power as the determinate sentencing model shifted power away from judges. The tough on crime coalition solidified when many Democrats took tougher policy stances by the late 1980s.

In reality, the criminal justice system shows a complex, nuanced picture. Every actor in a policy subsystem will not belong to or share each one of the major policy beliefs within each coalition. A criminologist, for example, may be indifferent to deep policy disputes but nonetheless participate in the process because of a certain skill—for example, statistical modeling of complex crime data (Meltsner 1976). Professionals working in public agencies may see themselves as neutral observers that bring objectivity to the policy process. Yet conservative Republicans and their base supporters in the 1980s clearly identified with the volitional theory of crime, the flawed science of rehabilitation, and the immoral underpinnings associated with crime and drugs. Law enforcement members held similar beliefs but also came on board because of material benefits that ensued with the prison boom. Moderate Democrats, however, shifted their views out of political expediency rather than a deep conviction for volitional theories of crime. Yet not all moderate Democrats equally joined the fight. For instrumental reasons, a moderate Democrat serving in a more conservative legislative district or state probably took a tougher stance on crime than a similarly positioned Democrat (in ideological space) representing a more liberal

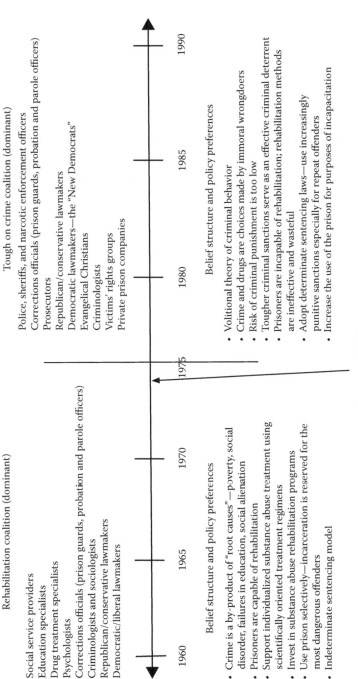

FIGURE 2.1

The dynamic nature of criminal justice coalitions.

jurisdiction. Mona Lynch explains how penal welfarism came first, and received the strongest support in the Northeast and the Midwest, whereas more punitive trends developed in the sunbelt South and Southwest (Lynch 2009). In short, the contextual environment matters.

Chapters 6 through 8 will explore the importance of these subnational forces on the smart on crime reform movement in greater detail. The next chapter outlines some general policy changes that characterized the get-tough period, propelled at the federal level and in many states by the newly dominant tough on crime coalition. The consequences of the coalition's policies, as evidenced by a variety of indicators that came into the policy subsystem over time, serve as crucial contextual backdrop to the smart on crime movement in the 2000s.

3

Crisis and Opportunity in the American Penal System

A public problem reaches the crowded governing agenda only after a sufficient number of policy makers recognize its existence. In his sweeping study of agenda setting and policy change, John Kingdon illustrates the important role that "policy indicators" play in alerting policy makers to signs of trouble (Kingdon 1995). Policy indicators take several forms. A drop in gross domestic product or a spike in the unemployment rate might signal the beginnings of an economic slowdown. Steep increases in families' health insurance costs might point to problems with anticompetitive health insurance markets. A dramatic "focusing event," such as an airline crash, alerts officials to deficiencies in air safety regulations. Advocacy groups constantly employ problem indicators to drive attention to their pet issues while petitioning policy makers to adopt favored policy solutions.

The story of how smart on crime policy reforms rose onto the governing agenda does not match the drama of an airline disaster. Rather, this chapter highlights how a slow but inexorable growth of knowledge about the *consequences* of punitive policies adopted during the tough on crime era presented lawmakers during the 2000s clear signs of an American penal system in crisis. In political systems, mere evidence of a problem does not guarantee that policy makers will take action. Political actors can ignore important public problems when other competing issues and groups constantly vie for attention. Exogenous shocks to a policy subsystem are often required to quicken the pace of policy learning and policy change. This chapter offers initial clues into how economic, social, and institutional forces combined to shape a political environment favorable to the interests of reformers.

TO THE VICTORS GO THE SPOILS

Policy represents the prize for the winners of political struggle. As the tough on crime coalition gained power and influence, no part of the criminal justice system escaped its reach. We can begin with examining changes at the front end of the criminal justice system where dramatic increases in law enforcement officials' drug interdiction efforts exemplified one of the most striking departures from past practice. After Ronald Reagan declared his war on drugs in 1982, the pace of drug arrests grew rapidly, tripling between 1982 and 2007. In 1982, law enforcement officials recorded 676,000 drug arrests. By 2007 the number of drug arrests climbed to 1,800,000 (Mauer and King 2007). Since 1980, law enforcement officials have made more than 31 million arrests for drugs. Few cities escaped the drug war's grip. Despite little or no evidence that the public consumed more drugs, forty of the nation's forty-three largest cities experienced growth in drug arrests from 1980 to 2003. Six states saw drug arrest rates increase more than 500 percent (King 2008).

As the number of drug arrests grew, the likelihood that a person served prison time after an arrest increased as well. According to research conducted by sociologist Bruce Western, the likelihood of a prison sentence upon an arrest for drugs (for crimes such as manufacturing, delivery, sale, and trafficking of controlled substances, in addition to possession or use of a controlled substance) grew sixfold from 1980 to 2001 (Western 2006, p. 44). The same general pattern held for violent and property crimes (Western 2006, p. 50).

Dramatic changes in sentencing laws ensured that people imprisoned served longer terms. State governments restructured sentencing laws that allowed prosecutors to try more juvenile offenders as adults—a process that guaranteed juveniles harsher and more punitive treatment. Lawmakers also increased the number of death penalty–eligible offenses and replaced indeterminate sentencing structures with harsher determinant sentencing laws that abolished parole (or severely narrowed parole officers' discretion) in favor of mandatory minimums for drug, firearms, and a whole variety of violent offenses.

During the mid-1990s, more than thirty states enacted "truth-in-sentencing" laws requiring violent offenders to serve a larger share of their maximum sentence. These laws varied from state to state, but worked largely through eliminating (or severely curtailing) prisoners' abilities to secure early release (Nicholson-Crotty 2004). President Clinton's 1994 Violent Crime Control and Law Enforcement Act helped diffuse truth-in-sentencing laws across the states. The law committed over $9 billion in federal dollars for new prison construction; yet to secure the funds, the law required state officials to enact truth-in-sentencing laws forcing violent offenders to serve no less than 85 percent of their prison sentence (Tonry 1996).

Truth-in-sentencing laws took their most punitive form in "three strikes and you're out" policies adopted by dozens of states and the federal government. Designed to impose tougher punishments on repeat offenders, three-strikes laws took their most extreme form in the western states. Until California voters softened its three-strikes law in 2012, a person convicted of any new felony but who already had a "serious" or violent felony charge on their record, received a "second strike" and a prison sentence double the length normally required by law. A person charged with a third strike received a sentence of twenty-five years to life (California Legislative Analysts Office 2005).

Ostensibly to achieve greater uniformity and consistency in federal sentencing outcomes, Congress passed the Sentencing Reform Act (SRA) in 1984. The law transformed the entire federal sentencing structure. First, the SRA eliminated parole in the federal system. Second, the SRA created an independent U.S. Sentencing Commission that promulgated presumptive federal sentencing guidelines.

When Congress created the Sentencing Commission, several states, including Washington, Oregon, and Minnesota, had already established well-functioning sentencing commissions whose presumptive sentencing guidelines helped reduce unwarranted racial disparities (Tonry 1996). The U.S. Sentencing Commission, however, shared few of these commissions' characteristics. Ronald Reagan's first appointees to the U.S. Sentencing Commission in 1985 saw the imposition of punishment as the primary goal of the new federal sentencing guidelines (Tonry 1996, pp. 12–13). The Commission created a mechanical and complex set of sentencing guidelines by dividing federal crimes into forty-three different categories (whereas most states had ten to twelve categories), but then made no effort like officials in Minnesota did, to tie sentencing decisions to correctional resources. The guidelines required judges to reject nearly all attributes of the indeterminate sentencing model. Judges could only consider a defendant's prior criminal record and the severity of the offense in their sentencing decisions. No other criteria, including a defendant's severe poverty or prior drug, alcohol, or sexual abuse, could inform judges' sentencing decisions. Offenders given sentences of a few months or years in many state systems would face much longer sentences if prosecuted under the federal guidelines (Tonry 1996, p. 15).

Congress also enacted long mandatory minimum sentences for violent, weapons, and drug offenses. The most notorious, the Anti-Drug Abuse Act adopted in 1986, added new mandatory minimums for cocaine trafficking. Congress made key distinctions between powder and crack forms of the drug. The law imposed much stiffer prison sentences on the latter. A person charged with trafficking 500 grams (more than a pound) of powder cocaine faced the same mandatory minimum five-year sentence as someone charged with 5 grams (less than one-fifth of an ounce) of crack cocaine. Congress intensified the disparity in punishments two years later when it passed the Omnibus Anti-Drug Abuse Act. The Act levied a five-year minimum prison sentence on anyone charged with possession of 5 grams of crack cocaine, even first-time offenders with no intent to sell.

After the implementation of the sentencing guidelines, the average length of federal sentences, when considering all offense types, more than doubled (Lynch 2012). The average drug trafficking sentence nearly tripled, increasing from thirty months to about eighty months in the first seven years of implementation (Lynch 2012). Today, about 50 percent of federal prisoners are serving time for nonviolent drug charges. At the state level, a report conducted by the Pew Center on the States reveals the aggregate effect of sentencing changes in the get-tough era. The report found that the average length of stay for offenders released in 2009 increased 36 percent from 1990, to a term of nearly three years. Several states were well above the average; Florida saw its length of stay increase 166 percent, Virginia 91 percent, North Carolina 86 percent, Oklahoma 83 percent, and Michigan 79 percent. Criminal sentences lengthened across all major categories of criminal offenses. Length of stay for violent crimes grew an average of 37 percent. Stays for drug offenses increased 36 percent; property crimes grew by 24 percent (1.8 years to 2.3 years) (Pew Center on the States 2012a).

One common misperception that people have of the American penal system is that most inmates serve very long sentences. Traditionally, however, a large share of people enter prison only to leave relatively quickly. The number of prisoners serving short sentences, however, has declined in recent decades. This trend served as an important factor behind the slow but inexorable increase in the average length of stay. With the advent of mandatory sentencing, the number of people serving short sentences of six months or fewer decreased from about 26 percent of the prison population in 1990 to about 14 percent by 2005 (Clear 2010). Moreover, far more prisoners did real hard time. Life sentences without the possibility of parole (LWOPs) tripled between 1992 and 2008. By 2008, 41,000 prisoners were serving LWOPs, or about 29 percent of the 141,000 prisoners serving life sentences (Nellis and King 2009).

More than imposing stringent criminal sentences and increasing time served, the tough on crime coalition transformed prison culture. The "no frills" prison movement, a euphemism for policy makers gutting prison rehabilitative programs and turning prisons into what Jonathan Simon calls "waste management systems," grew popular in the 1990s (Simon 2007, p. 142). Library amenities, counseling services, and "yard" or exercise time were removed from prisons or curtailed. Texas and Arizona were the first states to adopt policies that charged prisoners for medical treatment, electricity, and exorbitant rates for collect telephone calls to family and loved ones (Gipson and Pierce 1996). The first "supermax" prison, chiefly designed to segregate prisoners in some of the most austere conditions imaginable, first opened in Arizona before quickly spreading to other states—particularly western states—and the federal penal system.

Policy changes to probation and parole made it more difficult for people with criminal records to exit the system. The parole system, for example, moved from its original goal of helping released offenders transition back into their communities to a system focused exclusively on surveillance (Petersilia 2003). This contributed to a high rate of recidivism as parolees were returned to prison in large numbers because of technical violations (Petersilia 2003). Parole practices in many jurisdictions became uprooted so dramatically that nationally, parole violators comprised 35 percent of state prison admissions by 1999, up from 17 percent in 1980 (Travis 2005, p. 49). Congress and many states governments enacted laws that Jeremy Travis, the former head of the National Institute of Justice, calls "invisible punishments" (Travis 2002, pp. 15–36; Travis 2005). These are civil penalties imposed outside the traditional criminal sentencing process that strip criminal offenders of their rights to many federally funded health and welfare benefits such as food stamps, public housing, and federal education assistance. Other invisible punishments restrict a person's right to become an adoptive or foster parent, to vote, or obtain a driver's license. Collectively, invisible punishments contribute to offenders' second class status because they restrict access to social programs, limit job opportunities, and weaken ties to civic and social life (Rubinstein and Mukamal 2002, pp. 37–49; Travis 2005).

PROBLEMS ON THE GROUND: CONSEQUENCES OF THE TOUGH ON CRIME REGIME

More arrests, longer prison terms, and high rates of parole and probation revocations, not surprisingly, incarcerated more Americans over time. Figure 3.1 illustrates the growth in the U.S. prison and jail population from 1980 to 2009. As shown, the adult correction population in jail or prison increased fourfold from approximately 500,000 in 1980 to 2.3 million by 2009.

Prisoner numbers swelled at every level of government. The federal prison population increased from fewer than 25,000 in 1980 to 209,000 in 2009. State prisoners increased from 305,000 to nearly 1.4 million. Inmates in local jails grew from 182,000 to 767,000.*

Growth in the custodial population was not confined to the prison system. Community supervision represents the largest share of the custodial population (Kleiman 2009). Probation and parole systems now supervise twice as many people as prisons.

As Figure 3.2 illustrates, the number of probationers in the United States, shown on the left-side axis, increased from just over 1 million in 1980 to more than 4 million in 2009. The number of parolees, measured on the right axis, increased from 220,000 in 1980 to more than 820,000 by 2009. During the first term of the Reagan administration, according to a report by the Pew Center on the States, community corrections supervised one in every seventy-seven adults in America. By 2008, the rate had climbed to one in thirty-one, or 3.2 percent of all adults (Pew Center on the States 2009).

The realities that flowed from these statistics—the consequences of the regime—placed extraordinary pressure on criminal justice officials. Judges and local court officials confronted a flood of misdemeanor and drug offense cases that placed enormous strain on the system. Probation and parole caseloads grew so large that officers could impose sporadic sanctions. When they did impose sanctions, they were too often overly severe. The community corrections system in many jurisdictions became a mere feeder system for prisons and jails (Clear 2010).

---

* University of Albany, Hindelang Criminal Justice Research Center, *Sourcebook of Criminal Justice Statistics*, Table 6.1.2011.

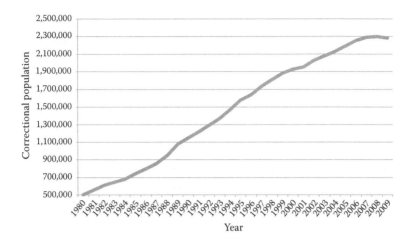

FIGURE 3.1
Growth in U.S. adult correctional population, 1980–2009. (From University of Albany, Hindelang Criminal Justice Research Center, *Sourcebook of Criminal Justice Statistics*, Table 6.1.2011.)

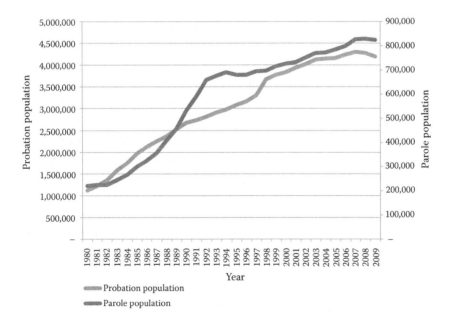

FIGURE 3.2
Probation and parole population, 1980–2009. (From University of Albany, Hindelang Criminal Justice Research Center, *Sourcebook of Criminal Justice Statistics*, Table 6.1.2011.)

Many prisons became overcrowded. The federal prison system operated 70 percent beyond its designed capacity by the late 1980s. Overcrowding eased in the 1990s after more federal prisons were built; however, by the early 2000s, many prisons remained 30 to 40 percent over their designed capacity (James 2013). In state prison systems, overcrowded conditions placed tremendous burdens on correctional staff. More prisoners led to higher inmate-to-guard ratios. Prisons are twenty-four-hour-a-day operations; the growth in the prison population meant (relatively fewer) prison officials had more people to feed, clothe, and house. Despite popular images of prisons full of nonviolent drug offenders, 53 percent of state prisoners were serving time for violent offenses—an increase from 1990.* More violent offenders, combined with overcrowded conditions, compounded threats of violence and persuaded many correctional officers to view risk management as their primary duty on the job.

Inmates' complex social characteristics and disorders further complicated work inside prisons. Correctional guards controlled larger inmate populations who were sicklier, less educated, and with greater substance abuse problems than the general population (Petersilia 2003). In the prison environment, tattooing, piercing, and unprotected sex have long been common; however, communicable diseases like hepatitis C, a lethal blood-borne disease, if left untreated, spread more quickly in crowded environments (Pew Center on the States 2008).

Federal and state prison officials faced new challenges in handling the growing number of aging prisoners—a by-product of long sentences that incarcerated offenders long past their most crime-prone years. Between 1992 and 2001, the number of state and federal inmates aged fifty or older grew 173 percent (Anno et al. 2004). Hearing and visual impairments, early onset of chronic disease, incontinence, and depression exemplify just some of the daily health challenges confronting correctional staff supervising an aging inmate population (Pew Center on the States 2008). These ailments help explain why the cost of caring for an older inmate averaged $70,000 per year by the mid-2000s—two to three times the cost for a younger inmate (Anno et al. 2004).

Politicians first elected in the 2000s faced a challenge their predecessors happily missed or simply ignored: what to do about increasing correctional system costs. State governments' corrections-related expenditures

---

* University of Albany, Hindelang Criminal Justice Research Center, *Sourcebook of Criminal Justice Statistics*, 2010, Table 6.0001.

increased 315 percent between 1987 and 2007, representing the fastest growing portion of states' general fund budgets except for Medicaid (Pew Center on the States 2008). In the federal system, per capita costs increased from $19,571 in 2000 to $26,000 in 2011 (James 2013). Total expenditures for the Bureau of Prisons (including costs for prison operations and capital budgets for new construction, repair, and modernization of facilities) increased from $330 million in 1980 to $6.6 billion in 2012. The Bureau of Prisons captured a growing share of the Department of Justice's (DOJ's) annual discretionary budget, moving from 15 percent in 1980 to 23 percent in 2010 (James 2013). An Urban Institute report estimated that even if the federal incarceration rate remains steady, the Bureau of Prison's share of the DOJ's budget would top 30 percent by 2020 (Mallik-Kane et al. 2012).

THE PENAL SYSTEM AND INEQUALITY

Policies of the tough on crime era had a devastating effect on blacks and Latinos (Pettit and Western 2004). Racial and ethnic minorities became overrepresented in all aspects of the penal system, comprising a disproportionate share of arrestees, inmates, probationers, and parolees (Pew Center on the States 2008). Whites' incarceration rate increased 6 percent between 1980 and 2000. The rate of incarceration for African American men—the most overrepresented racial subgroup in the penal system—increased twenty-sixfold (Muwakkil 2005). In 2008, the rate of incarceration for black men was six times the rate of white men (U.S. Department of Justice 2009). For the most economically marginalized minorities, the statistics present an even more distressing picture. Among blacks aged eighteen to thirty-four who failed to earn a high school diploma, one in three are now incarcerated (Tierney 2012).

As the carceral system grew, it developed into an instrument of social and economic exclusion. Individuals with a prison record experienced lower earning capacities, suffered from more physical and mental health ailments and destabilized family structures (Clear et al. 2001; Geller et al. 2006; Rose and Clear 1998). Felon disenfranchisement laws stripped felons of the most fundamental form of political expression in a democratic society—the right to vote (McCloud et al. 2003). This was most acutely felt in the African American community. Eight percent of the black voting-age population is now disenfranchised because of a felony conviction (Manza and Uggen 2006). Felon disenfranchisement laws combined with the compounding toll of the prison boom have reshaped the composition of the American electorate and the relationship between the people and the government. Individuals with greater contact with criminal justice officials and institutions become less likely to join civic groups, participate in elections, and have less trust in government (Weaver and Lerman 2010). The children of incarcerated parents represent perhaps the tough on crime era's greatest collateral damage. Between 1991 and 2007, the number of children with an incarcerated parent increased 80 percent (U.S. Department of Justice 2010). The number of children with a mother in prison grew 131 percent. Nationally, about one in forty children now have a parent in prison. Among black children, the number equals one in fifteen (Tierney 2012). Because these social patterns concentrate in poor communities of color, they have eroded social bonds and reduced minorities' chances of upward social mobility across generations.

DIMINISHING MARGINAL RETURNS OF MASS INCARCERATION

Crime rates in America have decreased significantly since the early 1990s. In fact crime in many American cities has reached depths not seen since the 1960s. New York City represents just one metropolis much safer today than two or three decades ago (Zimring 2008). America's greater reliance on the prison undoubtedly bears some credit for the great crime decline. The most careful studies attribute 10 and 25 percent of the overall reduction in crime to the prison boom—a relatively modest reduction considering the significant social and economic costs of the tough on crime era (Kleiman 2009). The law of diminishing marginal returns explains part of the prison boom's low rate of return. University of Chicago economist Steve Leavitt, who once strongly endorsed the benefits of incapacitation, now believes policy makers have gone too far.

> We know that harsher punishments lead to less crime, but we also know that the millionth prisoner we lock up is a lot less dangerous to society than the first guy we lock up. In the mid-1990s I concluded that the social benefits approximately equaled the costs of incarceration. Today, my guess

is that the costs outweigh the benefits at the margins. I think we should be shrinking the prison population by at least one-third. (Tierney 2012)

Even John DiIulio, who introduced the superpredator to the American crime lexicon, came to believe by the late 1990s that incarcerating more people was a mistake. In a *Wall Street Journal* article, DiIulio said the nation had "maxed out" the public safety value of incarceration. With close to two million people behind bars, "the value of imprisonment is a portrait in the law of rapidly diminishing returns" (DiIulio 1999).

CONDITIONS FACILITATING THE SEARCH FOR ALTERNATIVES AND POLICY LEARNING

Signs of the burgeoning corrections crisis seeped into the political system slowly over time. Yet policy makers routinely ignored signs of trouble or effectively doubled down on punitive policy approaches after the criminal justice policy debate remained grounded in dimensions favorable to the tough on crime coalition. Growing evidence of a problem rarely guarantees new political coalitions will form or that policy learning occurs within or across coalitions. Exogenous shocks and social changes emanating from outside elite circles of a policy subsystem can fracture political coalitions and cause policy makers to begin a search for new directions in policy. The next section examines these forces, beginning with the role of the economy.

ECONOMIC CRISIS

A 2009 *New York Times* article published under the headline "To Cut Costs, States Relax Prison Policies," exemplifies a popular narrative in the media about the causes behind recent criminal justice reforms. The article began this way:

> For nearly three decades, most states have dealt with lawbreakers in two ways: lock them up for longer periods, and build more prisons to hold them. Now many governments, out of money and buried under mounting prison costs, are reversing those policies and practices. (Steinhauer 2009)

This "economic thesis" unfolds in three interrelated parts. The first component recognizes the high cost of building and operating prisons. The second points to the impact of the Great Recession on the growth in state budget deficits. The third portrays policy makers as rational cost cutters; confronted with the twin challenges of expensive prisons and growing budget deficits, state officials quickly turned to less punitive and less expensive policy alternatives.

The prison is an expensive crime-fighting instrument. This has been true both now and in the past. If recent policy reforms and the incarceration rate's five-year decline merely represent by-products of a bad economy and the pragmatic decisions of cost-conscious policy makers, then similar patterns should be evident during economic recessions of the 1980s and 1990s.

From the unofficial start to the tough on crime period in 1980, to the Great Recession in 2007, the American economy fell into recession three times. Yet during each of these recessions, the U.S. prisoner population *increased* not decreased. During the 1981 to 1982 recession when the unemployment rate topped 10 percent, the prison population grew from approximately 360,000 to 402,000.* A milder recession ten years later saw the prison population grow from 792,000 to 850,000. During the 2001 to 2002 recession, which followed the September 11 terrorist attacks, the population increased from 1,330,000 to 1,367,000 (see footnote).

Advocates of the economic thesis remain stuck answering the question of why policy changed in the midst of the latest economic calamity but failed to change in previous recessionary years. The *severity* of the recent economic downturn—what many economists agree is the worst since the Great Depression—offers one possible answer. Despite the federal government's drastic monetary and fiscal stimulus efforts in 2009, severe cutbacks in consumer spending and cuts to state and local government budgets slowed economic growth and reduced demand for workers. The Great Recession pushed the official national unemployment rate to 10 percent; over 700,000 public sector workers lost their jobs. The number of long-term unemployed (the official statistic measures people out of work for more than twenty-seven weeks) more than tripled (Bureau of Labor Statistics 2012). Despite the slow pace of economic recovery and the deep level of economic pain the Great Recession levied on lower and middle

---

* University of Albany, Hindelang Criminal Justice Research Center, *Sourcebook of Criminal Justice Statistics*, Table 6.1.2011.

class Americans, if we examine incarceration trends dating back to the Great Depression, the *economic severity* argument looks less persuasive. The U.S. imprisonment rate increased from a rate of 98 per 100,000 in 1930 to 125 per 100,000 by 1940 (U.S. Department of Justice 1986).

THE CONTEMPORARY PRISON SYSTEM IS A DIFFERENT BEAST

The central issue is not that the economy plays an insignificant role in shaping the smart on crime movement, but rather analysts' predilections for viewing the economic recession as a singular, all-important force. Indeed, the economic crises during the 2000s mattered because they helped facilitate policy learning and reshaped political coalitions within the criminal justice policy subsystem. This argument becomes more persuasive after considering the broader policy and institutional context in which the economic crises occurred.

The size and complexity of America's twenty-first century penal system are far greater than the system circa 1980. For prison officials, policy makers, and communities across America, the nearly 1.5 million people in prison in 2008—the year numbers peaked—presented far more challenges than the roughly 300,000 prisoners did in 1980. The 830,000 people on parole, or the nearly 4.2 million on probation, proved far more difficult to handle than the 220,000 or 1.1 million people with the same disposition in 1980. Budget rules found in most state constitutions only added to the challenge. By states' constitutional designs, state lawmakers must pass balanced budgets, meaning officials cannot borrow money to help fill budget gaps or pay for needed services. When the post-9/11 recession emerged, followed by the far more damaging Great Recession, pressure intensified on state lawmakers to "do something" about the corrections crisis. Lawmakers, however, quickly found their choices severely constrained by stringent budgetary rules. They could not simply borrow and spend their way out of the problem. Few elected officials were willing to make further cuts to popular programs to fortify troubled corrections departments. For fiscal conservatives, the economic collapse helped them "rediscover" the prison issue and caused them to reevaluate their punitive positions. Chapter 7 will explore this process in greater detail using a case study of prison reform in Ohio.

EXAMINING CHANGES IN PUBLIC ATTITUDES ON CRIME AND PUNISHMENT

Changes in public attitudes toward punitive crime policy and changes in the crime rate itself are two additional forces that deserve consideration. In a majoritarian model of democracy, lawmakers are portrayed as delegates of the people who adopt policies that match popular public sentiments. Political science researchers have found strong relationships between public opinion and government policy outputs (Erikson et al. 1993). Indeed, in the crime policy arena, lawmakers routinely explained their tough on crime votes as their response to strong public demand for such policies (Beckett 1997; Cullen et al. 1985). If the public felt anxious about increasing crime rates or if an especially heinous crime captured the media's attention, politicians sought electoral benefits through tough on crime political posturing (Davey 1999; Tonry 1999; Warr 1995).

Crime rates in America, as discussed earlier, are declining. We might expect changes in the crime environment to affect public opinion in several ways—each with the potential to alter how elected officials view crime and the political and policy strategies they pursue. The first expectation is that Americans are now less fearful of crime. If true, crime should hold less political potency when politicians use crime as a political wedge issue. Similarly, we might expect the public to see crime as a less important problem relative to other more pressing concerns. A decline in the saliency of the crime issue may provide lawmakers political "space" to pursue alternative, less punitive policy approaches. Third, we might expect the public to hold less punitive attitudes on criminal punishment and criminal sentencing. Politicians may be more apt to pursue prison reform if their efforts are met with public support or, at worst, public indifference.

FEAR OF CRIME

Since 2001 the Gallup organization has routinely asked Americans how much "they personally worry about crime and violence." In a March 2001 survey, 62 percent of respondents worried about crime and violence a

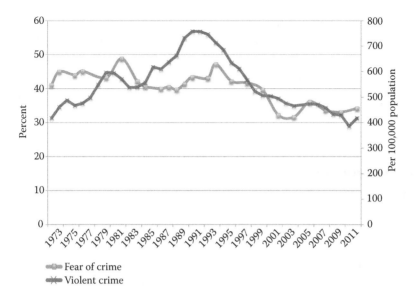

FIGURE 3.3
Americans' fear of crime, 1973–2012. (From Tom W. Smith, Peter V. Marsden, Michael
Hout, and Jibum Kim, *General Social Surveys*, 1972–2012 [machine-readable data file].
Principal Investigator, Tom W. Smith; co-principal investigators, Peter V. Marsden and
Michael Hout, NORC ed. Chicago: National Opinion Research Center, producer, 2005;
Storrs, CT: The Roper Center for Public Opinion Research, University of Connecticut.)

"great deal." By March 2014, this number had declined 23 to 39 percent.*
The National Opinion Research Center's General Social Survey has measured Americans' fear of crime dating back to the 1970s. Figure 3.3 examines the percentage of Americans who answered "yes" to the question, "Is
there an area, right around here—that is within a mile, where you would
be afraid to walk alone at night?," between 1973 and 2012.

Figure 3.3 also includes a measure of the U.S. violent crime rate to
assess how Americans' fear levels corresponded with changes in crime.†
Measured on the left-side axis, the percentage of Americans who reported
fearing crime reached a peak in 1982 when nearly 49 percent of survey
respondents answered "yes" to questions about feeling unsafe. Another
uptick occurred in 1994 when 47 percent of respondents reported a fear of
crime. Americans' fear levels tracked closely with the violent crime rate,

---

* Gallup Poll, March 6–9, 2014; March 5–7, 2001. Available at http://www.gallup.com/poll/1603
/crime.aspx.
† Violent crime data are drawn from the FBI's Uniform Crime Reporting Index. Violent crimes
include murder, forcible rape, robbery, and aggravated assault. Available at http://www.fbi.gov
/about-us/cjis/ucr/ucr.

although the relationship between the two was far from a perfect correlation. Violent crime, measured on the right-side axis, peaked in 1991 and declined in every subsequent year through 2012. Similarly, Americans' fear of crime dropped throughout the late 1990s and by 2002 had dropped 15 percentage points from 1994. Fear levels remained consistently lower through 2012.

SALIENCY OF CRIME

Have crime and law enforcement issues become less important to the public over time? We can answer this question using the help of two data sources. Gallup's "most important problem" (MIP) question asks survey respondents to offer what they believe is the most important problem facing the country.* Not surprisingly, Americans' responses have varied widely over time. Fortunately, researchers with the *Policy Agendas Project* have coded Americans' responses to Gallup's "most important problem" question into one of twenty-three major policy topic categories allowing researchers to gauge general trends across time. Topic categories include macroeconomic issues, education, the environment, and housing and community development, in addition to many others.† I place focus on the "law, crime, and family issues" policy category. Survey respondents who mentioned prisons, guns, family violence, drug trafficking and national drug control strategy, child abuse, or financial assistance to state and local law enforcement as "most important problems" facing the country are included in this category.

Figure 3.4 tracks change in the law, crime, and family issues policy category between 1972 and 2012. The figure presents the aggregate percentage of responses in this category. For example, a value of 3.4 in 1989 indicates that 3.4 percent of responses to the Gallup's most important problem question, aggregated across that year, mentioned a problem coded under the law, crime,

---

* Specifically, Gallup asks, "What Do You Think Is the Most Important Problem Facing the Country Today?" Available at http://www.gallup.com/poll/1675/most-important-problem.aspx.
† Visit the Policy Agendas Project website for a complete list of topic codes. Available at http://policyagendas.org/page/datasets-codebooks#codebook. The data used here were originally collected by Frank R. Baumgartner and Bryan D. Jones, with the support of National Science Foundation grant numbers SBR 9320922 and 0111611, and were distributed through the Department of Government at the University of Texas at Austin. Neither NSF nor the original collectors of the data bear any responsibility for the analysis reported here.

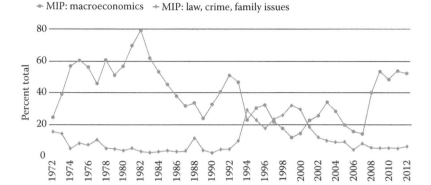

FIGURE 3.4
Political saliency of law, crime, and family issues, 1972–2012.

and family issues policy topic category.* For the purpose of comparison, I also present the percentage of responses that mentioned "macroeconomic issues." Public concern about economic growth, recession effects on state and local governments, unemployment, inflation, tax policy, the national budget and national debt, and industrial policy are issues included in this category.

Relative to macroeconomic concerns, the public expressed modest concern for crime-related issues during the 1980s. Only in 1988 did mentions of law, crime, and family issues climb above 10 percent. Macroeconomic issues dwarfed crime-related issues in most every year. During the 1981 to 1982 economic recession, for example, macroeconomic issues comprised nearly 80 percent of all responses to the most important problem question. A strong economy in the 1990s led to a significant decline in the macroeconomic concerns but then rebounded with the onset of the Great Recession. Crime became a more salient concern in the 1990s. In 1994, the year President Clinton's crime bill was debated and passed in Congress, crime-related issues were mentioned in 28.2 percent of all responses and actually surpassed macroeconomic concerns that year. Crime-related mentions remained at an elevated level through the 1990s. The saliency of crime-related issues dropped considerably, however, in the 2000s. They never rose above 10 percent of responses from 2003 to 2012, and between 2008 and 2011 they comprised less than 5 percent of responses.

---

* As reported in the Policy Agendas Codebook, these figures had to be normalized to account for the fact that some interviewers allowed respondents to give multiple answers to the most important problem question. See http://policyagendas.org/page/datasets-codebooks#codebook, for a more detailed description of the methods used.

We can also consider whether the public now holds less punitive attitudes on criminal sentencing. Tracking public opinion on specific policy issues over a decade or more requires pollsters to have asked the same (or similar) question(s) at regular time intervals. Many surveys, of course, do not ask questions about criminal justice issues. If they do, pollsters often field them irregularly. The General Social Survey offers a "Courts" question fielded at regular intervals dating back to 1972. While not perfect, the variable offers researchers a generalized measure of American's attitudes toward criminal punishment. Specifically, the question asks, "In general do you think the courts in this area deal too harshly or not harshly enough with criminals?" Response categories included (3) "not harsh enough," (2) "about right," and (1) "too harsh."

Generalized questions like this risk measuring people's "top of the head considerations," and researchers have criticized the "Courts" variable and others like it for artificially inflating public support for punitive policy.* These are valid criticisms. Research shows the public holds complex attitudes on criminal punishment. Americans support tough retributive policies—especially for violent criminals—but also support rehabilitation (Roberts and Stalans 1997). People's attitudes become more nuanced when they learn more about a criminal offender or the type of crime in question. For example, when people understand an offender's criminal behavior to be a product of a substance abuse problem or a disadvantaged upbringing, support for lengthy punishment declines (Cullen et al. 2000).

A priori, however, there is no reason to expect respondents processed the "Courts" question wording differently over time. Hence, Figure 3.5 traces public responses to the courts question between 1972 and 2012. My greatest interest lies in examining change in the percentage of respondents who expressed the view that courts are "not harsh enough" given that the indicator serves as a rough proxy for the public's appetite for increasingly punitive crime policies. The violent crime rate and the percentage of respondents who answered "too harsh" are included as well.

As shown, from the late 1970s through the early 1990s, 85 to 90 percent of the public consistently expressed the opinion that criminal sentencing was "not harsh enough." In 1994, 89 percent of the public supported harsher punishment for criminals. Over the next eighteen years, however, public support for harsher punishment steadily declined and again tracked

---

* For a review of people's "top-of-the-head" considerations, see Zaller and Feldman (1992) and Cullen et al. (2000).

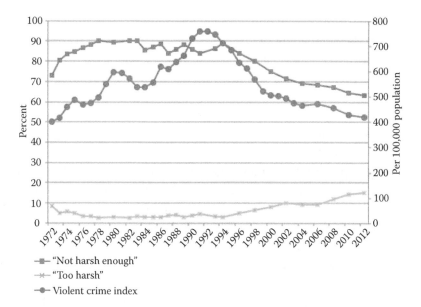

FIGURE 3.5

Public opinion on punitive criminal sentencing, 1972–2012. (From Tom W. Smith, Peter V. Marsden, Michael Haut, and Jibum Kim, *General Social Surveys*, 1972–2012 [machine-readable data file]. Principal Investigator, Tom W. Smith; co-principal investigators, Peter V. Marsden and Michael Hout, NORC ed. Chicago: National Opinion Research Center, producer, 2005; Storrs, CT: The Roper Center for Public Opinion Research, University of Connecticut.)

closely with the decline in the violent crime rate. By 2012, public support for harsher punishment had decreased nearly 27 percentage points from their peak levels in 1978.

The public opinion and crime data all point in the same general direction. As crime rates have declined, Americans' fear of crime, the political saliency of the crime issue, and Americans' support for punitive criminal justice policies have all decreased. We must be cautious in our interpretations of causation. Research finds little evidence that public opinion shapes crime policy in the same manner a majoritarian model of democracy predicts. Mass opinion seems to react to elite discourse on crime rather than the reverse. Katherine Beckett, for example, found that increased media attention and politicians' "get tough" speeches on crime and drugs in the 1970s and 1980s predated the public's elevated fears about crime and support for punitive policy (Beckett 1997). In a study of public opinion and capital punishment, Barbara Norrander finds greater public support for capital punishment in states with preexisting capital punishment laws. Capital punishment policy and public opinion are mutually reinforcing forces (Norrander 2000).

As we turn in the next chapter to examine the politics of prison reform in specific policy debates and institutional contexts, beginning with the prisoner reentry movement and the Second Chance Act, it will become clear that the rise of the smart on crime coalition and the shift toward smarter, less punitive criminal justice policy is a process driven and shaped by policy elites. Bureaucratic experts, practitioners, elected officials, and interest groups with deep knowledge of the issues and a big stake in policy outcomes are the primary instigators of change. Yet major indicators of public opinion on crime and punishment all point to a decidedly different political environment in the 2000s. Policy makers now have space to consider less punitive alternatives knowing that public outrage will not meet every misstep along the way. For lawmakers willing to take a chance on prison reform, public opinion can serve as a positive reinforcement. If reform-minded officials turn a concerned eye to public opinion, what they will find, in most jurisdictions, is a public supportive of less punishment or, at worst, a public that judges reform with a collective shrug.

Section II

The Smart on Crime Movement in National Politics

4

Prisoner Reentry and the Politics of the Second Chance Act

The congressional agenda is a crowded place. Organized interest groups and issues constantly compete for time and scarce resources. It was no small achievement then in the late 1990s when Congress and officials in the Department of Justice (DOJ) became focused on the tens of thousands of prisoners who were returning to their communities each year.

The emergence of the prisoner reentry movement begins our first detailed examination of smart on crime politics at the national level. The prisoner reentry movement, as we will document ahead, culminated with the passage of the historic Second Chance Act (SCA) in 2008. The SCA marked the federal government's first major effort to confront the challenges of prisoner recidivism and the growing number of prisoners behind bars since the beginning of the get-tough era. The SCA authorized more than $300 million in new investments in prisoner reentry related programs, services, and research.* State and local governments and nonprofit organizations, including faith-based organizations, could compete for federal grant money to improve housing, education, job, and mentorship programs for returning prisoners. The SCA sought to establish specialized "reentry" courts and facilitate new research on improving evidence-based risk assessment tools. The SCA offered incentive grants to expand both in-prison and community-based drug and alcohol treatment programs, and counseling services for incarcerated parents with minor children. State, local, and tribal governments were required to develop reentry plans with measurable performance outcomes (O'Hear 2007). To assist in the future

---

* It is important to make a distinction between authorization and allocation. If Congress authorizes spending, it does not guarantee Congress will fund programs to the authorized level. In many cases, in all areas of policy, funding is below what is authorized. The actual dollar amount allocated is decided in the yearly budget process.

development of evidenced-based reentry policies, the SCA established a National Offender Reentry Resource Center that now disseminates "best practices" research and training to federal, state, and local government officials across the country.

The SCA was, and continues to be, an important if not imperfect cog in the federal government's effort to reduce recidivism and, over the long run, chip away at the gargantuan size of the U.S. custodial population. Yet for our purpose, the SCA's greatest offering is in what it teaches us about the changing politics of crime and how a newly emergent smart on crime coalition enacted a policy nearly unthinkable during the height of the get-tough period. The SCA, and the nearly decade-long debate that preceded it, offers a front-row view of the smart on crime coalition emerging in national politics after federal officials answered cries for help from county and state correctional officials. Moreover, by placing reentry policy at the center of our analysis, we see more clearly how political institutions, the economy, and developments in policy research mattered, how and why policy learning occurred, and the strategic arguments made by politicians and bureaucratic experts along the way.

PRESSURE FROM THE BOTTOM UP

In the late 1990s Reginald Wilkinson, the director of the Ohio Department of Rehabilitation and Corrections (ODRC), had a growing problem on his hands. The Ohio correctional system had become the state's de facto mental health ward. Almost a third of its prisoners suffered from mental illness. Wilkinson was hardly alone. In his role as president of the Association of State Correctional Administrators (ASCA), a national organization representing the interests of correctional administrators, Wilkinson heard similar stories from colleagues across the country. Their prisons and jails were filling fast. Offenders increasingly entered prison with an array of substance abuse problems and physical and mental health disorders that correctional officials felt ill equipped to handle on a mass scale.

The growing set of problems in Ohio and elsewhere had important public safety implications. With many correctional systems lacking a detailed prisoner release plan except for offering inmates $50 gate money and a bus ticket, many inmates, without sufficient services when they returned to their communities, quickly committed new crimes.

By the late 1990s correctional officials on the front lines began to mobilize. Their mobilization efforts differed from correctional officials' standard routine in the 1980s when overcrowded conditions were met with administrators calling for more resources and more prisons. This time, however, correctional officials were not chiefly interested in securing more resources nor did they call for more prisons. Instead, they mobilized around a shared recognition that the current model was unsustainable. Recalling his time as president of the ASCA, Reginald Wilkinson noted, "There was an awful lot of discussion through the American Correctional Association and the Association of State Correctional Administrators who were all thinking that we need to create a new infrastructure—a new philosophy" (Wilkinson 2010). Prison officials were not the only ones mobilized. Groups representing the interests of parole and probation officials, including the Adult Probation and Parole Authority, the International Association of Parole Authorities, and the International Corrections and Prisons Association, also joined the conversations (Wilkinson 2010).

CONCEPTUALIZING PRISONER REENTRY

The chatter coming up from the states and counties eventually reached the top levels of the Justice Department. During the mid-1990s DOJ officials seemed at least aware of problems brewing at the subnational level; however, in an era when the costs and complexities of mass incarceration were largely an afterthought, officials lacked comprehensive information. This began to change in the spring of 1999 when Attorney General Janet Reno asked Jeremy Travis, the Director of the National Institute of Justice (NIJ), and Laurie Robinson, the Assistant Attorney General for Justice Programs, a seemingly straightforward question: "What are we doing about all the people coming out of prison?" In his response Travis said that they "didn't know." Reno told Travis and Robinson to report back in two weeks with more information. As Travis recalled,

> There was very little attention paid to that question. It's remarkable in hindsight that the nation had gone through such a remarkable buildup in the prison population without paying attention to that question, without asking what's the consequence of many more people in prison and out of prison for institutions and societal realities on the outside. (Travis 2011)

Travis convened staff within the DOJ to help answer the Attorney General's question. He first turned to statisticians with the Bureau of Justice Statistics (BJS) to help gain a sense of how many prisoners were actually returned to their communities each year. The number, it turned out, was 585,000. Upon hearing the news, Travis recalls that DOJ staff sort of "fell off their chairs" (Travis 2011). A few more data runs by BJS statisticians indicated that about 80 percent of prisoners nationwide were released on parole, but an additional 20 percent were released without any supervision at all. With these numbers in hand, Travis acknowledged early in DOJ deliberations that what they were talking about was not simply about parole. In one of the first DOJ meetings on the topic, Travis put forward the term "reentry" as a way to express the idea of prisoners transitioning back into their communities after their release from prison and jail. This proved to be a crucial early decision. "The framing of the issue worked on a couple levels," Travis said (Travis 2011). "Yes, there is an issue that we haven't paid attention to. And it's big. And we haven't quantified it. And it wasn't about parole and how we supervise. It wasn't just the 80 percent. The word reentry then became something of a shorthand term" (Travis 2011).

Around the same time of Reno's inquiry, Jeremy Travis along with Larry Meachum, the Director of the Corrections Program Office, had been coincidently organizing executive-session-style meetings on the topic of sentencing and corrections. First developed by researchers at the Kennedy School of Government, executive-style sessions assemble leading scholars and practitioners, typically two to three times a year over several years, to discuss the state of a problem or policy area. Afterward, session participants often write position papers reflecting on what they learned.

Meachum and Travis assembled some of the country's leading thinkers on sentencing and corrections policy. Michael Tonry, a law professor at the University of Minnesota, suggested to Travis that he author a paper. The end result was a paper titled, "But They All Come Back: Rethinking Prisoner Reentry," published by the NIJ (Travis 2000). Informed by deliberations during the executive sessions and the internal discussions about reentry within the DOJ, Travis's paper expounded the prisoner reentry concept and introduced an innovative proposal for "reentry courts"— specialized problem-solving courts in the same mold as drug courts—to assist in the management of reentry efforts. Over time the framing of the issue became more focused. "To help people understand the frame of the policy discussion we were having," Travis recalled, DOJ officials focused on what they saw as three crucial elements of reentry. The first two elements focused on what reentry was not. Reentry was not a program nor was it a form of supervision. "It's not like we do reentry," Travis said. "It's a personal experience of leaving the state of incarceration." The third element offered a simple but memorable aphorism: "reentry is not an option." Except for inmates who die in prison, the rest come home (Travis 2011). Travis called this the "iron law of incarceration."

Furthermore, DOJ officials worked hard to separate their inquiry from the long-running debate about the purpose of punishment or drug treatment interventions inside prison. Travis argues that distinguishing reentry from rehabilitation brought political and tactical advantages.

> It allowed us to focus on the inevitable consequence of incarceration and put aside whatever ideological differences there might be in a room or at conference about what people go to prison, why we punish, how long they go—all the debates. I can then walk into a room and say we have people of different ideological persuasions in this room, but we're talking about the inevitable consequences of our decision as a society to put people in prison … it became pragmatic very quickly; very results oriented; very non-ideological. It was also understandable. (Travis 2011)

As the conversations continued, a Reentry Development Team formed within the Justice Department. Headed by Travis, Larry Meachum, and Joe Brann, who directed the Office of Community Oriented Policing, the team quietly convened with stakeholders from outside Washington. The team's main goal in these sessions was to test different ideas. The team asked corrections officials, parole officers, and community leaders how they thought about reentry, if they thought about it at all. Initially some stakeholders took a defensive posture. Corrections officials understood their job to keep prisoners safe while in prison but expressed concern about being held responsible for outcomes after a prisoner's release. Parole officials grew concerned that candid discussions about prisoner recidivism would reflect negatively on their work (Travis 2007).

Undeterred, the Reentry Development Team introduced a project they called Reentry Partnerships. They solicited calls for concept papers on developing community-level reentry partnerships and reentry courts, as well as a reentry demonstration project to be managed by the DOJ. On October 14, 1999, Reno and Travis formally announced the project in a joint press conference. As Travis recalled,

This was the first time we'd gone above the radar. This was the first testing in a political sense of the idea. We didn't know what the reaction would be. We got one skeptical reaction from the *Wall Street Journal* basically saying, "There they go again." Other than that the reaction was overwhelmingly positive. A lot of head scratching—what is this all about? There was an immediate seeding of the ground. (Travis 2011)

The Attorney General brought the Reentry Partnerships project to the attention of officials on the Domestic Policy Council (DPC), a relatively small policy shop that coordinates domestic policy for the White House. In the waning months of the Clinton Administration, White House officials became interested in reentry from a budgetary standpoint. In coordination with the DPC, the Departments of Justice and Labor, and the National Institutes of Health each made formal requests for reentry funding in the 2001 fiscal year budget. President Clinton even placed reentry spending on his "veto list"—essentially a list of "must haves" in the budget bills sent from Congress, lest he would issue a veto. Congress authorized money to develop eight reentry test sites.

During the spring of 2000 Travis left the NIJ for a senior fellowship position at the Urban Institute. From his post at Urban, Travis convened a Reentry Roundtable. The Roundtable included leading academicians, practitioners, policy makers, former prisoners, community leaders, victims-rights groups, and social service providers. The team met eight times over four years. They further refined and conceptualized the topic. They surveyed research and looked for gaps in knowledge. They held meetings on the nexus between reentry and problems related to employment, housing and homelessness, family life, community policing, and civil society. The group fostered a first-of-its-kind four-state longitudinal study, *Returning Home*, which tracked the experiences of returning prisoners.

OHIO PLAN

In any given policy subsystem, policy-making activity often occurs simultaneously at all levels of the federalist system. Down at the state level the Council of State Governments (CSG), which would play an even larger role in facilitating prison reform later in the decade, had begun work on reentry. The CSG, together with the ASCA, the American Probation and

Parole Association, the Urban Institute, the National Association of State Alcohol/Drug Abuse Directors, the National Association of State Mental Health Program Directors, and other partner organizations formed the Reentry Policy Council. The Reentry Policy Council had a three-part mission: assist state officials struggling with the release and transition of thousands of prisoners, issue a core set of principles to help policy makers evaluate reentry processes in their own jurisdictions, and disseminate reentry "best practices" to practitioners around the country. After a dozen meetings with over 100 stakeholders, the Reentry Council published a 600-page report, "Charting the Safe and Successful Return of Prisoners into the Community," in 2003. The report offered hundreds of recommendations.

Around the same time the Reentry Policy Council compiled its report, Reginald Wilkinson was leading a groundbreaking reentry effort within the Ohio Department of Rehabilitation and Corrections. Wilkinson's effort was officially called the "Ohio Plan for Productive Offender Reentry and Recidivism Reduction," but colloquially officials called it "The Ohio Plan." The Ohio Plan outlined a systemic approach to reentry. Prison staff needed to begin reentry planning immediately after an offender's admission to prison. The plan called for more in-prison treatment programs, more family involvement, improvements in job training and discharge readiness, stronger community partnerships, and community supervision levels determined by a released prisoner's relative risk of reoffending.*

When officials circulated drafts of the Ohio Plan, some called it "parole reinvented" or a "fad." Others thought it would just go away. The plan defied an easy label because it *was* something different. It was transformative in one major sense: it represented, as Wilkinson notes, "a philosophy, not a set of programs" (Wilkinson 2010).

Wilkinson himself had been a participant in the executive sessions on reentry in Clinton's DOJ and then served on the Urban Institute's Reentry Roundtable. As president of the American Correctional Association, Wilkinson had a bully pulpit of sorts. He used it to raise awareness among correctional administrators that prisoner reentry was not simply a set of programs. It was, as Wilkinson said,

> An underpinning of what's important. If you are really embedded in a reentry philosophy then it drives not only the process of releasing prisoners to the community, it drives your operational perspectives of the entire

---

* Reginald Wilkinson, testimony before the House Committee on Government Reform, February 5, 2005.

correctional agency ... [In Ohio] we tried our best to institutionalize the importance of successfully getting persons back into the community. (Wilkinson 2010)

For Wilkinson this meant front-line staff needed to think beyond their narrowly (but no doubt important) focused role of keeping the peace behind prison walls. How could they prepare inmates for their inevitable release back into the community? Correctional agencies needed to be less insular. Treatment and social service providers needed to see themselves not only as savers of human lives but as crime fighters who made meaningful contributions to community public safety efforts. Civic and religious leaders needed to view returning prisoners as valued members of the community. The Ohio Plan evolved over time. As Wilkinson remembers,

We were talking about restorative justice and community justice, and we were talking about victims' rights earlier than we were talking about the notion of reentry per se. Back then (the 1990s) we were talking about reintegration, pre-release readiness, discharge planning—all those kinds of things ... [But] Before it was more or less what do you do to prepare a person to go home—certainly not what you do several weeks or several months before their imminent release. (Wilkinson 2010)

A big effort was made to collect the best information available. The ODRC, dating back to 1991 when Wilkinson had first become director, had (unlike many states) wanted to know more about the characteristics of the state's inmates. Who among the people the agency had behind bars were violent, nonviolent, and who was more likely to respond to rehabilitation? Staff members also relied on outside sources. They consulted reports from the National Institute of Corrections and the NIJ in addition to the latest research from University of Cincinnati's School of Criminal Justice. Researchers at the University of Cincinnati had examined the effectiveness of Ohio's halfway houses and community-based correctional facilities. Wilkinson notes,

We got a lot of information about halfway houses and how we can use them. We found that it was a waste of money to put super low-level people in them and that people that benefited most was medium to high-level offenders. So we changed our approach about who needed what in terms of community supervision, in terms of how we would expend our resources on supervision and treatment programs. Over time we learned more and more about the people we had under our supervision—whether it was in the community or in our institutions. (Wilkinson 2010)

Drafters of the Ohio Plan first tried to identify areas and problems that the ODRC had the institutional means to address. "We started to look at all the reasons related to why people were returned to prison and we started eliminating them," Wilkinson said (Wilkinson 2010). The parole system, and specifically the problem of parolees returning to prison on technical violations including simple drug possession charges, was one area that quickly drew officials' attention. If first time simple possession of marijuana was not enough to put someone in prison, why should it be enough to return someone to prison? In later planning sessions the ODRC reached out to community stakeholder groups who helped advance additional policy recommendations. What could they do in the areas of employment, drug treatment, housing, and family life? These were all relevant questions.

Neither rank-and-file members of the agency or elected officials in Columbus offered much pushback. The general acceptance among corrections officials can best be explained by the collaborative nature of the process and the consistent messaging that came from the top. Reentry was not a program but a philosophy. Moreover, Wilkinson noted, "This wasn't a soft on crime approach but 'smart on crime' approach" (Wilkinson 2010). For elected officials the newfound emphasis on reentry was understood through a cost containment lens. "We didn't have to ask for any money to do it. If we asked for a new line item to do reentry in the state, it may have been different," Wilkinson said. "We robbed Peter to pay Paul. We got creative" (Wilkinson 2010).

Ohio officials formalized the Ohio Plan in 2001. It was shopped widely within the correctional community and the broader network that began mobilizing in 1999. "There was a synergy in the 2000s as reentry became part of the corrections vernacular," Wilkinson recalled. "We started to nationalize. We started singing from the same hymnal of sorts" (Wilkinson 2010).

DEVELOPMENTS IN CORRECTIONS POLICY RESEARCH

In 2002, the BJS published the agency's most comprehensive study to date on prisoner recidivism (Langan and Levin 2002). After collecting data on over 272,000 prisoners released in fifteen states in 1994, the study offered empirical confirmation of what many corrections officials already knew;

the country faced an alarming rate of prisoner recidivism. Six months after their release from prison, 30 percent were rearrested. The number increased to 44 percent after one year, nearly 60 percent after two years, and after three years 67 percent of released prisoners were rearrested for at least one new offense. Of course, not all rearrests led to conviction. Nonetheless, the study found almost half (46.9 percent) were convicted of a new crime and 25 percent were sent to prison for a new conviction.

One of the study's most important findings was that an offender's risk of rearrest varied across time. The highest rate of rearrest occurred within the first six months after a prisoner's release. The BJS study also found crucial variation in *who* was rearrested with the cohort. Prisoners with a long criminal record (in this study, individuals with forty-five or more crimes) represented just 6.4 percent of the 1994 release cohort but were responsible for 14 percent of the cohort's total charges. Those less criminally active but who were still busy (those with twenty-five to forty-four previous crimes) accounted for 24 percent of the released cohort but 52 percent of its rearrests (Langan and Levin 2002). A relatively small share of the released cohort, then, committed a high percentage of the new crimes. Collectively, these results informed policy makers in two primary ways. First, the initial months right after a prisoner's release posed the greatest risk to public safety. Second, accounting for an offender's prior criminal history, along with other risk factors such as an offender's age, allowed policy makers to improve how they targeted scarce reentry resources.

No less important to the strength and viability of the reentry movement, once it reached the halls and committees of Congress, was the quiet revitalization of prisoner rehabilitation research. Francis Cullen, one of the leading criminologists of his generation, points to a dozen scholars (a number that Cullen himself admits is artificially low) who worked in a "loosely coupled network ... fighting back the ideas that offenders were beyond redemption and that corrections was a uniformly and inherently bankrupt exercise" (Cullen 2005). One of these was Ted Palmer, who, as discussed earlier, was one of the earliest challengers of Robert Martinson's claim that "nothing works." Cullen himself, along with Karen Gilbert, published *Reaffirming Rehabilitation* in 1982 (Cullen and Gilbert 1982). The book rallied rehabilitation supporters because it laid out the dangers of wholly discrediting rehabilitation while showing that the public's appetite for rehabilitative approaches remained strong.

Paul Gendreau and Robert Ross, in an exhaustive review of the treatment literature published in the post-Martinson years, published two major compendiums, the first in 1979 and the second in 1987 (Gendreau and Ross 1979, 1987). One of their central arguments was that criminal behavior was learned. This was an important insight because it challenged the hegemonic belief that criminal offenders were incapable of relearning socially acceptable behavior. Moreover, they found that many ineffective treatment programs were not inherently flawed but were just poorly implemented. Correctional staff and drug treatment officials, in Ross and Gendreau's view, needed to incorporate empirical evidence into their programming. Officials who designed interventions on personal experience alone risked committing "correctional quackery" by exposing offenders to scientifically unproven interventions (Gendreau 1999).

North of the American border, two Canadian psychologists, Don Andrews and James Bonta, made critical advancements in "effective correctional treatment theory" (Andrews 1995, pp. 35–62; Andrews and Bonta 2003). Their work formed the basis for what officials now commonly refer to as the "what works" literature. Over time, Andrews and Bonta identified four major principles of effective treatment intervention. First, programs needed to place greater emphasis on high-risk offenders. This may seem obvious in retrospect, but for years correctional officials ignored higher-risk offenders. Treatment interventions often populated low-security institutions, which automatically excluded high-risk offenders. In many correctional institutions administrators would exclude high-risk inmates from treatment to maintain community support. Self-selection effects also played a role when only the most self-motivated inmates—often the lowest-risk offenders—sought out programming.

Second, rehabilitation programming needed to target what criminologists now call "criminogenic" factors, or the risks and needs that cause offenders to recidivate. Some criminogenic factors are immutable. Criminologists have long known, for example, that crime is a young man's game, yet clearly no program exists that changes an offender's age. Moreover, it is often said that today's criminal is yesterday's crime victim. An offender may commit a crime today because he himself suffered abuse in the past; yet we cannot reverse time to erase horrific life events. Researchers now recognize, however, that a variety of factors are subject to change. Antisocial attitudes, poor impulse control, association with criminally-prone peer groups, low levels of education, and poor vocational skills all represent malleable criminogenic factors.

Third, and related to the second, offenders needed responsive treatments that match their risk factors. Cognitive behavior therapies proved effective in this regard. They emphasize action, motivation, goal setting, and "correct" thinking patterns. Therapies inserted into drug treatment programs, life skills classes, or anger management courses orient offenders toward the present and future. Unlike psychoanalytic therapies, cognitive behavior therapies do not attempt to identify the "root" causes of an offender's behavior.

Finally, rehabilitation programs required institutional support. Programs needed adequate funding, designs focused squarely on recidivism reduction, and motivated staff that understood the benefits of rehabilitation programming.

Without considering the broader context of the tough on crime era, these four principles of effective intervention appear rather pedestrian. Yet among the prison rehabilitation programs that managed to survive in the 1980s, few systematically focused on reducing prisoner recidivism. Correctional institutions had an eclectic mix of rehabilitative programs that evolved over time. Prison administrators often accepted invitations from well-meaning individuals or nonprofit organizations who came offering their own boutique programs. Although these often kept inmates engaged and posed little cost to prison administrators, they suffered from unpredictable funding and lacked a standardized curriculum.

Researchers also made important advancements in what works at the back end of the criminal justice system. During the 1980s intensive supervision programs (ISPs) were a popular response to the recidivism problem. Policy makers believed close supervision of parolees and probationers would act as a deterrent.

The problem, researchers determined over time, was that intensive supervision failed as a deterrent. Joan Petersillia and Susan Turner used a random experiential design to measure effects of intensive community supervision in fourteen different sites. They found, "at no site … did ISP participants experience arrest less often, have a longer time to failure, or experience arrest for a less serious offense" (Petersilia and Turner 1993, pp. 310–311). Military-style "boot camps" were another tactic popularized in the 1990s. Exposing offenders to boot camps would "break down offenders and build them back up" (Cullen et al. 2004). These too, however, produced disappointing results (MacKenzie 1993; MacKenzie and Souryal 1996, pp. 287–295).

This is not to say supervision has no value. Supervision strategies, when smartly designed like the Hawaii Opportunity Probation and Enforcement (HOPE) program, show impressive results. One of the key insights from

HOPE, as Mark Kleiman documents, is that officials need not impose severe penalties on parole (or probation) violators in order for supervision to act as a deterrent. Instead, penalties for a parole violation must be swift and certain (Kleiman 2009). For example, if a parolee misses a drug test, parole officials must apply a punishment—usually a short stint in jail—within twenty-four to forty-eight hours of the offense. By imposing swift sanctions, parolees see a clear link between their unwanted behavior and the consequence of their actions. Any significant delay reduces the deterrent effect.

Researchers now know that if sanctions are swift, and if they are imposed every time a parolee violates their conditions of parole—the certainty principle—then over time most parolees will self-comply (Kleiman 2009). When parole officials no longer have to closely supervise a given cohort of parolees because they learned bad choices bring real consequences, officials can then target a new high-risk cohort just beginning their transition into the community. In short, smart supervision strategies make efficient use of scarce correctional dollars.

As we will see in later parts of this chapter, the advancements in knowledge about what works in prisoner reentry had an important *political effect* over time. In the debate over the SCA, members of Congress who supported greater investments in prisoner reentry services used the smart on crime theme as rhetorical shorthand to communicate their effectiveness. Caustic "soft on crime" arguments from reentry opponents could be challenged with an equally penetrating claim in return: "prisoner reentry is smart on crime. It works." Evidence from the academy gave political fence sitters just a bit more courage.

CONSERVATIVES BEGIN THE PUSH FOR PRISONER REENTRY

The State of the Union, presented once a year to a joint session of Congress, offers presidents one of their best opportunities to set the national policy agenda. Presidents' views on the macro economy or issues of war and peace are part of almost every State of the Union speech. Presidents also reserve time for less salient issues. Funding for HIV/AIDS, poverty and homelessness, foreign aid, energy, and transportation issues all come to mind. For interests groups and political actors who organize around specific policies and social causes, a State of the Union mention of a pet issue, even if just a few sentences, helps build political momentum.

When a president lays out a policy agenda in big speeches, he cannot force Congress to go along. Congress is a coequal branch of government with different structural incentives than the occupant of the White House. Specific mentions of policy, however, provide a window into a president's legislative priorities and how a president and his party think about a problem. It was significant then when the prisoner reentry issue found its way into President George W. Bush's 2004 State of the Union address.

> In the past, we've worked together to bring mentors to children of prisoners, and provide treatment for the addicted, and help for the homeless. Tonight I ask you to consider another group of Americans in need of help. This year 600,000 inmates will be released from prison back into society. We know from long experience that if former prisoners can't find work, or a home, or help, they are much more likely to commit more crime and return to prison…. America is a land of second chance, and when the gates of the prison open, the path ahead should lead to a better life. ("Text of President Bush's 2004 State of the Union Address" 2004)

President Bush's view of America as a "land of second chance" proved a remarkable assertion. Not at any time during the tough-on-crime era had a sitting president, let alone a conservative Republican president, given such a high-profile imprimatur to extending policy benefits to prisoners. By mentioning the tens of thousands of people released from prison each year, the barriers prisoners faced when they returned home, and the nexus between recidivism and public safety, the speech signaled a changing political landscape. The reentry groundwork laid by officials in President Clinton's DOJ, the executive-style sessions, the roundtables, the process improvement groups in Ohio and elsewhere, and the growth in knowledge about "what works" not only helped the reentry issue reach the national agenda; they also helped shape the president's course of action.

Deeper ideological forces were also at play. Bush had run for president as a "compassionate conservative"—a politician who putatively mixed conservative philosophies and policies to assist the poor and needy. Bush also sought to expand the role of faith-based organizations in American life. After overcoming his own personal struggle with alcohol abuse, Bush came to believe that religious faith, especially Christianity, could help cure social ills. Faith-based organizations, Bush believed, could play a critical role in this mission. Even more important for the long-term success of the conservative project, faith-based organizations could expand the privatization of social service delivery (Plotz 2000). Prisoner reentry investments that offered criminal offenders a chance at redemption but likewise called for a prominent need for social services could help achieve both of these fundamental goals.

On prison reform issues, no organization had a stronger influence on the president's thinking than the Prison Fellowship Ministries. Bush's relationship with the Prison Fellowship dated back to his Texas governorship. As governor, Bush signed legislation making it easier for Texas's faith-based groups to apply for and receive state and federal funding.* By this time the Prison Fellowship had built a robust national operation, complete with an army of 50,000 volunteers who preached the gospel and taught bible study classes in prisons in all fifty states (Plotz 2000). Bush encouraged a deeper involvement in Texas. He asked the Fellowship's founder, Chuck Colson, to establish a full-fledged faith-based prerelease program in Texas, later to be named the InnerChange Freedom Initiative, or IFI.

In January 1996, the Prison Fellowship introduced to the Texas Legislature the concept of a program expressly Christian in orientation. It emphasized "restorative justice where the offender works through several phases of treatment to reshape his value system" (Johnson and Larson 2008, p. 6). Just over a year later the program opened its doors in the 378-bed Carol Vance Unit in Richmond, Texas. The public–private partnership represented the first of its kind in the Texas criminal justice system—a full-scale "around-the-clock" Christian-centered program that contracted directly with the Texas Department of Criminal Justice (Johnson and Larson 2008, p. 6). The IFI combined biblical teachings with life skills training, group counseling, and personal accountability classes in a program that began sixteen to twenty-four months before a prisoner was released and then continued in the postrelease period (Kellner 2003).

The significance of what the Texas program, along with additional IFI programs in Iowa, Kansas, and Minnesota, meant for the larger role of faith-based organizations was not lost on Chuck Colson. In a 2003 radio interview he remarked (in reference to a lawsuit filed against the Fellowship in Iowa on First Amendment grounds) on the Prison Fellowship's place in the larger conservative project. "What's at stake is not just a prison program, but how we deal with social problems in our country. Do we do

---

* State of Texas, Executive Order GWB 96-5, May 2, 1996; State of Texas, Executive Order GWB 96-10, December 17, 1996; House Bill 2482 75R; House Bill 2481 75R; House Bill 2017 76R.

it through grassroots organizations or big government? We know what works" (Shapiro 2007, p. 139).

Motivated by his desire to expand opportunities for faith-based organizations, Bush wanted reentry programs in dozens of states, not just a selected handful called for under the Clinton administration's Reentry Partnerships project. Bush's DOJ, in partnership with over a dozen federal and state agencies, launched "Going Home: The Serious and Violent Offender Reentry Initiative," or SVORI, in 2002. SVORI allocated $120 million to assist all fifty states in developing new evidence-based prisoner reentry programs. Not surprisingly, SVORI programs required close collaboration with faith-based organizations.

Once in Washington, Bush continued his work with the Prison Fellowship Ministries. Bush invited Chuck Colson and a team of researchers to the White House in June of 2003 to present the findings of a research study that seemed to indicate Texas IFI participants had lower rates of recidivism than a control group.* These discussions, as well as early lessons gleaned from SVORI, led to the announcement of President Bush's Prisoner Reentry Initiative during that same State of the Union address in 2004. Under the Prisoner Reentry Initiative, the Department of Labor issued thirty new grants to faith-based and community organizations tasked with helping released offenders in urban communities find work. These grants complemented a number of preexisting job training, education, and transitional services programs within the Labor Department. Funding also helped coordinate a growing number of reentry services in the sprawling federal bureaucracy. Over a dozen agencies, including Housing and Urban Development, Health and Human Services, Veterans Affairs (the Incarcerated Veterans Transition Program), and the Internal Revenue Service (which oversaw the work opportunity tax credit), had at least some connection to prisoner reentry programs.[†]

---

* This study came under scrutiny for its flawed methodology and overinflating the benefits of the IFI program. Mark Kleiman notes the study suffered from severe "selection bias." Of the 177 prisoners in the sample it reported on only those 75 offenders who "graduated" and completely ignored the 102 offenders that dropped out. For a more complete treatment of the study's methodological flaws, see Kleiman (2003).

[†] Mason Bishop, testimony before the Senate Judiciary Committee, September 21, 2006.

INTRODUCTION OF THE SCA

These small-sized reentry initiatives developed and nurtured in the executive branch marked important victories for reentry advocates. In a polarized political environment, executive-style policy making may present policy advocates their only viable option, but rarely does it present the best route. Policy gains become vulnerable to the vagaries of internal agency politics. Policy advocates often achieve superior policy gains and greater certainty if they pass desired legislation in Congress. The introduction of the SCA in Congress in 2004 can be viewed through this lens. Supporters of the SCA not only sought to protect reentry programs and services already won, but hoped to broaden their victory by helping reentry policies scale.

One of the SCA's initial sponsors in the House of Representatives was a Republican—Rob Portman of Ohio. Portman was a close friend of President Bush. After witnessing Reginald Wilkinson and the ODRC formulate the Ohio Plan, Portman understood the strain recidivism and crowded prison environments placed on Ohio correctional officials. Joining Portman were cosponsors Mark Souder, an Indiana Republican, and two Illinois Democrats, Danny Davis and Stephanie Tubbs-Jones. The Bush administration gave the SCA its immediate blessing. In a statement issued June 23, 2004, the White House said,

> Today, Representatives Rob Portman (R-OH) and Danny Davis (D-IL) introduced the Second Chance Act of 2004, which includes key elements of the president's prisoner reentry initiative. The president strongly supports their efforts, and commends the Congressmen for their leadership. We urge the House and Senate to work in a bipartisan way to get legislation passed this year that is consistent with what the president outlined. (Office of the Press Secretary 2004)

When Portman introduced the legislation to the House Subcommittee on Crime, Terrorism, and Homeland Security, Portman referenced President Bush's State of the Union speech. This serves as another indicator of the importance of that speech in creating political momentum for the reentry movement among conservatives in Congress. Portman stated,

> President Bush made a case for the need to address our reentering population in his State of the Union address. He put this issue in perspective,

"America is the land of the second chance, and when the gates of the prison open, the path ahead should lead to a better life … This [legislation] is an important aspect of our federal response to reentry … ."*

Portman framed the bill by advancing both pragmatic and moral dimensions of the smart on crime movement. "We need to be both tough and smart on crime," Portman said. "Tough in keeping dangerous felons from returning and committing new crimes, but also smart in making sure that those who are coming home are given the most basic chance to start a new life and turn away from crime" (see footnote).

PRISON FELLOWSHIP MINISTRIES

Along with the White House, the Prison Fellowship Ministries mobilized on behalf of the bill. Pat Nolan, president of the Justice Fellowship, the public policy arm of the Prison Fellowship Ministries, would lead the effort. Nolan had experienced both sides of the criminal justice system. On the one side Nolan crafted criminal justice policy during his fifteen-year tenure in the California Assembly, four of which he spent as a Republican leader. After he was first elected to the Assembly in 1978, Nolan quickly gained a reputation for his tough on crime credentials and his strong advocacy for victims' rights. Nolan was one of the lead sponsors of California's Proposition 15, a victim's rights initiative passed by voters in 1984. That work earned him the Parents of Murdered Children "Victims Advocate Award." He was the floor manager for an Assembly bill that funded California's only "Supermax" prison—Pelican Bay. Despite shepherding dozens of tough on crime bills through the Assembly during his tenure, Nolan's most personal experience with the criminal justice system came during his twenty-five-month term in a federal penitentiary after he pleaded guilty to a racketeering charge in 1994 (Lehner 2004).

Seeing prison from the inside affected Nolan's views about inmates. "You wonder if anyone remembers or cares about you. The prisons I was in, thousands of times in the two years I was there they [the correctional officials] said, 'you ain't got nothing coming.' It's said with hate. The

---

* Rob Portman, testimony before the Subcommittee on Crime, Terrorism, and Homeland Security, October 7, 2004.

implication is: you came from nothing, you are nothing, you're worthless" (Cusey 2012). After being released from prison he struggled to adjust community life; even ordering off a restaurant menu proved difficult. "While you're in prison, all control is taken away from you. For two years I hadn't a choice of what to eat" (Cusey 2012).

It is often said that when one proverbial door of opportunity closes, another opens. Prison has to rank at the bottom of places where one would expect to find a new professional opportunity (a licit one, anyway). But for Nolan, whose elected career was over, his prison experience led him down a new professional path. He first became acquainted with the Prison Fellowship after volunteers with the Fellowship's Angel Tree program had sent Christmas gifts to Nolan's children while he was incarcerated. Nolan joined a church choir; he read the Bible, and, as it happened, read one of Chuck Colson's books.

Nolan first met Colson in 1995 after a prison chaplain brought a group of inmates to hear Colson talk at the prison. Their first encounter blossomed into a deeper relationship over time. Colson's belief in Nolan's political acumen, along with his new outlook on prison life, made Nolan an ideal candidate to head the Justice Fellowship. After his release from prison in the fall of 1996, Colson offered Nolan the job of president of the Justice Fellowship. Colson remarked that Nolan "had practical experience in politics and in prison, is a proven leader and a growing Christian disciple. Pat will be a powerful voice for biblical justice around America" (Gladstone 1996). The next year would mark the Justice Fellowship's first significant foray into congressional politics under Nolan's leadership.

FIGHT TO PROTECT INMATES' RELIGIOUS FREEDOM

Political scientist David Truman argued long ago that groups become politically mobilized after "disturbances" in the political system (Truman 1951). When groups feel their self-interests are threatened, they are more likely to get involved. The "disturbance" for the Prison Fellowship came in the form of a 1997 Supreme Court ruling, *City of Boerne v. Flores*. The decision struck down key provisions of the Religious Freedom Restoration Act (RFRA) passed by Congress with strong majorities in 1993. From the Prison Fellowship's perspective, the ruling threatened the very role of religion behind prison walls.

At issue was the Free Exercise Clause in the Constitution's First Amendment and the meaning of the phrase: "Congress shall make no law respecting an establishment of religion, or the free exercise thereof." Before *Boerne v. Flores*, any number of court decisions had ruled that overt attempts by the government to suppress a person's ability to practice their religion constituted a clear violation of the First Amendment. One remaining legal dispute involved the constitutionality of laws that were neutral on their face but nonetheless interfered with a person's freedom of religious practice. Antidrug laws that banned the use of peyote, or local zoning ordinances that prevented churches from expanding, exemplify laws that did not ostensibly target religious exercise rights but have thus been challenged for violating the First Amendment.

In a long history of case law, the Supreme Court generally applied strict scrutiny (the highest standard the court brings to the actions of government) to government actions that placed a substantial burden on a person's religious exercise rights. When a generally applicable law—a law that did not specifically restrict a person's actions engaged in for a religious reason—was challenged on free exercise grounds, the court's standard up to 1990 held that religious practice must be accommodated under the First Amendment unless the government could show a burden that poses the "least restrictive means" of achieving some "compelling state interest." This was the standard until *Employment Division v. Smith*. In this decision, the court curtailed free exercise protections by restricting the instances where the government had to show a compelling interest before it could prohibit religiously motivated conduct.* *Smith* effectively gutted the compelling interest doctrine in free exercise cases.

Congress had passed the RFRA in 1993 in response to anger expressed by many religious groups following the court's *Smith* decision. The RFRA compelled the Supreme Court to use strict scrutiny in free exercise cases. Under the RFRA, a burden placed on free exercise rights could only happen if the government satisfied two conditions. First, the burden could

---

* Two plaintiffs, Alfred Smith and Galen Black, who were both members of the Native American Church, brought the *Employment Division v. Smith* case. After they were fired from their jobs in a drug treatment clinic for use of peyote, then illegal under Oregon law, they sued for unemployment benefits. Because peyote use was part of their religious practice, Smith and Black argued for an exemption from Oregon's anti-peyote statute. A key part of this case, as it made its way to the U.S. Supreme Court on appeal, was the law's general applicability—the law did not target any one religion. Justice Antonin Scalia, who wrote the court's majority opinion, noted that the Free Exercise clause did not require religious exceptions to facially neutral law. Religious exceptions were not guaranteed by the First Amendment.

only be placed if it furthered a "compelling government interest." Second, the burden had to represent the "least restrictive" way to further that interest.

But as a result of *City of Boerne v. Flores*, major portions of *this* Act were ruled unconstitutional after the court ruled Congress had overstepped its enforcement powers in Section 5 of the Fourteenth Amendment. The Prison Fellowship Ministries saw the court's decision to strike down the RFRA as direct assault on prisoners' free exercise rights. In a 1997 testimony before a House Judiciary subcommittee, Chuck Colson told Congress that too often prison administrators cut off prisoners from religious activities, citing security concerns, retribution, or in some cases no reason at all. "I've spent the last twenty years working in prisons," Colson said. "I've seen the door slam shut to religious services on the whim of administrators. Immediately after the *Smith* decision, prison administrators and prison officials were able to prevent Jewish prisoners from wearing yarmulkes, deny Catholic prisoners access to a priest, and restrict Bible studies for evangelical prisoners."*

Colson framed the issue as one larger than the personal religious rights of prisoners. The fight was also about a "societal interest." Colson linked the right of free religious practice to a prisoner's rehabilitation prospects to help make the point.

> Religious observance by prisoners is strongly correlated with successful rehabilitation. While it is pretty clear the First Amendment would prohibit the government from overtly pressuring prisoners to practice religion, it is sheer social folly to place any obstacles in the way of the many prisoners who, on their own initiative, seek out ministers, priests, rabbis, Bible studies, and so forth. Yet, I myself have talked with wardens ... who have told me that if it were not for prisoners' legal ability to sue for the denial of free exercise, they would withhold even ordinary, mainstream, non-controversial forms of religious accommodation. (see footnote)

The Prison Fellowship working with the Baptist Joint Committee, the Family Research Council, and the Christian Legal Society wanted new legislation. They wanted a bill similar to the RFRA that could provide insurance against the Supreme Court, an unelected body that, as they understood it, attacked a fundamental right in the wake of the *Smith* and

---

* Chuck Colson, testimony before the House Subcommittee on the Constitution, July 14, 1997.

Boerne decisions. The eventual legislative solution would come with the Religious Land Use and Institutionalized Persons Act (RLPA).

The RLPA was introduced by two political heavyweights in the Senate—Ted Kennedy of Massachusetts and Orin Hatch of Utah—two close friends who held opposite ideological beliefs but somehow found ways to collaborate on important legislation. Crafting the bill more carefully within the spending and commerce powers of Congress (with the hope the legislation survived any future challenges before Court), the bill returned strict scrutiny to cases where incarcerated individuals' free exercise rights were substantially burdened. It forced the government to show a "compelling state interest"; it reestablished the "least burden" standard, and extended these standards to "generally applicable" laws and regulations.

The Prison Fellowship believed passage of the RLPA was fundamental to their core mission. "Under the protection of RLPA, the Prison Fellowship and other ministries will have new opportunities to minister to thousands of men and women, giving true rehabilitation through the power of the cross," Pat Nolan told Congress. "If Congress does not pass RLPA this session, we will be left with no statutory protection for our first freedom, religious liberty; and, grave damage will have been done to our ability to legislate in accordance with our moral traditions."*

Law enforcement organizations and state attorneys general expressed concerns that expanding the free exercise rights of prisoners would bring junk lawsuits. Their opposition found a legislative voice in Senator Harry Reid who not only represented a state (Nevada) with a growing number of prisons, but he also had close ties to unionized correctional officers. When the RFRA was debated in 1993, Reid had offered an amendment prohibiting the applicability of the RFRA to incarcerated individuals. He claimed his main reason was a high volume of lawsuits filed by federal prisoners against prison officials and the costs these imposed on the state. That amendment failed, but now years later Reid still held his concern about what extending strict scrutiny to religion cases filed by prisoners would mean for corrections officials. "Many prisoners will use any excuse to avoid searches and avoid security to protect prison personnel and the general public from harm."† Reid also expressed concern that strict scrutiny would cause prisoners and the courts to second-guess prison officials' decision making.

---

* Pat Nolan, testimony before the House Subcommittee on the Constitution, July 14, 1998.
† Harry Reid, remarks made in congressional debate, July 27, 2000.

Kennedy countered Reid's claim, citing the number of lawsuits filed by federal prisoners under the RFRA. "According to the Department of Justice, among the 96 federally run facilities, housing over 140,000 inmates, less than 75 cases have ever been brought under the Act [the RFRA], most of which have never gone to trial. On average, over seven years, that's less than 1 case in each federal facility. It's hardly a flood of litigation or a reason to deny this protection to prisoners."*

Kennedy had another tool at his disposal: The Prison Litigation Reform Act. The Prison Litigation Reform Act, adopted between the time Congress passed the RFRA and began debate on the RLPA, placed new constraints on prisoners' procedural rights to sue. Kennedy made it clear that no provision in the RLRA could be construed to amend or repeal the Prison Litigation Reform Act. "Based upon these protections and the data on prison litigation," Kennedy stated, "it is clear that this provision in our bill will not lead to a flood of frivolous lawsuits or threaten the safety, order, or discipline in correctional facilities" (see footnote).

Kennedy and Hatch had one final argument. Sounding the same themes advanced by the Prison Fellowship, they tied religious practice to a prisoner's rehabilitation prospects. "Sincere faith and worship can be an indispensable part of rehabilitation, and these protections should be an important part of that process," Kennedy said. Still not wholly convinced, Reid nonetheless saw enough benefits in the bill to help push the legislation through the Senate.

FRAMING THE MEANING OF THE SCA

All of this is to say that by the time the SCA reached the congressional agenda, the Prison Fellowship Ministries had already notched a significant political victory. It would later become a key player in passing the Prison Rape Elimination Act in 2003. In a short period the Prison Fellowship had established itself as far more than a bit player in the rough-and-tumble politics of Congress.

The Prison Fellowship invested significant resources on the SCA's behalf. Nolan traveled to dozens of states and testified no less than four times

---

* Remarks made by Ted Kennedy in congressional debate, July 27, 2000.

before Congress between 2004 and 2008.* In his congressional testimony Nolan (like Portman before) stressed the bill's public safety aspects while calling for a new way of doing things.

> The fact of the matter is most of the inmates we have released do commit more crimes. Over the last thirty years, the rate of re-arrest has hovered stubbornly around sixty-seven percent. If two-thirds of the patients leaving a hospital had to be readmitted, we would quickly find a new hospital. We must find a better way to prepare inmates for their release if we are to have safer communities.†

Nolan drew attention to the moral failures of mass incarceration, the lives ruined in its wake, and the inherent dignity of each person behind bars.

> As the number of people released from prison and jail increases steadily, we cannot afford to continue to send them home with little preparation. These policies have harmed too many victims, destroyed too many families, overwhelmed too many communities, and wasted too many lives as they repeat the cycle of arrest, incarceration, release and rearrest. (see footnote †)

Nolan continued,

> While many people would never associate the word 'love' with prisoners, love is precisely what has been lacking in the lives of many of these men and women. They have gone through life without anyone caring about them or what they do, nor caring enough about them to coach them as they confront life. Many inmates are emotionally overdrawn checkbooks. We must make deposit, after deposit, after deposit before we will see any positive balance. (see footnote †)

For conservatives in Congress who had little interest in or knowledge of criminal justice policy, Nolan offered one final but no doubt important pitch. Prisoner reentry, and the SCA more specifically, advanced

---

* House Committee on Government Reform, February 2, 2005, CIS # 2005-02-02 titled, "Confronting Recidivism: Prisoner Reentry Programs and a Just Future for All Americans"; House Subcommittee on Crime, Terrorism, and Homeland Security, November 3, 2005, CIS # 2005-11-03 titled, "Offender Re-entry: What Is Needed to Provide Criminal Offenders with a Second Chance"; Joint Economic Committee, October 4, 2007, CIS # 2007-10-04 titled, "Mass Incarceration at What Cost?"; Senate Subcommittee on Corrections and Rehabilitation, June 8, 2006, titled, "Findings and Recommendations of the Commission on Safety and Abuse in America's Prisons."

† Pat Nolan, testimony before the House Subcommittee on Crime, Terrorism, and Homeland Security, November 3, 2005.

conservatives' goal of expanding the role of faith-based organizations. Advancing the idea that even prisoners, the "worst of the worst" in many peoples' minds, need love and support, it was then but a short step to see how reentry work was ideally suited for the church and religious organizations. Nolan remarked,

> It does not have to be this way. Fortunately, there are many things that the government in partnership with the community, and in particular our churches, can do that increase the likelihood that inmates will return safely to our communities. One of the most important provisions of the Second Chance Act will provide grants to community and faith-based non-profits to link offenders and their families with mentors.

CORRECTIONAL ASSOCIATIONS

While members of the Religious Right were busy pushing the legislation along several different angles, corrections officials also made their preferences known, not in their overwhelming presence, but in what they had to say about recidivism, crime reduction, and reentry. In the eight hearings held on prisoner reentry and the SCA between 2004 and 2008, only five out of forty-five total witnesses (or 11 percent) were prison, probation, parole, police, or sheriffs' officials. Witnesses from nonprofit or religious organizations comprised the largest cohort, totaling nineteen. Despite correctional officials' relatively low presence, at least in official hearings, we know from Lisa Miller's work that their expertise earns the respect of Congress. What they say matters.

When the SCA was first introduced, corrections officials quickly expressed their support and stressed the importance of the federal government helping to innovate and scale reentry efforts across the nation. Ashbel Wall, testifying on behalf of the Association of State Correctional Administrators, told Congress,

> It is the role of the federal government to call attention to these emerging models, to stimulate additional innovation, and to research and evaluate these programs and policies. Indeed, the safety and stability of our communities and families, and integrity of the justice system, depend on such federal leadership. The re-entry legislation before this committee puts us

on that path, and we look forward to working with this committee toward its passage.*

Stefan LoBuglio, Chief of the Pre-release and Reentry Services Division of the Montgomery County, Maryland, Department of Correction and Rehabilitation, offered similar views. "Reentry is sound corrections," LoBuglio told members of the Senate Judiciary Committee.

> There are leaders at all levels in corrections—from line officers, sergeants, lieutenants, shift commanders, sheriffs, wardens—who are ready to embrace reentry. We need some assistance. We need some good models. We are ready to do the task. Those facilities and those systems that incorporate reentry are among the cleanest, the most humane, and the ones that best use their bed space. Reentry has a great advantage, not only in public safety, not only to community well being, not only to victims, but also to the correctional professionals who staff our thousands of correctional facilities, and those that monitor the millions of individuals in community supervision. It can literally transform how we do corrections to the betterment of those in the correction field.

Corrections officials understood the broader public safety benefits attached to the reentry movement. But their support, as LoBuglio mentioned, was chiefly motivated by self-interest. The reentry movement offered help to corrections officials looking to better manage their workload and cope with the demands and challenges of a profession where the workplace had became more crowded and dangerous. Richard Stalder, head of the Department of Public Safety and Corrections in Louisiana, reinforced this point in testimony before the Commission on Safety and Abuse in America's Prisons, a specialized prison reform panel established by the Vera Institute in 2005. Stalder, who spoke on behalf of the Association of State Correctional Administrators and the American Correctional Association, told the Commission, "We share a common goal. And that is to advocate for safe and stable and productive and organized and disciplined correctional environments in America. That is what we want." Stalder continued,

> I think from our perspective, particularly from my perspective as an administrator, overcrowding means, do you have more inmates than your

---

* Ashbel Wall, testimony before the House Committee on Crime, Terrorism, and Homeland Security, October 7, 2004.

resources can support? The question then becomes, how do we make those resources stretch to accomplish our goals? In my mind the best way to do this is to quit putting so many people into the system, which means we need to pay more attention to prevention ... we need to put more resources into basic education in our prisons. We need to put more resources into substance abuse. Let's teach job skills.*

The significance of corrections officials advocating for a reduction in the prison population and more resources to assist inmates was not lost on Stalder. Commission member Ray Krone, himself a former prisoner who spent more than a decade behind bars before DNA evidence cleared him, asked Stalder about staff line support for reform in light of the history of politicians who "are very reluctant to back any type of studies, any type of legislation that makes them appear soft on crime...." Krone said,

My question to you is you working on the inside, you know how the prisons work, your ideals and opinions of what needs to be done in there, how readily is that accepted by your co-workers, your peers, your other people in the profession in the other states? Do you recognize how much resistance there is or how much support is there for these types of changes that we're talking about here that need to be done to address this overcrowding issue?

Stalder responded,

Mr. Krone, there was more resistance a decade ago. Today there is very little resistance to the type of program that helps people leave prison and not come back for a very simple reason. If you were a legislative panel in Louisiana, I could sit before you like this and tell you the reality is every year 15,000 people leave Louisiana's prisons; within 5 years 43% of those will return, that's 7,000 people coming back to prison at a cost of $25,000 per bed to build the bed they sleep in, and at a cost of $35 a day or thirteen and a half thousand dollars a year in operating expenses for them to stay in prison.... What we do to teach job skills and basic education and what we do with substance abuse education and the values piece, keeps them from coming back. So that means ... Whether you are a Republican or Democrat, or whether you are a liberal or conservative, what that now means is that you can spend money on higher education, that you can spend money or roads or bridges, that you can spend on services for the elderly. (see footnote)

---

* Richard Stalder, testimony before the Commission on Safety and Abuse in America's Prisons, July 19, 2005.

SECOND CHANCE ADVOCACY IN THE SENATE

On the progressive side of the coalition, Democrat Joe Biden, the senior Senator from Delaware, introduced his own prisoner reentry bill to the Senate with bill S. 2923, "The Enhanced Second Chance Act of 2004." "We have tried, but simply cannot build our way out of this problem. We need tough-but-smart-strategies to stop the revolving door of prisoners being released from prison, only to re-offend and land right back behind bars. We simply can't be penny-wise but pound-foolish," Biden said after he introduced the bill.* That Senator Biden suggested the United States could not build its way out of the corrections crisis is worth noting. Biden had personified the "New Democrat" model championed by Bill Clinton. In a debate over President Clinton's major crime initiative in 1994, Biden took hard-line stances on the death penalty and three strikes. The crime bill gave Clinton and the Democrats a desperately needed victory following their weak showing on health-care reform. The bill itself is probably best remembered for helping fund an additional 100,000 new police officers. Prison reformers, though, point to the bill's nearly $10 billion for new prison construction; the increase in the number of federal crimes that qualified for the death penalty; and a new crop of mandatory life sentences for people convicted of three "violent" federal crimes.

Discussing the need for the SCA ten years later, Biden cited statistics that his own policies helped create: 650,000 returning prisoners each year, skyrocketing prison costs, and high rates of recidivism. He noted that in his own state of Delaware, 4,000 inmates were released each year. "Here's the kicker," Biden said, referencing the Bureau of Justice Statistics study on recidivism without citing it explicitly,

> A staggering 2/3 of these released state prisoners are expected to be rearrested for a felony or serious misdemeanor within 3 years of release. Two out of every three! You're talking about hundreds of thousands of reoffending ex-offenders each year and hundreds of thousands of serious crimes being committed by people who have already served time in jail. (see footnote)

Biden pivoted to the challenges that confronted returning offenders.

---

* Congressional Record, October 7, 2004, pg. S10717.

Unfortunately, it's not too difficult to see why such a huge portion of our released prisoners recommit serious crimes. Up to 60 percent of former inmates are not employed; 15 to 27 percent of prisoners expect to go to homeless shelters upon release; and 57 percent of federal and 70 percent of state inmates used drugs regularly before prison, with some estimates of involvement with drugs or alcohol around the time of the offense as high as 84 percent.

He then portrayed the damage the prison system inflicts on individuals, families, and society,

These huge numbers of released prisoners each year and the out-of-control recidivism rates are a recipe for disaster—leading to untold damage, hardship, and death for victims; ruined futures and lost potential for re-offenders; and a huge drain on society at large. One particularly vulnerable group is the children of these offenders. We simply cannot be resigned to allowing generation after generation entering and reentering our prisons. This pernicious cycle must come to an end.

The irony of Biden's rhetoric is palpable given his history on the issue. Yet it also illustrates how policy research on prisons and reentry began affecting elite thinking and discourse. Biden's bill had five cosponsors in the Senate, including two Republicans. Members of Congress routinely hail bipartisan bills. Members that successfully secure a cosponsor from the opposite party can increase the chance the bill is viewed favorably, especially among swing voters who do not hold hard-line positions. From a lawmaking standpoint, however, gaining a handful of opposite-party cosponsors often proves insignificant given the many ways a bill can die in Congress.

Sam Brownback

In this case, however, Senate Republicans' cosponsorship carried more than symbolic meaning. No Republican Senator was more crucial to the SCA's prospect of reaching the Oval Office than Sam Brownback of Kansas. Sam Brownback was raised in a farming family. He got his first itch for politics in high school when he served as the state president of the Future Farmers of America. While in college at Kansas State University, he volunteered for Ronald Reagan's failed 1976 presidential campaign and then again for his far more successful effort in 1980. After earning his law degree from the University of Kansas, he worked as an attorney in Manhattan, Kansas for four years before he was appointed secretary of the state's Board of Agriculture—a position he held until 1993.

Brownback first came to Washington in 1994 when he was elected to the House of Representatives as part of the Newt Gingrich–led Republican Revolution. His stint in the House was short. With strong support from evangelical voters Brownback was elected to Bob Dole's Senate seat, left vacated after Dole ran for president in 1996. Once in office Brownback had all the hallmarks of a card-carrying member of the contemporary Republican Party. He was staunchly pro-life; he voted for the controversial Bush tax cuts that benefited the wealthy; he supported oil drilling in the Arctic National Wildlife Refuge; he pledged to abolish the federal departments of Energy, Commerce, and Health and Human Services; and he voted for the use of military force in Iraq and the confirmation of both John Roberts and Sam Alito—two of the Supreme Court's most conservative jurists. Brownback held positions any Republican must take to be considered authentic in a party that, over the past generation, has moved much further to the political right.

What seemed to separate Brownback from the rest of the pack was his staunch advocacy for compassionate conservatism. Karl Rove, George W. Bush's chief political architect, pushed compassionate conservatism in the late 1990s in an effort to attract younger, more racially and ethnically diverse voters who felt largely abandoned by the Republican Party. Yet Brownback seemed to be a true believer. He was drawn to compassionate conservatism, he said, because of his deep religious faith, particularly the "love your neighbor as yourself" creed found in the Second Great Commandment (Eastland 2006). Brownback grew up Methodist before later joining the Topeka Bible Church, a nondenominational evangelical parish. In 2002 he converted to Catholicism, a move not without controversy among his supporters in the evangelical community (Copeland 2006). Brownback's "compassionate side" looked to America's past corrective postures for guidance. In a 2006 speech at his alma mater, he waxed nostalgic about "American exceptionalism" and America's "fundamental goodness" (Eastland 2006). America, Brownback noted, "often gets things wrong," but society eventually corrects its course because of "some movement based on goodness and fixing what's wrong. The abolitionist movement, the civil rights movement, these were both movements that sought to end a wrong." These were fights for "the inherent dignity" of every person and for "righteousness and justice."

By the end of Bush's first term, and after the president became engrossed with the war on terror, Brownback believed that compassionate conservatism had failed to reach its full potential. The movement had not reached the right people (Eastland 2006). Liberals had long made this point. Compassionate conservatism never succeeded because the policies attached to it were never very serious in the first place. Conservatives offered appealing rhetoric, but their actual policies hurt rather than helped the poor. Conservative-led cuts to social services and their push to privatize parts of Medicare and Medicaid threatened the social safety net developed in the New Deal and its progeny.

In prison reform and especially prisoner reentry, Brownback saw a renewed opportunity for compassionate conservatives looking to reenergize the cause. In April 2005 Brownback traveled to Kansas where he and Governor Kathleen Sebelius, a Democrat, would headline a convention to educate state lawmakers on prison issues and recidivism. Toward the end of his speech, Brownback laid down the gauntlet: "I want to see recidivism cut in half in this country in the next five years and I want it to start in Kansas" (Werholz 2009). "It was like 'game on' when he made that statement," recalled Roger Werholz, who served as Kansas's Department of Corrections secretary at the time. "It was something the governor had always been interested in even though she was a fiscally conservative Democrat—all of a sudden the electoral politics went out of this" (Werholz 2009).

Ironically, given his general resentment of federal power, Brownback wanted to see the federal government help bring reentry policies to scale. Brownback's effort to raise awareness in his home state was coupled with more intensive lobbying efforts inside Congress. Indeed, his lobbying efforts were making inroads. When Brownback reintroduced the SCA (S. 1934) in October 2005 with Joe Biden, the bill had thirty-seven cosponsors. Among the sponsors were moderate Republicans like Susan Collins from Maine and Arlen Specter of Pennsylvania. The list also included Orin Hatch and Robert Bennett—both from the deep red state of Utah—and Jon Kyl from the get-tough state of Arizona. Jim Talent of Missouri, Rick Santorum of Pennsylvania, and Mike DeWine of Ohio—all electorally vulnerable Republicans up for reelection in 2006—were also on board.

POLITICAL PROGRESS IN THE HOUSE

Similar progress unfolded in the House as the conservative coalition continued to grow in number, gaining key supporters like Howard Coble, a Republican from North Carolina, and Chairman of the House Crime, Terrorism, and Homeland Security Subcommittee. Given the power of a committee chairperson in Congress to kill legislation they oppose, Coble's support for the SCA was crucial to the bill's prospects in the House. When reintroducing the SCA to his committee during the 109th Congress (the original SCA introduced by Portman failed to make it out of committee and no votes were taken), Coble noted the bill offered "an enlightened departure" from the politics of "lock them up and throw away the key" (Suellentrop 2006).

Also in support was Republican and fellow Crime, Terrorism, and Homeland Security Subcommittee member Christopher Cannon. Representing Utah's Third District, one of the most staunchly conservative House districts in the country, Cannon's voting record seemed a perfect match. It earned him an almost perfect 96 rating from the American Conservative Union. Cannon supported the SCA because of his belief that the Republican Party had gone too far in the punitive direction. Prison reform was a moral issue. "The Republicans have taken a pretty harsh position. Just locking people up. And the system has a very strong tendency to change them for the worse. Everybody knows that, I think. Our current system is fundamentally immoral" (Suellentrop 2006).

Despite the growing number of conservative supporters, a markup session in the summer of 2006 would represent the closest thing to a poison pill introduced in the House. The dispute involved the role of faith-based organizations. Louie Gohmert, a Republican from Texas, had inserted an amendment that gave faith-based organizations guaranteed funding under the SCA. It was a popular idea among Republicans. For Democrats, however, Gohmert's amendment crossed a bright line. Democrats were comfortable with the idea of Christian groups competing for SCA money, but direct legislative authorization funding Christian organizations was a different matter. Behind the scenes Pat Nolan quickly tried to narrow the scope of debate. The Prison Fellowship sent a message to House Republicans: the SCA was centrally about reentry. It was important not to take hard-line positions on the much more explosive issue of public financing of faith-based organizations. In a crucial vote that kept up momentum for the bill, four Republicans including Coble and Cannon voted with Democrats to defeat the amendment (Suellentrop 2006).

ROADBLOCKS IN THE SENATE

In the Senate, Brownback continued his advocacy. In a September 2006 Senate hearing, Brownback again addressed the need to cut recidivism in half in five years. "We've got to hit the number. And it's important. It's important to society. It's important to these individuals. And I hope as well we can work with their families too."* He added arguments about the value of people behind bars, debt, and redemption.

> And I think, chairman, what the whole thing really requires us to just say is that these people have worth. Yes, they've committed a horrific crime. They've done a very bad thing. They owe a debt to society. They've got to pay that debt to society. Yet we've got 2 million people in prisons. At some point in time most are going to come out. And we don't want them to do it again … we won't shy away as well, saying, if you did the crime, you have a debt you will pay to this society. You shouldn't do that. It's wrong and you're going to pay a debt to that. But now, once you've paid it, we want to work with you to make sure you don't go back in to this system again.

Brownback was notably protective of his right flank. He felt it important to reiterate that the SCA was not "soft on crime" but legislation designed to scale up effective reentry policies.

> … And also it says to the rest of society at large, this [the Second Chance Act] isn't a soft-headed program, this isn't us just kind of being mushy on crime. It's being very realistic and it's being very hard-nosed and bottom line—we don't want these guys coming back to prison. We want them out, productive members of society. And if your program can produce that, God bless you. We're going to help support it. If you don't, we're not going to fund it—period.

---

* Comments made before a Senate hearing before the Senate Judiciary Committee, September 21, 2006.

Despite Brownback's cheerleading, in the closing weeks of the session Senator Tom Coburn, a former physician and influential fiscal and social conservative from Oklahoma, put a "hold" on the bill.

The U.S. Senate is often said to be the place where bills go to die. This is not because senators are particularly intransigent (although some are), but rather the institutional rules of the chamber make obstruction easy. A simple majority (fifty-one votes) will technically pass a bill in the Senate; however, just getting to a final vote requires overcoming a number of procedural hurdles. The filibuster is by far the most powerful dilatory tool used to obstruct because it allows a minority group of senators to prevent a bill from going to the floor for a final vote. To end a filibuster requires sixty votes. The "hold" is another common dilatory tactic. A single senator, for just about any reason, can tell the Senate leadership that they have a problem with the bill and want to place a hold on it.* The majority leader decides how long to honor a senator's hold; however, it is generally the case that once a hold is placed, progress stops on the bill until the issue's been resolved to the holding senator's satisfaction (Davidson et al. 2011; Sinclair 2013).

Coburn's hold was motivated by his concerns about new government spending rather than an ideological aversion to reentry services. As a former practicing physician, he often expressed support for drug treatment over incarceration. He was even on the record saying the SCA was a "good act" (Suellentrop 2006). When Coburn came to the Senate in 2004, he had quickly gained a reputation as "Dr. No" for his staunch opposition to any new federal government spending without adequate "offsets"—cuts to other (existing) federal spending programs to pay for spending on new programs. No new spending, however minor, seemed to avoid Coburn's gaze. The SCA, with its millions (and not billions) of dollars in new spending, amounted to a rounding error when viewed in the totality of federal budget. By placing his hold, Coburn wanted Senate leaders to terminate what he believed were duplicative federal reentry programs. Despite pleas from Pat Nolan, Brownback, and Specter to let the bill go to the floor, the Senate took no vote.

The fact that no final vote was taken on the SCA in the 109th Congress symbolized much of what ails the modern version of the institution. The

---

* Critics of the "hold" often focus on the secrecy surrounding it. Before reforms in the 112th Congress, senators could place a hold on a bill anonymously, which allowed a senator to obstruct the legislative process without the public or even fellow senators knowing who placed it. Rules now require a senator to make his or her hold public after two session days.

109th Congress had the fewest number of days in session than any Congress since World War II, and it failed to pass any number of salient measures, from a minimum wage increase to a comprehensive immigration reform package. So unproductive was the 109th, Democrats successfully labeled it the "Do-Nothing Congress." After twelve years of Republican rule in the House, Democrats took back control after gaining thirty-one seats in the November 2006 midterm elections.

CLOSING THE DEAL

The Democratic Party's takeover of the House did not increase the chances that the SCA would pass. The two parties had effectively converged on the reentry issue, making who controlled the chamber a negligible factor in the bill's final outcome. But with Democrats now chairing House committees and setting the terms of debate, the change in the balance of power offers one final glimpse into how progressive members of the smart on crime coalition framed the issue in the closing weeks. Robert "Bobby" Scott, a Democrat and member of the Congressional Black Caucus from the get-tough state of Virginia, and now new chairman of the Subcommittee on Crime, Terrorism, and Homeland Security, focused on the SCA's effect on public safety outcomes and cost savings. In a March 2007 hearing Scott said,

> The Second Chance Act provides a host of evidence-based approaches to reduce the high rate of recidivism…. The primary reason for doing this is not to benefit offenders, although it does. The primary reason to do this is because it assures that all of us and other members of the public will be less likely to be victims of crime due to recidivism and also will be much less likely to have to pay the high costs of incarceration as tax payers.*

Of course, Democrats like Scott knew the history of Republicans using the "soft on crime" label as a cudgel to bludgeon weak-kneed Democrats. This explains why Democrats immersed in the debate tended to empha-size public safety so as to leave no doubt they had public safety as their top

---

* Comments made before the House Subcommittee on Crime, Terrorism, and Homeland Security Hearing, March 20, 2007.

priority. Democrats largely avoided making broader arguments about how the SCA would begin to chip away at that moral ignominy mass incarceration represented.

In short, Democrats followed a cautious rhetorical strategy that matched their political experiences with the tough on crime era. The substance of Democrats' "closing arguments" was only made possible because of the slow but inexorable accumulation of knowledge about recidivism reduction. John Conyers of Michigan, the new chairman of the House Judiciary Committee who served in Congress when the politics on crime turned in the 1970s, relied on research findings to help frame the issue and explain reasons why he sponsored the bill.

> The statistics underlying the needs of our prison population are staggering. As detailed by many researchers these deficiencies included limited education, few job skills or experience, substance and alcohol dependency, and other health problems, including mental health. If we allow them to return to communities with few economic opportunities, where their family and friends are often involved in crime and substance abuse, we can only expect to extend the cycle of recidivism. For example, 57 percent of federal and 70 percent of state inmates used drugs regularly before prison, with some estimates of involvement with drugs or alcohol around the time of offense as high as 84 percent. Further, over one-third of all jail inmates have some physical or mental disability and 25 percent of jail inmates have been treated at some time for a mental or emotional problem.

Conyers continued,

> In the face of these statistics, I believe that we can be cautiously optimistic in the support of reentry programming. Researchers at the Washington State Institute for Public Policy have determined that programs employing "best practices" have yielded up to 20% declines in re-arrest rates. Spread across the thousands of arrests each year, these practices could yield a significant decline in recidivism, with a commensurate reduction in community and victim costs. (see footnote on p. 115)

Republican Randy Forbes, another Virginian and new ranking member on the Crime Subcommittee, also sounded themes about improvement in public safety outcomes and cost savings. But much more than Scott or Conyers, Forbes discussed the SCA's effect on prisoners' lives, their families, and second chances.

Public safety is essential of a free society. And criminals must be aggressively prosecuted and incarcerated to protect our communities. Once criminals are incarcerated, we have an obligation to make sure they are rehabilitated and treated humanely. A critical component to this is the need to plan and provide effective re-entry services. We can no longer release criminals with new clothes and a $5 bill and expect them to become productive citizens. The Second Chance Act creates a framework of strategic policy innovations to provide effective re-entry services.

Forbes continued,

States are being crushed by an overwhelming financial burden for correctional cost. We need to ensure that governments have in place appropriate programs to ease the transition of offenders, to bring families together again, and to make sure that offenders get the necessary support, so that they can truly have a second chance to live a law-abiding life. (see footnote on p. 115)

Scott's subcommittee held a final markup session that offered members another chance to offer amendments. Congressman Gohmert again offered several but each was defeated in committee. The bill's passage became imminent in the House.

In the Senate, Biden, Brownback, Specter, and Patrick Leahy reintroduced the SCA, S. 1060, in late March 2007. By August the SCA had passed the Senate Judiciary Committee. That October the Congressional Joint Economic Committee held a hearing on the causes and consequences of rising incarceration rates. It was a hearing nearly unthinkable a decade earlier. It is important to take note of the witnesses: Pat Nolan; Bruce Western and Glenn Loury, two leading prison reform advocates in the academy; Michael Jacobson, director of the Vera Institute, a prison and criminal sentencing reform organization; and Alphonso Albert of the Second Chances nonprofit. Each witness testified in favor of the SCA. Notable in their absence were any of the usual suspects: prosecutors and law enforcement agents.

On November 13th, the SCA passed the House of Representatives by a wide 347–62 margin. Of the 347 yea votes, Republicans cast 129.* Free of any holds or filibuster threats, the Senate passed the House bill by unanimous consent the next March.

---

* Thomas, House Roll Call 1083, 2007.

In his remarks at the signing ceremony in April 2008, President Bush spoke of dignity, hope, and renewal that were all part of his State of the Union speech four years earlier. "I'm about to sign a piece of legislation that will help give prisoners across America a second chance for a better life," Bush said. "This bill is going to support the caring men and women who help America's prisoners find renewal and hope" ("President Bush Signs H.R. 1593" 2008). Bush continued,

> The country was built on the belief that each human being has limitless potential and worth. Everybody matters. We believe that even those who have struggled with a dark past can find brighter days ahead. One way we act on that belief is by helping former prisoners who've paid for their crimes—we help them build new lives as productive members of our society.... The Second Chance Act will live up to its name; will help ensure that where the prisoner's spirit is willing, the community's resources are available. It will help our armies of compassion use their healing touch so lost souls can rediscover their dignity and sense of purpose. ("President Bush Signs H.R. 1593" 2008)

5

Fair Sentencing Act of 2010

The Second Chance Act represented a remarkable achievement for national policy makers who for decades raced to see who could be the toughest crime warrior. An overlapping struggle to reform federal cocaine sentencing laws would prove just as important, if not more. From a political standpoint, the fight to pass the Fair Sentencing Act (FSA), a bill signed into law by President Obama in August 2010, carried even greater consequence. The Second Chance Act addressed problems at the back end of the criminal justice system. Offenders received policy benefits only after they had served prison or jail time. The FSA, in contrast, required lawmakers to weaken criminal penalties at the front end of the criminal justice system. The legislation marked the first time in forty years that Congress reduced a criminal punishment for a federal drug offense. In so doing, Congress took a significant step toward achieving greater justice and fairness in America's federal criminal sentencing system.

POLICY CONTEXT

The Anti-Drug Abuse Act passed by Congress in 1986 was a perfect reflection of its time. In adopting an array of new mandatory minimums and strengthening punishments for drug use and drug trafficking, Congress made it certain that in the nation's fight against drugs, the prison would play a starring role. The law's most notorious provision—and indeed, the provision that became central to the fight over the FSA—involved its differential treatment of powder and crack cocaine. The law penalized the selling or trafficking of crack at a level 100 times that of the powder form of the drug. For example, a defendant convicted for 5 grams of crack cocaine (about the equivalent of two sugar packets—a quantity that yields 10 to 50 doses) faced a mandatory five-year prison sentence. With powder cocaine, a defendant would need to possess 500 grams (an amount that yields between 2,500 and 5,000 doses) to receive the same sentence (Federal Crack Cocaine Sentencing 2010). This 100-to-1 disparity ratio remained in place even as the quantity of drugs involved grew. A defendant convicted with 10 grams of crack cocaine, for example, faced the same mandatory sentence—10 years in prison—as someone convicted for possession of 1,000 grams of powder cocaine. In 1988 Congress went further by adding penalties for simple possession. A person convicted of possessing 5 grams of crack cocaine, without the intent to sell, faced a mandatory five-year sentence.

The Anti-Drug Abuse Act's stiff penalties and the decision of drug enforcement agents to focus their sweeps in poor, urban communities of color caused a staggering number of blacks to find themselves incarcerated for long periods. Prison reform advocates like Michelle Alexander view the law as another element in conservatives' long-running effort to use the criminal justice system as a tool of black subjugation; only this time the effort fell under the guise of Ronald Reagan's war on drugs. Reagan's drug war, officially announced in 1982, weaved imagery and rhetoric on race, drugs (especially crack), and crime to help drive a moral panic. By the mid-1980s, airwaves and glossy magazines were filled with stories, many of them racially coded, with captions or headlines that mentioned "crack whores," "crack babies," and "gang bangers." The death of star basketball player Len Bias from a cocaine overdose just two days after being drafted by the Boston Celtics stoked fear about a growing epidemic.* In 1986, *Time Magazine* named crack cocaine the biggest story of the year (Alexander 2010, p. 51).

Not all liberal-leaning academicians agree with the premise that politicians ginned up the war on crack for political purposes. David Kennedy, a prominent criminologist who has worked in some of the nation's most gang-infested neighborhoods for his groundbreaking Operation Cease Fire project, calls the claim "bullshit."

> It's become fashionable these days to say that crack sparked a 'moral panic': that it was never really that bad, that the public and political and law enforcement was just a fevered overreaction. Crack blew through America's poor black neighborhoods like the Four Horsemen of the Apocalypse had traded their steeds for supercharged bulldozers. It is now genuinely true, I think, that you

---

* Later it was revealed Len Bias did not die from a crack overdose but rather the powder form of the drug.

had to be there. … More than anything else, the moral panic nonsense misses the mark because it's all about *use*. Crack use, drug use, has never been the real drug problem. Crack markets, drug markets, are the problem. I'd rather be in a crack market than be, say, held at gunpoint, or have boiling oil poured on me. Short of that, things don't get much worse. (Kennedy 2011, p. 27)

Scholars need not waste time debating what is not a zero sum proposition. There were too many similarities between conservatives' race-baiting antics and the larger racialized war on crime to suggest politics played no role in the targeting of crack cocaine. It was also a (flawed) policy response to the very real problem of drug market violence that swept though America's poorest urban neighborhoods after the bottom fell out of the urban labor market; joblessness swept through inner-city black America, and drug dealing became more enticing and violent. Nonetheless, Congress should have known better (Tonry 1995). Congress should have known that drug enforcement efforts that targeted inner-city drug use would disproportionately ensnare black Americans and the poor. This is the tragedy of that era. Our elected leaders did not care enough to lessen the harm on America's most marginalized citizens.

Congress was putatively motivated by several beliefs when it passed the law. Many members believed crack cocaine was more addictive. We now know that, pharmaceutically, crack is about identical to powder cocaine. Crack allows users to inhale the drug. This offers users a faster high but also allows them to use less of the drug.* During a debate on the Anti-Drug Abuse Act, Congress heard expert testimony from Johnny St. Valentine Brown, a well-respected police investigator and "resident narcotics expert" of the Superior Court in Washington, DC. Brown told Congress that possession of 20 grams of crack cocaine was just as dangerous as having 1000 grams of powdered cocaine (Beaver 2010). Brown's testimony was dubious at best. He was later convicted for fabricating his professional credentials. Researchers had not developed a comprehensive understanding of the chemical compounds of cocaine or the relative harms of crack cocaine to the powder form (Beaver 2010). Eric Sterling, former counsel to the House Judiciary Committee, recalled that period: "There was also the notion that crack was a freakish demon drug—that it was many times more addictive, a trigger for violence, and infinitely more dangerous than powder in virtually every way" (Cose 2009).

---

* Crack is made by taking powder cocaine and cooking it with baking soda and water until it forms a hard rocky substance. The "rocks" are broken into small quantities and sold. It earned the street name "crack" because of the crackling sound it makes when smoked (Beaver 2010).

When Congress debated the bill just two weeks before the 1986 midterm elections, hyperbolic rhetoric about the addictiveness of crack cocaine spread through the chamber. Representative James Traficant (who himself would later be sentenced to federal prison for his part in a campaign finance scandal) said, "Crack is reported by many medical experts to be the most addictive narcotic drug known to man ... I am relieved that provisions I coauthored ... [will] create new stiff penalties for dealing with crack cocaine" (Beaver 2010, p. 2546). Democrat Patrick Leahy of Vermont, who would, over two decades later become a leading sponsor of the FSA, reported that crack was "sweeping the nation" because of its wide availability and addictive qualities. Senator Lawton Chiles, a Florida Democrat said, "If you try it once, chances are that you will be hooked. If you use it up to three times, we know that you will become hooked, and it's the strongest addiction that we have found" (*Report to Congress: Cocaine and Federal Sentencing Policy* 2002, p. 9).

Beyond crack's addictiveness, Congress also became concerned about its effect on America's youth. Senator Leahy remarked that "crack is available to the young, and it will be in the schools this fall. I have heard stories of children as young as nine who are already crack users. The sellers also use these children as lookouts and as workers in houses that manufacture crack" (*Report to Congress: Cocaine and Federal Sentencing Policy* 2002, p. 10). Senator Chiles raised concern about crack and youth-committed crime. "Crack can turn promising young people into robbers and thieves, stealing anything they can to get the money to feed their habit," Chiles noted (*Report to Congress: Cocaine and Federal Sentencing Policy* 2002, p. 10). Congress was also alarmed about prenatal exposure to crack cocaine. So-called crack babies faced inevitable prematurity, threats of multiple birth defects, early death, and lifelong struggles with disabilities.

Many of these concerns turned out to be false or overblown. Joe Biden apologized to the Senate Judiciary Committee years later. "Our intentions were good," Biden remarked, "but much of our information was bad" (Cose 2009).

CHALLENGING THE UNIQUE DANGERS OF CRACK COCAINE

Of course, Biden's apology came only after the law ravaged urban communities of color. How did policy makers come to the conclusion that they were wrong? To begin to answer this question, we again must delve into the world of policy research.

As part of the Sentencing Reform Act of 1984, Congress gave the U.S. Sentencing Commission a research directive. Specifically, the commission was charged with making "recommendations to Congress concerning modification or enactment of statutes relating to sentencing, penal, and correctional markers that the commission finds to be necessary to carry out an effective, humane, and rational sentencing policy" (*Report to Congress: Cocaine and Federal Sentencing Policy* 2002, p. 1). As we will see, the Commission's research on the effectiveness of crack sentencing would prove pivotal to the eventual adoption of the FSA.

The commission's work on the subject can be traced to President Clinton's 1994 Crime Bill. A little noticed provision directed the Sentencing Commission to begin examining the effectiveness and consequences of cocaine sentences. A year later the commission issued its first major report. The Sentencing Commission admonished Congress for its sweeping adoption of punitive cocaine sentences despite having only limited anecdotal evidence when it formulated the policy. "Despite the unprecedented level of public attention focused on crack cocaine," the commission stated, "a substantial gap continues to exist between the anecdotal experiences that often prompt a call for action and empirical knowledge upon which to base sound policy" (*Report to Congress: Cocaine and Federal Sentencing Policy* 1995, p. vi).

Moreover, the commission began challenging the belief that crack cocaine was especially addictive. Crack reached the bloodstream much quicker and thereby reached its maximum psychotropic effect faster than snorting the powder form, but the "high" also dissipated much quicker (twenty minutes as opposed to about sixty minutes using the powder form). There was no evidence that either form of the drug was physiologically addictive. Both, however, were psychologically addictive.

The commission's report also addressed crack-related violence. Crack cocaine markets contributed to a higher degree of "systematic violence," mostly involving turf battles in poor urban neighborhoods. But the commission found no evidence that crack cocaine itself invoked violent behavior. "Neither powder nor crack cocaine excite or agitate users to commit criminal acts and that the stereotype of the drug-crazed addict committing heinous crimes is not true for either form of cocaine" (*Report to Congress: Cocaine and Federal Sentencing Policy* 1995, p. vii).

The commission then laid out in alarming terms how the 100-to-1 disparity disproportionately affected blacks. Drawing on data from 1993, the report found that blacks accounted for 83.3 percent of federal crack cocaine convictions, Hispanics 7.1 percent, and whites constituted a meager 4.1 percent. The rate of crack cocaine use across racial and ethnic subgroups, however, looked much different. Results of a 1991 Household Survey showed 52 percent of the people who reported using crack were white, 38 percent were black, and 10 percent were Hispanic. "Federal sentencing data leads to the inescapable conclusion that blacks comprise the largest percentage of those affected by the penalties associated with crack cocaine," the commission said (*Report to Congress: Cocaine and Federal Sentencing Policy* 1995, p. xii). Yet when it came to the issue of whether racial prejudice played a role in the law's enforcement, the commission treaded lightly. It noted, for example, that the law applied equally to defendants regardless of race. "Nevertheless," the report read, "the high percentage of blacks convicted for crack cocaine offenses is of great concern" (*Report to Congress: Cocaine and Federal Sentencing Policy* 1995, p. xii).

Finally, the commission advised Congress that if it wanted to penalize the two forms of drug differently, one form had to be more dangerous to public health or safety. "In assessing the relative harms posed by the two forms, the aim is to arrive at a penalty differential that approximates the increased dangers posed by the more harmful drug" (*Report to Congress: Cocaine and Federal Sentencing Policy* 1995, p. xii). The commission said that distinctions (or risks) between the two "may warrant higher penalties for crack," but it did not the support the 100-to-1 ratio (*Report to Congress: Cocaine and Federal Sentencing Policy* 1995, p. xiii). "… Given its review of the subject, the Sentencing Commission cannot support the current penalty scheme. The factors that suggest a difference between the two forms of cocaine do not approach the level of a 100-to-1 quantity ratio" (*Report to Congress: Cocaine and Federal Sentencing Policy* 1995, p. xiv).

In May 1995 the Sentencing Commission made a formal policy recommendation to Congress. It called for a one-to-one ratio with enhancements for offenders who used a dangerous weapon or committed other harmful acts while trafficking drugs. Congress rejected the commission's recommendation out of hand. It did, however, tell the commission to revisit the issue, but with one important caveat: any future recommendation had to include more punitive sentences for crack.

In 1997 the Sentencing Commission published a second report. The commission stood by its earlier call to reduce the crack/powder disparity; only this time it offered Congress several policy proposals that carried disparity ratios ranging from two-to-one to fifteen-to-one. Most important, the report emphasized the injustice of the 100-to-1 disparity.

One of the issues of greatest concern surrounding federal cocaine sentencing policy is the perception of disparate and unfair treatment for defendants convicted of either possession or distribution of crack cocaine. Critics argue that the 100 to 1 quantity ratio is not consistent with the policy, goal, and mission of federal sentencing—that is to be effective, uniform, and just. While there is no evidence of racial bias behind the promulgation of this federal sentencing law, nearly 90 percent of the offenders convicted in federal court for crack cocaine distribution are African American while the majority of crack cocaine users is white ... The current penalty structure results in a perception of unfairness and inconsistency. (*Report to Congress: Cocaine and Federal Sentencing Policy* 1995, p. 8)

Congress again rejected each of the commission's recommendations. Congress also rejected a number of reform bills introduced into both the House and Senate mostly by letting them languish in committee. Charlie Rangel, for example, the Democratic Congressman from Brooklyn (and original supporter of the Anti-Drug Abuse Act), offered crack sentencing reform legislation in every Congress during the 1990s (*Report to Congress: Cocaine and Federal Sentencing Policy* 2002).

By the early 2000s, however, the commission's efforts were aided by several factors. First, Congress's worst fears about crack-addicted babies had never materialized. Testifying before the U.S. Sentencing Commission in February of 2002, Dr. Deborah Frank, a professor of pediatrics at Boston University, called the image of the "crack baby" a "grotesque media stereotype and not a scientific diagnosis" (Federal Crack Cocaine Sentencing 2010, p. 6). In another report to Congress that same year, the commission stated that the "negative effects of prenatal exposure to crack cocaine are identical to the effects of exposure to powder cocaine and are significantly less than previously believed" (*Report to Congress: Cocaine and Federal Sentencing Policy* 2002, p. 21). "In fact, the negative effects from prenatal cocaine exposure are similar to those associated with prenatal tobacco exposure and less severe than the negative effects of prenatal alcohol exposure" (*Report to Congress: Cocaine and Federal Sentencing Policy* 2002, p. 22).

Second, data continued to show teenage use of crack cocaine remained low. Nor was there evidence that America's youth played a major role in cocaine trafficking. Crack-related violence was also on the decline. The rate at which crack offenders or unindicted coparticipants used a weapon had declined 35 percent between 1995 and 2000 (*Report to Congress: Cocaine and Federal Sentencing Policy* 2002, p. 53). Three quarters of federal crack offenders in 2000 (the most recent data available to the commission in

2002) had no personal weapon. In only 2.3 percent of cases was a weapon discharged. The commission stated, "The extent that the 100-to-1 drug quantity ratio was designed in part to account for this harmful conduct, it sweeps too broadly by treating all crack cocaine offenders as if they committed those more harmful acts, even though most crack cocaine offenders in fact had not" (*Report to Congress: Cocaine and Federal Sentencing Policy* 2002, p. vii).

It became broadly apparent that crack cocaine was not, as Representative Traficant said in 1986, the "most addictive narcotic drug known to man" (*Report to Congress: Cocaine and Federal Sentencing Policy* 2002, p. 8). Moreover, the gravest concerns about crack-induced violence, crack-addicted teenagers, or crack-addicted babies had either waned or were discredited by new research. "Revising the crack cocaine thresholds would better reduce the [sentencing] gap than any other single policy change, and would dramatically improve the fairness of the federal sentencing system," the commission told Congress (*Fifteen Years of Guidelines Sentencing* 2004, p. 122).

PROPOSALS FOR CHANGE

When combined over time, these forces began to affect members of Congress, most notably conservatives. Just before Christmas in 2001, Jeff Sessions, a conservative Republican from Alabama, introduced a bill (S. 1874) titled the Drug Sentencing Reform Act. Although Sessions's bill eventually died in committee, it was important because it helped structure the dimensions of the policy debate inside Congress for the rest of the decade. The congressional debate shifted in subtle, yet important ways; Congress became focused not on whether it should reduce the disparity, but rather how much, and what mechanisms, Congress should use to do it. Sessions's bill reduced the disparity to a twenty-to-one ratio. This was achieved in two ways. First, the bill increased from 5 to 20 grams the quantity of crack cocaine required to trigger a five-year minimum sentence. Second, and more controversial, it *increased* the penalties for powder cocaine by lowering the quantity needed for a five-year sentence from 500 to 400 grams.

As a former prosecutor, Sessions saw virtue in the Anti-Drug Abuse Act. He credited the bill for reducing drug use and crime—a claim countered, justifiably so, by progressive groups. Yet even he recognized its flaws, especially the law's undeniable effect on blacks.

My experience does lead me to conclude, however, that where an over-whelming majority of those convicted of crack offenses are African-American, and the penalties for crack offenses are the most severe, we should listen to fair-minded people who argue that these sentences fall too heavily on African-Americans.*

Sessions continued,

As data from the Sentencing Commission became available during the mid-1990s, many federal and state officials, including myself, began to doubt whether the 100-to-1 ratio between powder and crack cocaine continued to be justifiable ... To date, however, Congress has declined to address the issue. Many say it is because of a fear of being called 'soft on crime'. Regardless, we can wait no longer. (see footnote)

But wait Congress did. In the meantime, many federal judges became vocal critics of the overly rigid drug sentencing process. Lawsuits brought by defendants challenging mandatory sentences under the federal sentencing guidelines began making their way through the federal courts. To place these legal challenges in proper context and to understand how they shaped the politics of crack sentencing reform, it is necessary to delve a bit deeper into how the federal sentencing process works.

LEGAL CHALLENGES TO THE FEDERAL SENTENCING PROCESS

When Congress passes a new criminal law, it issues a statutory maximum punishment; that is, it specifies the longest punishment a person *can* receive if convicted. Congress may also choose to adopt a mandatory minimum penalty, which specifies the lowest level of punishment a person *must* receive. In effect, Congress's mandatory minimums create a floor and statutory maximums set a ceiling for punishment ("How Federal Sentencing Law Works" 2013).

As noted earlier in the book, following the adoption of the Sentencing Reform Act in 1984, the U.S. Sentencing Commission codified federal criminal laws into a set of federal sentencing guidelines. The guidelines

---

* Remarks made in Senate, December 21, 2001, CR S13961–S13965.

created forty-three different base offense categories ranging from least to most severe. Federal judges sentencing a defendant under the guidelines considered two primary factors: the seriousness of the offense as defined by congressional statute and the defendant's criminal history. After a judge paired the seriousness of the offense, which determined the "base offense level" under the guidelines, with a defendant's criminal history, the guidelines specified a sentencing range, in months, within which the judge could sentence the defendant.

Sentencing for drug crimes operated in the same manner. In these cases the base offense level was tied to the quantity and type of drug involved and a defendant's criminal record. As just one example, suppose a defendant was convicted for possessing an amount of marijuana greater than 60 kilograms but less than 80 kilograms. According to the federal guidelines this would trigger a base offense level of 20. A defendant with no prior criminal record (e.g., Criminal History Category 1 in the Federal Sentencing Table) at base offense level 20 would receive a guideline sentence in the range of thirty-three to forty-one months. A defendant convicted of the same drug offense but with a longer criminal record (e.g., Criminal History Category 3) would receive a longer guideline sentence of forty-one to fifty-one months.

Until 2005, when the Supreme Court ruled in *United States v. Booker*, a sentence range determined by the sentencing guidelines, like that described above, was mandatory. Judges grew frustrated because they had no discretion to go above or below a guideline sentence.[*]

Despite the rigidity of federal sentencing guidelines, judges did retain some control over a defendant's sentence insofar as they had to consider a number of facts in a case. In a drug trafficking case, for example, a judge would need to ask: how much cocaine did the defendant carry? Did the defendant have prior convictions? Did the defendant carry a weapon while committing the crime? Federal judges not only held the power to make these findings of fact but also could lawfully issue a sentence based on their conclusions.[†]

---

[*] There are exceptions to this statement including when a "departure" was justified under federal "safety valve" rules, or if Congress had imposed a mandatory minimum. In the latter case, a statutory mandatory minimum with a longer punishment than a guideline sentence forced a judge to impose a sentence above the guideline allowance.

[†] The above section relies on the work of Ken White who writes about federal sentencing and legal matters at the legal blog. Available at http://www.popehat.com.

By the late 1990s, the Supreme Court began to consider whether the U.S. Constitution's Sixth Amendment—which states that in "all criminal prosecutions, the accused shall enjoy the right to a speedy and public trial, by an impartial jury"—also extended to federal sentencing decisions. As detailed by legal writer Ken White, the court asked, "When a statute imposes different punishments based on different levels of culpability, must a judge or jury determine that level of culpability?" (White 2013).

The court first answered this question in 2000 in the case of *Apprendi v. New Jersey*. The court ruled that when a statutory factor increased a defendant's maximum sentence, the longer sentence must result from a jury's decision (or a defendant's guilty plea), not a judge. Judges could not (by themselves) make findings of fact that increased a defendant's sentence. In *United States v. Booker*, the Supreme Court extended its holding in *Apprendi* to the entire federal sentencing guidelines. The guidelines were unconstitutional, the court ruled, because judges (and not juries) determined the factors that contributed to longer sentences. For example, for a defendant who faced a ten-year sentence for drug trafficking but saw his sentence increased to fifteen years because he held a weapon, a judge (and not a jury) would make the factual determination of whether the defendant carried a weapon. The process violated a defendant's Sixth Amendment right to trial by jury. As a result, the court made a crucial determination that the sentencing guidelines were only advisory (White 2013).

Two years later the court dealt explicitly with federal guideline sentences for crack cocaine in *Kimbrough v. United States*. The defendant, Derrick Kimbrough, was indicted in 2004 on several drug charges: conspiracy to distribute crack and powder cocaine, possession with intent to distribute more than 50 grams of crack cocaine, and using a firearm in "furtherance" of a drug distribution. Kimbrough pleaded guilty to each charge. Under the federal sentencing guidelines, he faced a sentence of nineteen to twenty-two and a half years.

U.S. District Court trial judge Raymond Alvin Jackson called the sentence "ridiculous." He argued that if Kimbrough's drug crimes had only involved powder cocaine, his sentence would have been much shorter. Citing the Sentencing Commission's reports disparaging the 100-to-1 ratio, Kimbrough's limited criminal record, and his steady job history, the district court departed from the sentencing guidelines and sentenced Kimbrough to a more lenient 180-month (or 15 year) sentence. But the Fourth Circuit Court of Appeals soon vacated the decision. The district court could not sentence outside the sentencing guidelines, the Fourth

Circuit Court argued, merely because judges opposed Congress's more stringent crack cocaine policy.

On appeal the U.S. Supreme Court reversed. The court ruled that crack cocaine guidelines, like all other guidelines post-*Booker,* were only advisory. Judges must consider the federal guidelines at the time of sentencing, but they may also determine in particular cases that a "within-guidelines" sentence is "greater than necessary" to serve the objectives of sentencing.*

Kimbrough was significant because it gave federal judges new powers to deviate from the federal guidelines in cases involving cocaine. But it was the larger message emanating from the *Booker* and *Kimbrough* decisions that served a greater political purpose; Supreme Court gave credence to sentencing reform advocates' major point: federal cocaine sentences were deeply flawed. Some reformers were ecstatic with the decisions; they saw the cases as posing a major gash in the armor of punitive sentencing advocates. Others, however, were less sanguine. What exactly the court's ruling meant for federal sentencing *in practice* moving forward remained uncertain.

NEW PROPOSALS FOR CRACK SENTENCING REFORM

Under federal sentencing rules, the U.S. Sentencing Commission can offer amendments to the federal sentencing guidelines. Unless Congress rejects the changes, they become law. By November 2007, the Sentencing Commission, seemingly tired of waiting for Congress to act and sensing an opportunistic political environment, presented an amendment to the crack cocaine sentencing guidelines. At the time, a defendant convicted for possession of 5 grams of crack cocaine was sentenced under base offense level 26—which carried a guideline prison term of sixty-three to seventy-eight months.† The commission's amendment (706) reduced sentences by two offense levels for each threshold quantity level of "cocaine base" listed under the Drug Quantity Table. Under the new rules, that

---

* *Kimbrough v. United States*; 06-6330: 5–21.
† This calculation is independent of any prior criminal record (or any aggravating or mitigating circumstances) that may result in a different guideline sentence.

same 5 grams of crack cocaine would be sentenced under a base level of 24—with a guideline sentence of fifty-one to sixty-three months. The commission estimated the change would reduce the average sentence by fifteen months.* In March 2008, the Sentencing Commission made the Amendment retroactive, allowing some 20,000 offenders the opportunity to seek reduced sentences under the new guidelines (Crowell 2010).

The Sentencing Commission itself saw the amendment as a temporary, less-than-perfect fix. In fact, in the early going, many offenders seeking shorter sentences were denied, especially those who were convicted under a "career offender guideline" (Crowell 2010, p. 960). Commission members continued to compel Congress to make a more definitive fix by passing new legislation (Crowell 2010, p. 960).

As the 110th Congress convened early in 2007, Republican Senator Orrin Hatch introduced a new crack sentencing reform bill. Like Sessions had six years earlier, Hatch's bill proposed to reduce the crack/powder disparity to twenty-to-one. It completely erased the five-year mandatory minimum for first time possession. It raised the mandatory five-year trigger on crack cocaine from 5 to 25 grams; most important, however, it did not raise punishments on powder cocaine as Session's bill did.

Hatch secured cosponsors in moderate Republican Arlen Specter, Democrat Dianne Feinstein of California, and the liberal stalwart from Massachusetts, Ted Kennedy. Kennedy, recall, was a leading proponent of the federal sentencing guidelines during the 1980s. Now, more than twenty years later, Kennedy noted how new evidence had changed his views on cocaine sentencing.

> When these laws were enacted, there was widespread belief in the extraordinary dangers of crack cocaine. It was viewed as highly addictive and likely to cause violent behavior. We know much more about crack cocaine now than we did 20 years ago. The rationale that crack is more dangerous or more addictive than powder is not supported by research. In fact, research has demonstrated that the effects of crack cocaine are much like the effects of powder cocaine.

---

* In practice, the amendment narrowed the disparity between crack and powder cocaine, moving the ratio from the draconian 100-to-1 to a range of 25-to-1 to 80-to-1, depending on the offense level—see *Kimbrough v. United States*; 06-6330: 16–18.

MOBILIZING SUPPORT FOR CRACK SENTENCING REFORM

Hatch's bill never became law. Its greatest impact was felt in driving the movement forward by giving reform advocates in Washington something to organize around. As legislation made its way through the Senate, organized groups on both the left and right side of the smart on crime coalition intensified their mobilization efforts and solidified their arguments. On the progressive side, national-level civil rights and liberties organizations like the National Association for the Advancement of Colored People (NAACP) (who worked closely with members of the Congressional Black Caucus) and the American Civil Liberties Union (ACLU) were active. So too were sentencing reform organizations such as the Open Society Foundation, the Vera Institute, Families Against Mandatory Minimums, the Sentencing Project, and the Drug Policy Alliance, among others.

Progressive members of the coalition had began their push for reform around the time the Sentencing Commission issued its first major report on crack sentencing in 1995. Their strategy was effectively twofold: continue to shift the dimensions of the policy debate to more favorable grounds and build a broader-based coalition of support inside Congress.

No advocacy organization had a larger effect on shifting the terms of debate than the Sentencing Project, a Washington, DC–based nonprofit. Directed by Marc Mauer, one of the most respected voices on sentencing reform in the country, the Sentencing Project published an impressive number of reports on crack cocaine and the effects punitive sentencing laws had on individuals, families, and state and federal budgets.

An advocacy organization's influence is only equal to its ability to get noticed. This is a constant challenge for advocacy groups working in a Washington policy environment saturated with information. It is difficult to cut through the noise. The Sentencing Project was more successful at getting their work noticed than others. National media like the *New York Times* routinely published the findings of the Sentencing Project's reports and vignettes about individuals suffering under prolonged sentences. As one staff member of the Sentencing Project said, "We've been good at getting coverage ... we've built good relationships with reporters and the press. That goes a long way. Staffers on the hill read the [*New York*] *Times*, the [*Washington*] *Post*, and regional papers. The media is critical to our work" (Gotsch 2009).

While news coverage and op-eds began to line up against long drug sentences, the second part of advocates' strategy required a sustained lobbying campaign inside Congress. These efforts were, and remain, a grind. Kara Gotsch, who served as the Director of Advocacy for the Sentencing Project, explained the challenges of making the sale inside Congress. "The 'soft on crime label' is always in their [members of Congress] thinking. Even those who have unbeatable credentials of being tough on crime are worried about it," Gotsch noted. The novelty of reducing drug sentences also did not help. "The idea of lower penalties for anything just doesn't happen," Gotsch said. "They [Congress] just don't do that. There is no history behind it" (Gotsch 2009).

Lobbying required a high degree of coordination among progressive organizations. They drafted press releases, developed "target lists," and scheduled strategy meetings or conference calls. "All the work I do is done in coalition," Gotsch said. "We go in big groups and go into these offices as a coalition. From my perspective we know that just going in as the Sentencing Project is not going to be as effective as going in with the ACLU, the American Bar Association, or Families Against Mandatory Minimums. It's important for them [Congress] to understand that we are all united in our position and its not just one organization that believes this. It's all of us. That is critical particularly for the kinds of policies we are trying to advance which are controversial and not politically popular" (Gotsch 2009).

On the conservative side of the coalition, the Prison Fellowship made its first major public engagement with the debate when Pat Nolan testified before the U.S. Sentencing Commission in 2007. At the time the commission was in the process of considering making its amendment to the federal sentencing guidelines retroactive. The commission had already faced opposition to the move from several House and Senate Republicans.*

Nolan quickly tried to appease Republican opponents. The Anti-Drug Abuse Act's ostensible goal of targeting drug traffickers was never realized, Nolan argued. The law instead ensnared too many small-time dealers. Nolan even told a story from his own prison experience to further his point. His federal penitentiary bunkmate named Jody, who served ten years for crack distribution, "was no Mr. Big," Nolan said. "He could have hardly organized a two-car funeral, let alone a crack conspiracy." Nolan also cited the Sentencing Commission's own statistics.

---

* Testimony of Pat Nolan before the U.S. Sentencing Commission, November 13, 2007.

> Only 7 percent of federal cocaine cases are directed at high level traffickers. Instead, federal authorities squander huge amounts of resources on small cogs in the cocaine distribution network: one third of all federal cocaine cases involve an average of 52 grams—the weight of a candy bar. This is a terrible misuse of the time and effort of federal law enforcement and prosecutors. Plus, it has filled our prisons to overflowing. (see footnote on p. 133)

Nolan, of course, was preaching to the choir; the commission had made many of the same arguments in their reports to Congress. Nolan and the Prison Fellowship likely had another audience in mind: risk-averse conservatives in Congress.

* * *

Nolan's political concerns were justified because the 110th Congress ended in December 2008 with no bill. In fact, Hatch's bill had never even made it out of committee. Much of the delay could be traced to narcotics officers. Narcotics officials fought hard to keep the debate headed along dimensions favorable to their cause, telling Congress that reducing crack cocaine sentences posed a threat to public safety. The testimony of Bruce Bushman, the vice president of the National Narcotics Officers' Associations' Coalition (NNOAC) (an organization that represents over 55,000 law enforcement officers across the nation), before the House Subcommittee on Crime, Terrorism, and Homeland Security in spring of 2009, provides a window into their thinking. Bushman defined narcotic agents' work as crucial in a threatening world. "In human terms, as we speak," Bushman said, "there are police officers, sheriff's deputies, state and federal agents working to protect our communities from predators who greatly profit by selling and distributing poisons to our kids."* Mandatory drug penalties, he went on to suggest, were a by-product of public demand.

> Citizens demanded tough measures to bring the situation (crack and violence) under control, and the current laws related to sentencing crack offenders were a direct response to the desperate pleas of law abiding citizens and their families. (see footnote)

---

* Testimony of Bruce Bushman before the House Subcommittee on Crime, Terrorism, and Homeland Security, May 21, 2009.

This was an effective line of reasoning if it was made in 1986. But now as the 111th Congress progressed, the political landscape became less and less favorable to organizations and interests trying to maintain the policy status quo.

The Sentencing Commission's stance, and the authority by which it spoke, aided the efforts of progressive reformers. Marc Mauer of the Sentencing Project used the commission's research to bring attention to the costs of locking up low-level drug offenders in his own testimony.

> The data from the Sentencing Commission have shown us over many years, roughly 60 percent of crack cocaine cases are in the lower levels of the drug trade … It costs conservatively $25,000 a year to incarcerate someone in federal prison, so every time a judge is required to impose a mandatory five year sentence, that's $125,000 of taxpayer resources. If we care about resources, if we care about addressing the problem, dealing with these low level cases in federal prison does not seem to be a very wise strategy.*

Addressing the issue of crack-related violence, Mauer urged policy makers to examine the problem in light of historical trends. New drugs entering the market often caused a surge in violence as dealers battled for turf. Mauer said,

> Is violence associated with crack? Yes, but it's about markets, just like powder cocaine. Most of this, in regard to crack, took place in the late 1980s, when crack first made its appearance in many urban areas. There was some belief at the time it was due to the drug itself. We now know, of course, these are battles over turf and young people, in particular, having easy access to guns, all of that coming together. We also know that the majority of crack cases do not involve violence in terms of offenders who actually use a weapon. (see footnote)

Advancements in research also helped Mauer and progressive reformers to discredit arguments from law enforcement groups that tougher drug sentences were responsible for the declining rates of drug use and crime in America. The following committee hearing exchange among Democratic Representative Bobby Scott, Bruce Bushman, and Marc Mauer offers enlightening evidence.

---

* Testimony before the House Subcommittee on Crime, Terrorism, and Homeland Security, May 21, 2009.

> Congressman Scott (to Bruce Bushman): Do you know of any studies that show drug use has been lowered in those areas with more severe penalties?

Bushman then appeared to evade the question directly. Instead he turned to anecdotal evidence on incarceration.

> Well, I can tell you that, based on my personal experience, when we've been able to prosecute and remove organizations and high-level dealers from the neighborhoods, the amount of violence has gone down. The numbers of our shootings have gone down. The number of murders in the communities that were running rampant with crack dealing has gone down.

In response, Congressman Scott again pressed Bushman on the research.

> Do you have any studies to show that the longer sentences, not the fact that you caught people and incarcerated them, but the longer sentences, were responsible for the reduction in crime?
> Bushman: I've seen some, but I don't have any here to cite for you.

Congressman Scott then asked the same question to Mauer.

> Mr. Mauer, Do you have any studies to show that the longer sentences actually reduce crime?

Mauer, in contrast, did not feel it necessary to evade the question because he knew what the research said and he knew it supported his position.

> Most of the deterrence literature in criminology suggests that any deterrent effect the system has, which it does, is more based on the certainty rather than severity of punishment. In other words, if we can increase the prospects that a given person will be apprehended, that at least some people will be deterred from committing crimes. But merely increasing the amount of punishment we impose for people who don't expect to be caught, and unfortunately, most people don't expect to be caught, has relatively little effect on adding to deterrence. (see footnote on p. 135)

New research, declining rates of drug-related violence, and sustained lobbying efforts of reform organizations all worked against the interests of narcotics officials. As it became clear the tide had turned, enforcement organizations began finding ways to support sentencing reform while also attempting to limit their losses.

To do so required a pivot of sorts. On the one hand, organizations like the NNOAC wanted to push a hard line. On the other hand, they needed to publicly recognize the damage done to minority communities. To do otherwise risked looking insensitive and threatened the image of the law enforcement profession. Bruce Bushman of the NNOAC told Congress,

> While we believe that the existing law has been a valuable tool in reducing the impact of crack cocaine on communities, we also realize that it has had a negative impact on some people's perception of law enforcement. So, while we agree that it is appropriate for Congress to review the law, we also believe that Congress should consider a solution to narrow the disparity between crack cocaine and powder that includes lowering the threshold quantity for powder cocaine. We do not believe that the best approach is to dramatically increase the threshold amount of crack that triggers the minimum penalty. (see footnote on p. 134)

The NNOAC was not alone. The National District Attorney's Association (NDAA), the largest organization representing state and local prosecutors, the National Association of Police Organizations (which represents over 240,000 law enforcement officers across the United States), and the Federal Law Enforcement Organizations all held the same position. They agreed that the 100-to-1 disparity needed amending but opposed a 1-to-1 ratio, citing concerns about violence in crack cocaine markets. As a representative from the NDAA warned Congress, "a random adjustment will have severe negative consequences as to the effects of the nation's prosecutors to remove the destructive effects of crack and violence from our communities."*

During the 111th Congress, leaders of the Congressional Black Caucus who worked doggedly (but fruitlessly) over the years to reform crack cocaine sentences introduced a new set of bills that erased the disparity outright. Representative Bobby Scott's bill (H.R. 3245) was the first to get successfully reported out of committee. But the vote reflected the remaining divisions between the two party caucuses. All sixteen Democrats on the Judiciary Committee voted in favor of the bill. The Republicans, nine in total, voiced the concerns of prosecutors and narcotics organizations and voted no.

---

* Testimony of Scott Patterson before the House Subcommittee on Crime, Terrorism, and Homeland Security, May 21, 2009.

In the Senate, Dick Durbin, the Chairman of the Senate Judiciary Subcommittee on Crime and Drugs, and Patrick Leahy, the Chairman of the Senate Judiciary Committee, introduced S. 1789, the Fair Sentencing Act. Like Representative Scott's bill in the House, it eliminated the crack/powder disparity outright. It would be a modified version of the Durbin/Leahy FSA that would eventually be signed into law. Durbin sounded the smart on crime theme as he introduced the legislation.

> Drug use is a serious problem in America and we need tough legislation to combat it. But in addition to being tough, our drug laws must be smart and fair. Our current cocaine laws are not. The sentencing disparity between crack and powder cocaine has contributed to the imprisonment of African Americans at six times of the rate of whites and to the United States' position as the world's leader in incarceration. Congress has talked about addressing this injustice for long enough; it's time for us to act.*

Elections that shift the balance of power in Washington can serve as important exogenous shocks to a policy subsystem (Sabatier and Jenkins-Smith 1988). It is important not to overlook what the 2008 election of Barack Obama meant for the chances that a crack reform bill in the mold of Durbin and Leahy's FSA would finally clear Congress. No previous presidential administration had publicly supported repealing the crack/power disparity. Even George W. Bush stopped short of endorsing crack sentencing changes. While campaigning for the presidency, Barack Obama voiced support for eliminating the disparity; he called it "fundamentally unfair" and remarked how the law "disproportionately filled our prisons with young black and Latino drug users" (Eckholm 2010). Once Obama took office in January 2009, Durbin's subcommittee heard testimony from Obama's assistant attorney general, Lanny Breuer, that the Justice Department favored elimination of the crack/powder disparity.

Durbin and Leahy found political divisions in the Senate similar to those surrounding Representative Scott's bill in the House. Jeff Sessions, the ranking member of the Senate Judiciary Committee and, recall, one of the first Republicans to introduce a sentencing reform bill in 2001, remained an obstacle. Sessions said the FSA "was pretty close to good policy," yet he would not support a full repeal. "I will not favor alterations that massively

---

* October 15, 2009, 155 Cong Rec S 10488.

undercut the sentencing we have in place … I oppose anything that represents a 50, 60, 70, or 80 percent reduction in penalties, but a significant rebalancing of that would be justified."* Orrin Hatch also opposed a full repeal.

Sessions and Hatch's unwillingness to support parity was no doubt the same reason voiced by Republicans sitting on the House Judiciary Committee: the reservations of law enforcement to go "all in." Kara Gotsch of the Sentencing Project noted how she and others on the progressive side of coalition continued to push Sessions and Hatch to go further, only to have them respond, "This is the best we can do. People are starting to say we are soft on crime" (Gotsch 2009).

Sponsors of politically difficult legislation who gain the support of a handful of leaders (e.g., the support of a committee chairman, a majority or minority leader, or a congressional member who holds specialized expertise in a given policy area) can often "unlock" additional votes from "fence sitters" of the same political party or ideological persuasion. Many Senate Democrats believed that if Sessions and Hatch could climb aboard they would likely bring with them the "yes" votes of Republicans John Cornyn of Texas, Chuck Grassley of Iowa, and Lindsey Graham of South Carolina. But with Sessions and Hatch having moved as far to the left as they seemingly wanted to go, the fate of the FSA would not be decided until that next spring.

* * *

For their part, the Prison Fellowship Ministries lobbied for the FSA by working on a number of fronts. The Prison Fellowship continued to benefit from a law enforcement community that, as a whole, had become increasingly fractured. The American Correctional Association (ACA) and the Association of State Correctional Administrators—both major backers of the Second Chance Act—now publicly favored sentencing reform.

The same self-interested dynamic that caused correctional guards to support prisoner reentry initiatives also played a part in their support for sentencing reform. Their main motivation: prison and jail overcrowding. The ACA supported mandatory minimums and truth-in-sentencing laws in the 1980s and 1990s. It had supported Clinton's 1994 Crime Bill. But as lawmakers continued to expand the use of mandatory minimums, the ACA grew concerned about their effect on guards' workloads. James

---

* Statement by Jeff Sessions, October 15, 2009, 155 Cong Rec S 10488.

Collins, then chair of the ACA's Legislative Affairs Committee, warned Congress in 1995 that as the movement to lengthen sentences continued, "offender populations and related costs will dramatically increase in decades to come."* Collins said the ACA opposed policies that would "impair corrections officials in the day-to-day management of their facilities or their ability to manage their inmates populations in a safe and secure manner" (see footnote *).

Of course we now know that prisons, just as the guards warned, did become unmanageable. In 2005, Pat Nolan heard firsthand about the stresses guards faced on the job when he served as a member of the Commission on Safety and Abuse in America's Prisons. James Marquart, a former correctional guard who now teaches at the University of Texas at Dallas, spoke before the commission.

> When I look at the correctional landscape, I think one word sums it up, and that's the word 'pressure'. The working environment for the average American prison officer is constantly laden with pressure. They're constantly working under strain and that strain is growing; finding housing, medication, recreation activities, showers, and human interaction on a daily or hourly basis.[†]

Former California Corrections Secretary Roderick Hickman told the commission that overcrowding was the biggest cause of violence in that state's overstuffed prison system. Vincent Nation, a leading expert on prison crowding said,

> The difficulties that administrators face in attempting to maintain safe institutions, to maintain staff morale, to prepare prisoners for re-entry, which is a fundamental responsibility of the state, to accomplish anything constructive, is made so much more difficult by the inability to do anything but respond to the daily crisis in the form of violence, in the form of staff response, in the form of deterioration of physical facilities, and all the problems that result from an overcrowded environment. (see footnote [†])

It is not a stretch then to see why corrections organizations supported crack sentencing reform. The FSA had the potential to lessen prison overcrowding. Most important, they believed it would help them cope with

---

* Testimony of James Collins before the Senate Judiciary Committee, July 27, 1995.
† Testimony before the Commission on Safety and Abuse in America's Prisons, July 19, 2005. Available at http://www.vera.org/files/public-hearing-3-day-1-corrections-officers.pdf, p. 73.

the day-to-day realities of working in crowded and dangerous correctional institutions.

The Prison Fellowship did not shy away from making instrumental arguments on behalf of others. Given the credibility of corrections officials in Congress, the Fellowship most certainly knew the political benefits of advancing their cause. In their closing pitch, the Prison Fellowship sold the FSA as an opportunity to tackle the problem of prison overcrowding. Reducing prison overcrowding, the Fellowship said, was the Commission on Safety and Prison Abuse's number one recommendation to curb prison violence (Prison Fellowship Ministries 2010).

The Prison Fellowship also sounded what were by then familiar themes. Nearly a quarter century had passed since the mandatory minimums took effect and "sadly, it has not worked," the Prison Fellowship told Congress. The "crack trade still thrives in our cities. Despite the substantial cost to taxpayers and society, the crack–powder ratio has resulted in no real impact on the cocaine trade—and has diverted precious federal resources from stopping drug kingpins to chasing after low-level, local offenders" (Prison Fellowship Ministries 2010). The Fellowship noted the "harsh penalties for crack powder have had an enormous, racially discriminatory impact on black communities." Citing the 2002 Sentencing Commission's report, they said revising crack sentencing laws would "reduce the sentencing gap between blacks and whites more than any other single policy change" (Prison Fellowship Ministries 2010).

Behind the scenes Nolan continued to solidify the conservative side of the coalition. Ward Connolly, a prominent conservative who led the fight against affirmative action programs in the 1990s, joined in support. So too did the American Conservative Union—a powerful grassroots organization that advances conservative causes—and religious organizations such as the National Association of Evangelicals and the United Methodist Church.

But perhaps the most prominent and powerful conservative to endorse the FSA was Grover Norquist of Americans for Tax Reform (ATR). Since heading ATR—an organization that traces its roots to the Reagan administration—Norquist has become one of the most effective antigovernment crusaders in Washington. His goal, as he once described it, was to reduce the federal government "down to the size where you could drain it down the bathtub" (Hacker and Pierson 2010, p. 493). Any policy he construes to increase the size of the federal government or even hint at raising taxes, he tries to foil.

Norquist's primary tool of choice is the so-called taxes pledge. He asks political candidates and national and state office holders to make specific promises not to support tax increases (Hacker and Pierson 2010, p. 493). ATR then plays hardball to keep politicians in line. Along with other Republican backers like the Club for Growth, ATR focuses its efforts on expelling RINOs—Republicans in Name Only—by supporting hard-line conservative candidates in primary elections and recruiting them for open seats. For nonincumbent candidates, signing the pledge has become a prerequisite to a serious run for Republican office. Moderates who hope to protect their right flank routinely sign the pledge as well (Hacker and Pierson 2010, p. 493).

Prison and sentencing reform seems far removed from the antigovernment crusading that motivates Norquist and other antitax zealots. But when Norquist was looped into conservative criminal justice reform efforts in Pat Nolan's "conservative working group" meetings in Washington, Norquist was persuaded that the prison system's largess, in terms of its costs and the increasingly tangled web of state and federal criminal statutes (what Norquist calls "creeping centralization"), spoke directly to his aversion of a big, activist government (Conant 2011; Woodruff 2014). What Norquist's stance meant for conservatives' willingness to support the FSA cannot be understated. Because of ATR's hardball tactics, conservatives in Congress routinely look for his blessing before voting on all types of controversial or even semicontroversial legislation. Norquist's endorsement of the FSA, then, served as a crucial informational shortcut; conservatives had yet another reason to join with Democrats and progressive organizations in support of the FSA.

* * *

Progressive groups made their final push with national lobby and call in days designed to flood Capitol offices with calls from reform supporters. By spring 2010 a compromise agreement on the FSA emerged from the Senate Judiciary Committee after several months of behind-the-scenes negotiations between Durbin and Sessions, and later joined by Orrin Hatch, Lindsey Graham, and Tom Coburn. A full repeal of the crack/powder disparity was removed; in its place was a crack/powder disparity ratio of eighteen-to-one. Possession of 28 grams of crack—an amount the U.S. Sentencing Commission associated with "wholesaler" operators—would now be required to trigger a five-year mandatory minimum (Federal Crack Cocaine Sentencing 2010). A ten-year mandatory sentence required possession of 280 grams of crack, up from 50 grams. For powder cocaine the trigger remained 500 grams.

With the compromise deal in hand, the FSA passed the Senate Judiciary Committee on a nineteen-to-zero vote. It passed the full Senate by unanimous consent two days later. Eighteen senators were present for votes on both the Anti-Drug Abuse in 1986 and the FSA in 2010.* All eighteen had voted in favor of the Anti-Drug Abuse Act. Nearly a quarter century later these same thirteen Democrats and five Republicans voted to begin correcting a wrong they helped create.[†]

When the bill was sent to the House of Representatives, Republican Lamar Smith of Texas spoke out against the compromise legislation. "Why are we coddling some of the most dangerous drug traffickers in America? Why enact legislation that could endanger our children and bring violence back to our inner-city communities?," Smith said.[‡] By this time, however, Smith was a lonely voice. The legislation was adopted by the full House in a voice vote on July 28, 2010.

In a legislative struggle that began two decades prior, President Obama signed the Fair Sentencing Act on August 3, 2010, in a low-profile event in the Oval Office. Surrounded by many of the leading figures in the debate, President Obama offered no words as he signed the bill. But in a speech the week before, Obama noted the bill would "help right a longstanding wrong," and that it was the "right thing to do" (Baker 2010). After the signing ceremony the president's press secretary, Robert Gibbs, remarked on the unique nature of the coalition that produced it. "I think if you look at the people that were there at the signing, they're not of the political persuasions that either always or even part of the time agree. I think that demonstrates ... the glaring nature of what these penalties had ... done to people and how unfair they were" (Gotsch 2011).

Many long-standing advocates of crack sentencing reform, especially those on the progressive side of the smart on crime coalition, saw the

---

* The Senators present for both votes are as follows: Max Baucus (MT), Joseph Biden, Jr. (DE), Jeff Bingaman (NM), Thad Cochran (MS), Christopher Dodd (CT), Charles Grassley (IA), Thomas Harkin (IA), Orrin Hatch (UT), Daniel Inouye (HI), Edward Kennedy (MA), John Kerry (MA), Frank Lautenberg (NJ), Patrick Leahy (VT), Carl Levin (MI), Richard Lugar (IN), Mitch McConnell (KY), John Rockefeller IV (WV), and Arlen Specter (PA).

† Thad Cochran, Charles Grassley, Orrin Hatch, Richard Lugar, and Mitch McConnell were the Republicans in this group. The number would have been six if Arlen Specter had not switched to the Democratic Party on April 29, 2009. Specter was a Republican Senator when he voted for the Anti-Drug Abuse Act in 1986.

‡ Available at http://www.famm.org/Repository/Files/FLOOR%20PROCEEDINGS%20FAIR%20 SENTENCING%20ACT%20OF%202010%5B1%5D.pdf (accessed July 28, 2010).

FSA as a major policy victory. "This victory in drug sentencing reform is extraordinary; advocates have been fighting for nearly two decades to eliminate the egregious disparity between crack and powdered cocaine," noted Nkechi Taifa, a policy analyst for the Open Society Policy Center, a civil and criminal justice reform organization ("First Time in 40 Years" 2010).

Yet some progressive reformers lamented not getting a full bite of the apple. In an issue brief published for the American Constitution Society of Law and Policy, the Sentencing Project's Kara Gotsch classified the FSA as a "bittersweet victory" and said that more action was needed to ensure "fair and proportionate penalties" ("First Time in 40 Years" 2010).

This is fair assessment and begs the question of why Congress was unable to achieve a full repeal of the crack/powder disparity. The most persuasive evidence points to the concerns of law enforcement, particularly narcotics agents, had about a full repeal. Senate leaders said as much in a letter sent to House leaders just before the House of Representatives voted on the final bill. "This 18:1 ratio responds to the concerns raised by many in law enforcement who agree the 100:1 disparity is unjustified, but argue that crack is associated with higher levels of violence and therefore should be subject to tougher penalties" ("Senate Letter to House of Representatives Urging Passage of Fair Sentencing Act" 2010). Of course this is a debatable point. But weakened as law enforcement was, their position and influence remained strong enough that conservatives in Congress were not willing to get behind a full repeal.

Others on the left, however, including Julie Stewart, the founder and president of Families Against Mandatory Minimums, saw the FSA as the beginning of something new. Stewart said the law "signaled the beginning of a new bipartisanship" that could lead to more reform, including extending the rules to those already in prison (Baker 2010). As we will explore further in the final chapter, Stewart made a prescient point. In many ways the FSA represents only the first chapter in a sentencing reform story still being written.

Section III

The Smart on Crime Movement in the United States

6

Texas

INTRODUCTION TO THE PROBLEM ENVIRONMENT

In 2007 Texas faced a corrections crisis. The nonpartisan Texas Legislative Budget Board projected significant growth in the state's prisoner population. By 2012 the inmate population was projected to rise to 168,000, a number that would put the system 17,000 inmates above its operational capacity. One solution was to do what the state almost always did in the past: build more prisons. Between 1980 and 2004 Texas built a total of ninety-four (Perkinson 2010). The Texas Department of Criminal Justice (TDCJ) was prepared to build again. The agency submitted a $523 million budget request for new prison construction and an additional $184 million for "emergency" contracted capacity to rent space from county jails (Fabelo 2010b). All told, new prison construction costs were estimated to reach $2 billion by 2012.

Further west, California had its own crisis. California's inmate population had ballooned to a record high 173,000—200 percent above its designed capacity. In 2006 Governor Arnold Schwarzenegger took the extraordinary step to declare a "state of emergency" in the California prison system—a step that allowed the state to begin contracting with private or out-of-state prisons (Schlanger 2013). The state was under pressure from two federal class action lawsuits, *Coleman v. Wilson* (filed in 1990) and *Plata v. Davis* (2001). The suits alleged that the state offered prisoners constitutionally inadequate mental- and health-care services caused by prison overcrowding.* Federal District Judge Thelton Henderson laid out the grim facts in a 2005 court filing:

---

* The primary cause here is an important distinction because under the rules outlined in the Prisoner Litigation Reform Act, a three judge court could not enter a population order (or what the PLRA calls a "prisoner release order") without clear and convincing evidence that "crowding is the primary cause of the violation of a federal right." See Schlanger (2013, p. 171).

By all accounts, the California prison medical care system is broken beyond repair. The harm already done in this case to California's prison inmate population could not be more grave, and the threat of future injury and death is virtually guaranteed in the absence of drastic action ... It is an uncontested fact that, on average, an inmate in one of California's prisons needlessly dies every six to seven days due to constitutional deficiencies in the (California Department of Corrections and Rehabilitation's) medical delivery system. This statistic, awful as it is, barely provides a window into the waste of human life occurring behind California's prison walls due to the gross failures of the medical delivery system. (Schlanger 2013, p. 174)

To address the crisis a special three-judge federal district court panel was convened. By August 2009, after failed attempts at a settlement, the panel held that California must reduce its prison population to 137.5 percent of designed capacity (or about 110,000 prisoners) "in no more than two years." If achieved, the state's prison population would reach levels not seen since 1993. The problem was that this would require lawmakers to institute prison reforms they had repeatedly been unwilling or unable to make at any time during the tough on crime era.

In Ohio, prisoner numbers had also reached record levels. After declining for a period in the early 2000s, the prisoner population had increased 16 percent between 2005 and 2008, to more than 51,000. With a rated capacity of just under 39,000, Ohio prisons were 30 percent above their target. Prison costs were also on the rise. The Ohio Department of Rehabilitation and Correction's (ODRC's) budget grew 18 percent (or nearly $240 million) between 2000 and 2008. Looking ahead, no relief was in sight. If trends continued, the ODRC estimated the state's prison population would climb by another 5,000 by 2018. The state would need to spend an additional $925 million for prison construction and operating costs to meet the demand (Council of State Governments 2009b).

These three states provide a window into the kinds of pressures that built up in American states where tough on crime politics reigned. Texas, of course, has long been the poster-child of tough on crime politics. The state's relatively frequent use of the death penalty, its number one or two ranking on a host of variables—from its incarceration rate, the number of people housed in supermax or for-profit prisons, or the number of juveniles incarcerated in adult prisons—all paint a vivid picture of the state's punitiveness (Perkinson 2010).

California and Ohio's rate of incarceration, 471 and 442 per 100,000 (in 2007) respectively, placed them just above the national average (West and

Sabol 2008). Yet their tough on crime bona fides cannot be questioned. California's punitive turn was the most dramatic since it once had the most progressive-minded penal system in the country. Since that time, California has adopted dozens of laws mandating longer prison sentences, including its three-strikes law in 1994, widely regarded as the most punitive in the country. No other large state in America has seen its imprisonment rate increase like California's. Between 1977 and 1998 California's incarceration rate grew 500 percent (Simon 2014). After building no new prisons in the 1960s and 1970s, California built twenty-one of its thirty-three total prisons after 1984. In 1996 the Ohio General Assembly abolished the state's largely indeterminate sentencing structure under which the Ohio Parole Board had release authority and could offer administrative good time credit. After parolees committed several high-profile crimes and amidst concern about arbitrary decisions made by Ohio's unelected Parole Board, Ohio's new sentencing structure became almost entirely determinate in nature (Diroll 2007). Ohio prisoners serving time for violent offenses jumped from an average of 3.09 years to 7.57 years in just five short years between 1995 (the year before SB 2 was adopted) and 2000 (Pew Center on the States 2012c). Time served for property and drug crimes jumped from an average of 1.73 and 1.23 years, respectively in 1995, to 4.89 and 2.9 years in 2000 (Pew Center on the States 2012c).

Despite their tough on crime history, each state's corrections policies are now propelled by the emergence of the smart on crime movement that has ushered in a wave of reforms. Included are efforts to use nonprison sanctions for drug and low-risk offenders, to eliminate or curtail crack/powder cocaine disparities, and reclassify some low-level felonies to misdemeanors and expand administrative good time credits. Efforts are under way to reshape parole and probation supervision by relying less on the prison for punishing technical violations and incentivizing the use of graduated sanctions. New investments are improving risk assessment instruments as well as drug treatment, job training, and cognitive behavioral therapy programs. All are designed to cut prisoner recidivism and smooth reentry.

Yet the timing, path, and the eventual design of prison reforms are different in each state. As will be documented in the Chapters 6 through 8, these differences are explained by variation in the strength and breadth of the smart on crime coalition in each state. To what extent did conservative leaders advocate for prison reform in each state? How did political repositioning of politicians on the political right shape the actions of Democrats on the left? To what extent did support for smart reforms cut across actors from different institutions of state government? The nature of the smart on crime coalition, and with that, the nature of policy changes under way, are themselves a by-product of each state's contextual characteristics and the extent to which exogenous forces in the federal system helped structure policy decisions over time. Accounting for each state's institutional structures, past policy decisions, and political experiences, organized interests as well as federal court mandates, all combine to advance a more nuanced understanding of prison reform at the subnational level.

BRINGING AN ENGINEER'S PERSPECTIVE TO THE TEXAS PENAL SYSTEM

No one was more surprised than Republican Jerry Madden when House Speaker Tom Craddick, a hard-nosed fiscal conservative, appointed him to chair the Texas House of Representatives' Corrections Committee at the beginning of the Seventy-Ninth Texas Legislature in 2005. Madden came to the Texas House in 1993, but he was far from an expert on prisons. The Texas legislature, unlike many states (or Congress), is officially organized on a nonpartisan basis (this, despite the fact that officials are elected by partisan ballots). This means members of both parties can hold all-important leadership assignments. The lieutenant governor (who presides over the state senate) and the speaker (who presides over the state House of Representatives) both have wide latitude in the leadership selection process. When Craddick selected Madden to head the Corrections Committee, his relative inexperience on prison issues, ironically, was viewed as a plus. From Craddick's perspective, the prison system needed a new set of eyes. Madden was not hindered by past baggage. With a degree in engineering Madden seemed a perfect choice to consider how the moving parts of the criminal justice system combined into a comprehensive (but deeply flawed) whole.

The problem confronting Madden and the rest of the legislature was that the Texas penal system was once again full of prisoners—151,000 strong in 2005. As a temporary fix the state leased 700 beds from county- and private-run jails (Ward 2005b). Texas appeared destined to build more prisons; after all, this is what the state had done any number of times before. Prison overcrowding in the 1970s had led to strict federal oversight and hard population caps. When prisons filled up, Texas was quick to build new ones to meet the demand. Yet this time, as Madden recalled, Craddick came to him with a clear but wholly different directive: "Don't build more prisons—they cost too much" (Madden 2010).

With Craddick's directive in hand, Madden quickly teamed with Senator John Whitmire, a Democrat from Houston and the so-called dean of the Texas Senate, having served in the institution since 1973. Whitmire was no stranger to get-tough politics. As the chairman of the Senate's Criminal Justice Committee, just about every major crime bill enhancing time served went through his committee. Whitmire was once even held at gunpoint during a burglary attempt outside his Houston area home. It is a story he has repeatedly told as a way to foster credibility on the issue.

The Madden and Whitmire relationship would form the legislative backbone of the smart on crime coalition in the state. The nonpartisan organization of the Texas legislature made the Republican/Democratic pairing easier. Republicans held a majority of seats in the Senate yet Whitmire, the Democrat, with his long service record and unmatched expertise, still controlled the Criminal Justice Committee.

By the time Madden came on board, Whitmire had already begun work on a probation reform package designed to lessen the number of offenders coming into the system. Whitmire's plan shortened probation terms for some low-level offenders from ten to five years. It allowed counties to expand drug courts and create new community supervision programs. And it provided money to hire more probation officers to lower case loads. Whitmire was quick to say his plan was not just about saving money. "This is not an alternative to build more prisons because we don't have the money, because if we need to do that, we will find the money in the interest of public safety," Whitmire said. "What this is about is focusing our probation program to make sure people who are out there succeed ... so they can turn their lives around. This is not soft on crime. I want the toughest policy on probation in the country, but I want something that works ... the system we have now does not work" (Ward 2005a).

Whitmire's probation bill ran into immediate trouble with prosecutors. Prosecutors claimed the measure was written too broadly because it gave shortened probation terms and "early release" to people convicted of more serious crimes. There were also no specific appropriations for new revenue, relying instead on increased court fines to pay for new treatment programs. Prosecutors' concerns were enough to persuade Republican Governor Rick Perry. "I can only conclude their opposition stems from good cause," Perry said at the time of his veto. "Attempts to improve this legislation that would have provided greater public safety benefits were rebuffed, ensuring this flawed piece of legislation that would endanger public safety made it to my desk" (Ward 2005c).

"We didn't get it perfectly right, I'll tell you that," Madden said of the legislative defeat (Madden 2010). But in retrospect the defeat was a blessing in disguise; the package didn't include some of the financial gains they would win in the next legislative session. It also brought several immediate benefits. First, Madden and Whitmire now had legislation to build from in the next session. Second, in 2006, Texas lawmakers received updated figures of the worsening bed shortage. Estimates suggested the shortage would reach 17,000 by 2012 if current policy went unchanged. Third, the defeat bought time for further study. What exactly was driving corrections costs upward? What prison alternatives would work and what wouldn't? Madden immersed himself in the issue.

EMERGENCE OF NEW ORGANIZED GROUPS

The Texas legislature scores low on comparative measures of state legislature "professionalization." It meets only every other year, legislator pay is comparatively low, and money to hire a large staff that might otherwise conduct policy research is scarce. State legislators without expert staffs must turn to alternative sources for policy expertise. Professional lobbyists help fill the informational void as do outside interest groups and think tanks. Madden's search for information was aided by groups newly emergent in the Texas criminal justice policy subsystem. These groups not only supplied valuable expertise, but in the case of one organization, the Texas Public Policy Foundation (TPPF), its mere presence added legitimacy to "smart" data-driven reforms previously overlooked or undermined in Texas-style get-tough politics.

The TPPF calls itself a "nonpartisan" research institute, but one would have to be a political neophyte not to recognize its conservative slant. The TPPF was founded in 1989 after San Antonio–based "mega donor" James Leininger wanted an organization to provide some intellectual muscle behind a public school voucher program. For years the TPPF floundered in San Antonio. The operation was later moved to the Austin Capitol to gain more relevance. With new leadership and close ties to Governor Rick Perry and political upstarts like Ted Cruz, the TPPF's staff and budget grew. On its list of donors are many of today's major corporate backers of the conservative movement: oil, coal, and gas interests, including Koch Industries, ExxonMobile, Devon Energy, ConocoPhillips, the American Coalition for Clean Coal, big Texas utilities (Energy Future Holdings, formerly TXU), tobacco (RJ Reynolds), and private prison corporations (GEO Group). A diverse set of supporters, indeed, but all generally favor deregulation or market-based approaches to public policy (Wilder 2012). The TPPF, for example, promotes a partial privatization of the state's Medicaid program; it issues research papers attempting to muddle the science surrounding climate change; and it advocates for lower taxes on industry (Wilder 2014).

The TPPF and its financial supporters advocate for policies anathema to just about everything progressives stand for. But as it happened, one of TPPF's major funders was an oilman from Odessa, Texas named Tim Dunn. Dunn had taken a prominent interest in the criminal justice system. He was an evangelical Christian with a strong libertarian streak. Dunn admired the Prison Fellowship's work in Texas and elsewhere, and he became dismayed watching the Texas prison population climb (Hart 2011). "I had come to see our justice system as imperial, as intent on maintaining the authority of the king," Dunn said. "It was no longer communal or restorative" (King 2013). "It is not in our best interest to take someone who is a productive member of society and train them to be a hardened criminal. It's morally stupid" (Hart 2011). Dunn bankrolled a new foundation within the TPPF called the Center for Effective Justice. Mark Levin, an attorney and sitting board member of the TPPF, was named director.

When Levin and the TPPF dug into the Texas prisons debate, they were joined by the Texas chapter of the American Civil Liberties Union and the Texas Criminal Justice Coalition for Public Priorities, a left-leaning research organization focused on de-incarceration and equality in the criminal justice system. Despite their ideological differences, the groups shared in their belief that the prison was overused and too expensive. The groups emphasized to Madden the need to strengthen probation and return its core mission to rehabilitation and recidivism reduction. Treatment opportunities for parolees needed improvement. Better risk assessments were needed to separate low- and high-risk offenders. The groups also supported progressive sanctions that imposed swift, certain, but proportionate punishments to hold probationers and parolees accountable (Texas Criminal Justice Coalition 2007). "In listening to their testimony I found that you know what, once I threw away their extremes, in the middle they agreed on an awful lot," Madden said. There were ideas out there that were "smart" (Madden 2010).

House Speaker Craddick's "no new prisons" mantra caused Madden to carefully weigh the costs and benefits of prison alternatives. "A new medium or maximum security prison with 2,200–2,500 people might cost you $250 million," Madden said. "So I had a demand out there was $1.75 billion for 17,000 beds, plus ... if it costs us, say, $50 a day [to house a prisoner], and I am adding 17,000 prisoners, I am adding $850,000 a day in cost to the system. The question then became, 'What can I do about it?'. 'How can I change the equation that we have out there?'" (Madden 2010). Madden saw two primary options: (i) release prisoners or (ii) keep offenders from coming in the first place. For Madden the choice was clear. "Opening the door and letting prisoners out, is probably not going to be politically acceptable to the governor, it's probably not going to be politically acceptable to me, and it's probably not going to be politically acceptable to the legislature" (Madden 2010).

Work began with picking up the pieces of the vetoed probation bill. Texas had nearly 270,000 people on probation. Nearly 25,000 had their probation revoked every year, many of them on technical violations. If this group could be diverted, it could save scarce prison space. No sooner had Madden begun working on a new probation bill when he examined Texas's larger recidivism problem. About 30 percent of Texas's prisoners released from prison came back within three years. Madden recalled his thinking at the time,

> I've got 70,000, roughly, leaving TDCJ. I've got 21,000 or so are back within three years. How can we as a state intervene, to break that cycle? So we started to ask those kinds of questions ... What if I can change that down to 18,000 in three years? Is that too undoable? Can I change that down to 15,000 come back in three years? What do I do within the parole area when they leave? What if I reduce the rate of prisoners returning ... down to 20 percent? It doesn't sound like much but ... That's one or more prisons that I don't need to build. (Madden 2010)

Finding answers to these kinds of questions requires good data. None of the rethinking in Texas would have been possible without the technical assistance provided by the Council of State Government's (CSG) Justice Center. The Justice Center, a nonpartisan organization established in 2006, grew out of the CSG's Eastern Regional Conference Justice Program. Its mission is focused on spreading the use of evidence-based, consensus-driven strategies to improve public safety and strengthen communities. The Justice Center provides technical analysis; it helps disseminate best practices, and offers state-specific policy recommendations. During the prison build-up, policy makers in many states had only limited knowledge of the interworkings of their sprawling criminal justice systems. Some agencies and jurisdictions collected data, but not others. Rarely was criminal justice data used for any serious policy analysis. In some states, prisoners came in so fast state policy makers effectively drove blind. What types of offenders made up the lion's share of a state's prison population? To what extent were prisons filled with parole violators, drug offenders, or violent offenses? If policy makers were to design a more rational, effective, and humane penal system, these were important questions. Few if any, however, had answers.

Unlike many states, Texas's problem was not caused by a shortage of data. The state had long relied on its own agency, the Criminal Justice Policy Council, to provide sophisticated analysis. That was until 2003 when Governor Perry gutted the agency's $2.5 million budget using his line-item veto power. The move effectively killed the agency. At the time Perry reasoned the council was no longer needed. After all, the state's prison system had successfully recovered from the overcrowding crisis of the 1970s and 1980s. But by 2007, with a new impending crisis, it became clear Perry's decision was shortsighted. He had stripped the state's correctional system of an invaluable policy resource: expertise. As Senator Whitmire told *Texas Monthly Magazine*, "We've been handicapped for good information. We wouldn't be in this crisis about capacity if we had had good information. We've been hurt tremendously" (Burka 2007).

Texas's self-inflicted wound made the state a rich target for the CSG's Justice Center. If the Justice Center could advance reform in Texas, it might just happen anywhere. Moreover, Justice Center officials believed they had the capacity to make it happen. Tony Fabelo, its newly hired research director, was the former director of the Texas Criminal Justice Policy Council. He had provided research and analysis on criminal justice matters to five Texas governors on both sides of the aisle. As a statistician he knew the state's system better than anyone.

In January 2007, Whitmire and Madden held a rare joint session of the Senate Criminal Justice and House Corrections Committees. They heard from the Texas Sunset Advisory Commission, a legislative oversight body, which reported that the TDCJ needed to improve substance abuse treatment or it risked negating any of the state's other recidivism reduction efforts. They also heard from Lieutenant Governor David Dewhurst and county prosecutors who argued that the state's increasing prisoner population was simply a function of growth in the state's overall population. The state just needed to maintain prison capacity (that is, build more prisons) to avoid the shortfall (Fabelo 2010a).

Around this time, Justice Center staff had already begun digging deep into the state's data systems. According to their analysis, neither the state's population growth, nor the crime rate for that matter, were the main issues.* Fabelo, who led the effort, went straight to Whitmire (with whom he had had a longtime working relationship) with the Justice Center's assessment. Texas's problem, Fabello told Whitmire, "was directly linked to policy decisions" (Fabelo 2010a).

At Whitmire's urging Fabelo presented his findings to the state legislature. The goal of his presentation, as Fabelo recalls, was to fundamentally "reframe the issue" (Fabelo 2010a). Fabelo told lawmakers that three main drivers were causing the impending shortfall: (i) too few prisoners were released on parole; (ii) increasing probation and parole revocations; and (iii) reduced residential and community treatment capacity. On the issue of parole release, the Justice Center's analysis found the state's parole board was failing to follow its own guidelines. For low-risk offenders, state guidelines called for minimum parole approval rates of 51 percent. The actual rate was closer to 40 percent. A difference of 10 or 11 percent might seem inconsequential but in a prison system as large as Texas's, just one percentage point might equal 1,500 prisoners. In addition, state cuts to substance abuse and mental health services had reduced the number of treatment programs and facilities. In 2006 alone, over 2,000 prisoners eligible for release were put on hold because of capacity shortages. This meant that more low-risk offenders, who otherwise would have been released, remained incarcerated (Fabelo 2010b).

The Justice Center also presented the legislature with an analysis illustrating the source of the state's prison population. Criminologists in recent years have captured a better understanding of how a small number of neighborhoods often generate a disproportionate share of state prisoners. These so-called "million dollar" blocks reference a collection of blocks in mostly poor urban neighborhoods that impose a million dollars or more

---

* Specifically the Justice Center's analysis showed the state's population increased 61 percent between 1980 and 2005 but the incarceration rate increased over 300 percent. Crime rates had declined 1.9 percent from 2000 to 2005.

in incarceration-related costs on a state (Gonnerman 2004). In Texas, five counties alone accounted for more than half of those sentenced to prison at a cost of over half a billion dollars (The Council of State Governments 2007). Harris County, which includes Houston, contributed the most. Just ten of Houston's 88 neighborhoods contributed over $100 million to the state's incarceration costs. The implications of this were clear: if policy makers concentrated resources in areas that not only fed the prison system but that also received the lion's share of returning prisoners, they could improve public safety, reduce prison-related costs, and, most important, save lives.

JUSTICE REINVESTMENT

Knowing who was in prison, where they came from, and where they returned to were all crucial pieces of information for the Justice Center's "Justice Reinvestment" Initiative. The genesis of CSG's Justice Reinvestment work can be traced to a 2003 paper penned by Susan Tucker and Eric Cadora for George Soros's Open Society Institute (Tucker and Cadora 2003). The idea is fairly simple: A state invests in alternatives that reduces its prison population and then "reinvests" a portion of savings captured from (forgone) prison construction and operations costs into evidence-based treatment and community supervision systems. Drawing on much of the same research that shaped the prisoner reentry debates, justice reinvestment called on policy makers to consider risk, need, and responsivity principles. This meant placing tighter supervision on high- and medium-risk prisoners and more focus on criminogenic needs and cognitive behavioral health therapies. And given the distribution of crime patterns and the "million dollar" block phenomenon, the initiative called for reinvestments to be targeted in high-risk counties and neighborhoods that fed the system.

The CSG's analysis not only provided an overarching view of the moving parts of the state's criminal justice system, but it also presented a clear path forward. As Fabelo noted, lawmakers too often relied on anecdotes to inform policy choices. "Its very difficult for lawmakers to think about the big picture. They look at one bill or one line item" (Fabelo 2010a). The Justice Center showed the legislature estimates of tangible savings that would flow from a reinvestment policy strategy. As just one example, Fabelo illustrated how new investments in probationer treatment could net the state millions over the next five years. Additional spending of just over $78 million for expanded treatment opportunities would bring $144 million in savings between 2008 and 2012, for a net benefit of $65 million. All told, investments in treatment and prison diversion alternatives, in addition to canceling prison construction plans originally proposed by the TDCJ, were estimated to save $443 million.

The result was that Madden and Whitmire were able to think systemically. And by spring 2007 they continued to push legislation forward. They designed a policy directly targeting identified needs. On parole they introduced a bill establishing maximum caseloads for parole officers to improve supervision.* On probation they reintroduced a bill cutting terms for drug and property offenders from ten years to five.† Another provided financial incentives for counties to establish progressive sanction models for probation violators.‡ Drug courts and other specialty courts were also expanded in counties to assist placing low-risk offenders in treatment programs.§ They were also receiving encouraging signals from Governor Perry. In his February State of the State Address, Perry said "I believe we can take an approach to crime that is both tough and smart ... there are thousands of nonviolent offenders in the system whose future we cannot ignore. Let's focus more resources on rehabilitating those offenders so we can ultimately spend less money locking them up again" (Office of the Governor 2007).

Spending was geared around these new priorities: $10 million to local probation departments to add 3,000 slots in outpatient treatment; $21 million for an additional 1,000 slots for In-Prison Therapeutic Communities—an in-prison and postrelease intensive substantive abuse treatment program; $32 million for 800 new beds for probation residential treatment facilities; nearly $29 million for 1,400 new slots in Intermediate Sanction Facilities; $63 million for 1,500 beds in the Substance Abuse Felony Punishment program; and $5.6 million for 300 beds in parole halfway houses.⁵ In

---

* Texas Legislature, House Bill 3736, "An Act Relating to Establishing Parole Office Maximum Caseloads."

† Texas Legislature, House Bill 1678, "An Act Relating to the Operation of a System of Community Supervision."

‡ Texas Legislature, Senate Bill 166, "An Act Relating to a Prison Diversion Progressive Sanctions Program."

§ Texas Legislature, House Bill 530, "An Act Relating to the Operations and Funding of Drug Court Programs."

⁵ ISFs are detention centers for parole and probation offenders violating their terms of supervision. Facilities are used to sanction offenders in lieu of revocation to prison. The Substance Abuse Felony Punishment Program provides residential substance abuse and counseling services for probationers who violated the terms of supervision owing to substance abuse problems.

sum, the legislative package would add 4,500 new prison diversion beds and 5,200 new slots for treatment. Total spending to expand substance abuse treatment, mental health, and intermediate sanction facilities and programs reached $241 million in the budget bill (Fabelo 2010b; The Council of State Governments 2009a).

BROAD-BASED SMART ON CRIME COALITION

At the end of the 2007 session the entire reform package became law. Texas managed to avoid building new prisons but also, more profoundly over the longer run, pointed the penal system down a decidedly different path. The political coalition that enabled this was hardly narrow. The parole bill, SB 166, passed by a vote of 31–0 in the Senate. In the House the vote was 143–1 (Legislative Reference Library of Texas). The drug court bill, HB 530, passed by unanimous votes in both the House and Senate. HB 1, which added new funding for drug treatment and prison diversion programs, received positive votes from 139 out of a possible 181 legislators; ninety votes, or 64 percent of the total, came from conservative Republicans (Gupta et al. 2011).

We can now also begin to assess the popular narrative in the media that prison reform in Texas and elsewhere resulted from macroeconomic pressure. Tom Craddick's "no new prisons" platform was undoubtedly tied to his knowledge about the high costs of building and operating new prisons. Yet when Craddick appointed Madden to head the Corrections Committee, Texas was in the midst of a budget surplus. The state certainly had the capacity to build more prisons if it wanted. Moreover, if Jerry Madden's sentiments about the meaning of prison reform offer a window into the thinking of other conservative lawmakers, then the story in Texas was indeed about more than dollars and cents. As Madden said,

> In many cases you have sons, brother, school friends—they did some bad, stupid things—but inherently they are not all that bad. … When you go into a room and ask how many friends, uncles, daughters, husbands, wives (or whatever) have been in prison, struggled with addiction, or in some way have experience with the criminal justice system, few fail to raise their hands. It's become a more personal issue. It's a big deal … This [reform] is how you change lives, this is second chances. (Madden 2010)

TEXAS PENAL SYSTEM AND THE SHIFTING
DIMENSIONS OF POLITICAL DEBATE

What is critical for understanding prison reform in Texas is that the entire debate on prisons and corrections had shifted by the early 2000s. To examine this more systematically, this section presents results of a content analysis examining the tone of Texas newspaper coverage of the prison system between 1991 and 2009.*

The goal of the analysis is to determine whether news coverage of the penal system moved from periods largely supportive of a "tough on crime" frame to periods more supportive of a "smart on crime" frame. Evidence of a shift in the tone and dimension of prison coverage suggests that new opportunities for policy learning occurred along with a newfound receptiveness for policy change among policy makers.

Given time and resource constraints, I constructed a random stratified sample (by year) of newspaper stories on the prison system from two major Texas newspapers—the *Houston Chronicle* and the *Austin-American Statesman.*† The characteristics of the two papers vary in a couple of respects. The *Austin-American Statesman* (with a circulation of 173,000 in 2009) is located in the state capital and offers extensive coverage of public policy issues of relevance to state lawmakers. The paper's editorial page generally takes more progressive stances on criminal justice policy. The *Houston Chronicle* (circulation 470,000 in 2009) publishes in a more conservative contextual environment—a point reflected in its more conservative editorial positions on criminal justice matters (Baumgartner et al. 2008). Analyzing prison coverage in these two papers should adequately capture any differences in coverage shaped by contextual factors.

The overall tone of a story, of course, is subjective. Tone is evaluative in nature. It has both positive (supportive) and negative components (Baumgartner and Jones 1993). I used a coding method similar to that found in previous research conducted by Frank Baumgartner and Bryan Jones (1993). Coding followed a fairly simple rule: If you were a leader of the prison industry, law enforcement, or other organized group that wanted to see a continuation of punitive penal policies and a prominent

---

* 1991 was the earliest year of coverage available in the online archives.
† Search terms included "prison," "prisoners," and "inmates" in LexisNexis.

role for prisons in the criminal justice system, would you be pleased or unhappy to see the story?

Each story was then coded to reflect whether its tone supported dimensions broadly supportive of a tough on crime frame, a smart on crime frame, or whether the tone was neutral/uncodable.* A tough on crime frame included stories on incarceration and imprisonment, punitive criminal sentences, stories invoking fear of crime, or stories that depicted criminals and prisoners as violent in nature. Smart on crime stories were broadly focused on the failings of the prison system and prison management, the mistreatment of prisoners, or the high financial and social costs associated with prisons. Smart on crime-framed stories also included coverage of the benefits or effectiveness of evidence-based prison alternatives. Examples of the kinds of coverage placed in a "tough on crime" or "smart on crime" frame are presented in the chapter's Appendix. The tone of each story did not necessarily refer to any editorial stance of the paper or journalist, but rather whether the decisions, actions, events, or opinions portrayed in the article lent support to a tough on crime or a smart on crime frame (Baumgartner et al. 2008). The content analysis was limited to stories involving the U.S. penal system, but, overwhelmingly, the stories covered topics of relevance to the Texas prison system. To ensure each story had a sufficient depth in coverage, I limited the software to search only those stories at least 400 words in length.† A total of thirty-five stories were randomly sampled in each year for a total sample size of 665.

The main topic of each story was also placed into any one of seventeen different topical categories. Placing stories into different topic categories allowed the opportunity to track the relationship between a story's primary topic and the overall tone of a story. For example, an article covering the opening of a new prison (topic category, prison construction) was coded as "supportive" of the tough on crime frame given the act of building a prison lends to incapacitation and custodial control. A story about violence in prison (topic category, prison violence) that also mentioned the dangerous, threatening, or out-of-control nature of inmates—all common dehumanizing images and labels attached to

---

* The neutral or uncodable category was reserved for stories that had no clearly identifiable frame.
† Stories on the Guantanamo Bay detention facility had a significant presence in news coverage in 2002, 2003, and 2004. Because these stories dealt primarily with the treatment of detainees in the larger "war on terror," I excluded these stories from the analysis.

prisoners in the tough on crime era—was coded as supportive of the tough on crime frame.*

In contrast, stories on prisoner mistreatment (topic category, prisoner treatment/rights), or growing concerns over the financial costs of prisons (topic category, correctional budgets), were coded as supportive of the smart on crime frame. Additionally, stories discussing the benefits of new rehabilitation programs, the expansion of drug courts, or successful prisoner reintegration efforts (topic category, rehabilitation/prison alternatives) were coded as supportive of the smart on crime frame. A complete list of topic categories is presented in the chapter's Appendix.

Figure 6.1 presents a graph of the "net tone" of prison coverage in the two newspapers. The net tone of coverage, measured on the left-hand-side *y*-axis, is a measure of the percentage of total stories in a year that supports a tough on crime frame minus the percentage of stories that support a smart on crime frame. Positive values represent a net surplus of tough on crime stories; negative values represent a net surplus of smart on crime stories. The right-hand-side *y*-axis measures the state's prison population (excluding jail), which can be used to gauge how media coverage tracks with changes in the state's imprisonment rate.

Although the confidence intervals within each year are fairly high because of the small sample size, the results show that in 1991 tough on crime stories had a 52 percent net surplus over stories supportive of the smart on crime frame. This increased to a net surplus of 64 percent in 1995. Not surprisingly, the state's prison population grew dramatically over this same period. The size of the prison population increased nearly 100 percent in 1993 and 1994 when Democratic Governor Ann Richards took extremely punitive positions on crime in these years. She dramatically reduced parole and began a prison construction boom. This broader political environment is reflected in the media coverage here. By the late 1990s, however, the trend in media coverage began to reverse itself as the net surplus of tough on crime stories declined. News coverage appeared to completely shift during the 2000s. While not all years reached statistical significance (for example, in 2001 and 2004 the one-tailed hypothesis that the proportion of smart on crime stories is greater than tough on crime stories cannot be rejected), in most years during the 2000s the

---

* A story may be coded in more than one topical category. For example, a story focused on new funding for prisoner rehabilitation programs would be coded under the topical categories of corrections budget and rehabilitation/prison alternatives.

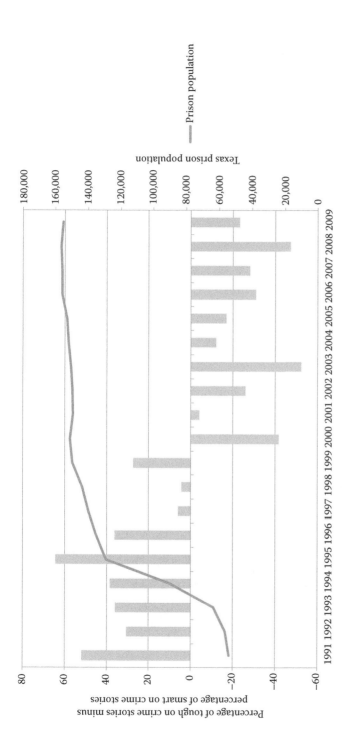

FIGURE 6.1

Net tone of *Houston Chronicle*'s and *Austin-American Statesman*'s news coverage of the Texas prison system. With the small sample sizes drawn in each year, 1997 and 1998 failed to reach standard levels of statistical significance. In these years a one-sided hypothesis that the proportion of tough on crime stories would be greater than the proportion of smart on crime stories in the more punitive era of the 1990s cannot be rejected. Likewise the 2001 and 2004 years also failed to reach statistical significance. In these cases we cannot reject the hypothesis that the proportion of smart on crime stories would be greater than the proportion of tough on crime stories.

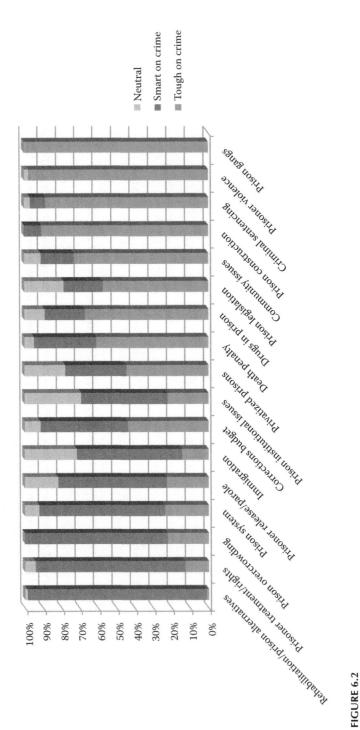

FIGURE 6.2
Topic determines the tone of media coverage on the Texas penal system.

media focused on the broad failings of the prison system, mistreatment of prisoners, and prison alternatives. As media coverage shifted to those dimensions of debate, the prisoner population held steady for the better part of the decade and then slightly declined.

Figure 6.2 shows the tone of different topics and whether for each of the seventeen coded topics, media coverage was more or less likely to resemble a smart on crime, tough on crime, or neutral tone. Some topics such as "institutional issues," had a relatively high percentage of neutral or uncodable stories, meaning they were less likely to have a clear frame. Many topics, however, had an almost built-in bias toward either the tough on crime or smart on crime frames. Stories covering topics like prison gangs, inmate violence, criminal sentencing, community issues, and drugs in prison all had a decidedly tough on crime tone. The rehabilitation/prison alternatives, prisoner treatment/rights, and prison overcrowding topics each had an overwhelmingly smart on crime tone.

Finally Figure 6.3 illustrates how the shifting nature of discourse on the Texas penal system was largely a function of a shift in the topics of debate. Specifically the figure shows the percentage of sampled stories in

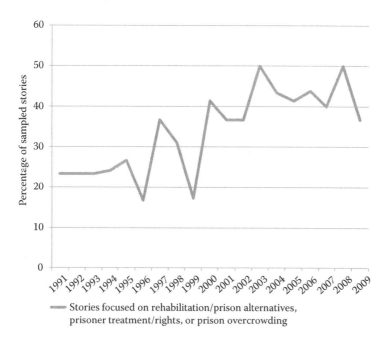

━━━ Stories focused on rehabilitation/prison alternatives, prisoner treatment/rights, or prison overcrowding

FIGURE 6.3

Growth in Texas newspaper coverage with the topic categories of rehabilitation/prison alternatives, prisoner treatment/rights, or prison overcrowding.

a given year that included coverage of any one of the three topic categories most strongly associated with the smart on crime frame in Figure 6.2—rehabilitation/prison alternatives, prisoner treatment/rights, and prison overcrowding. In the early 1990s these topics comprised only 20 to 25 percent of sampled stories in any one year. By the early to mid-2000s, they consistently reached 40 to 45 percent of all sampled stories, peaking at 50 percent in 2003 and 2008. In sum, the political debate on prisons in Texas changed because the topics changed. When the debate moved from the failures of the prison boom on the one hand, to the benefits of smarter prison alternatives on the other, it opened opportunities for policy learning and generated a new receptivity to reform.

The importance of this broader shift in political debate and the effect it had among conservatives in a historically tough on crime state like Texas was not lost on lawmakers like Jerry Madden.

> I think its easier for a red state conservative Republican to do this [reform] than it is for a blue state liberal Democrat. Because its harder for people to use the point on me that I'm not tough on crime when I've got a record that clearly indicates I'm tough in almost everything I am ... when for a blue state Democrat it puts them almost automatically for a target for somebody who says they don't have the voting record that says they're tough on crime. (Madden 2010)

Madden's change of heart and the support many conservatives showed for prison reform was needed to deliver the necessary votes in the Texas legislature. Yet conservatives' newfound receptivity to reform was also important because of what it signaled to Democrats. As Senator Whitmire noted, Democrats needed political protection in light of the political history surrounding the issue.

> For a Democrat you need political cover. I had to be tough and smart ... Republicans, especially in this state, tend to paint criminals with a broad brush. I don't take a back seat on being tough on the murderers, rapists, and child molesters—we lock them up. But we needed to do much better on nonviolent offenders. And to do this, to get smart, I also needed Republican support. (Whitmire 2010)

APPENDIX

Listed below is each of the seventeen topic categories used in the content analysis of Texas newspaper coverage of the prison system. Below each topic category is a list of the different types of stories coded as supportive of the "tough on crime" or "smart on crime" frames.

Topic Category

1. Rehabilitation/prison alternatives
   Tough on crime: stories on the failure of prisoner rehabilitation programs, community corrections, or in-prison education programs; stories on the inability of prisoners to be rehabilitated.

   Smart on crime: stories covering the benefits of any of the following programs: in-prison rehabilitation or community-based rehabilitation or education programs, community corrections services, drug courts; stories of individuals successfully reentering free society or "turning their life around."

2. Criminal sentencing
   Tough on crime: stories covering people sentenced to prison (not including capital punishment sentences).

   Smart on crime: stories covering advocates fighting against overly punitive criminal sentences including drug sentences; acquittals; judges overturning sentences deemed too harsh.

3. Prisoner violence
   Tough on crime: stories on prisoner violence, riots, and dangers inside prison; stories focused on crimes caused by released or paroled prisoners.

   Smart on crime: no stories on prisoner violence were identified as supportive of the smart on crime frame in the sample.

4. Prison system
   Tough on crime: stories covering specific academic or government-sponsored studies illustrating the growth in the size of the penal system or the public safety benefits of punitive criminal justice policies.

   Smart on crime: stories covering specific academic or government-sponsored studies that focus on the failures or shortcomings of the prison system including racial or ethnic disparities; stories on declining prison populations or declining racial biases or racial disparities in the system.

5. Prison gangs

   Tough on crime: stories covering growth in prison gangs, violent nature of prison gangs, or gang-related violence.

   Smart on crime: no stories on prison gangs were identified as supportive of the smart on crime frame in the sample.

6. Prison overcrowding

   Tough on crime: stories on prison overcrowding and linking overcrowding with the need to build more prisons.

   Smart on crime: stories focused on prison overcrowding leading to a planned prisoner release; stories linking prison overcrowding with poor conditions for prisoners or staff.

7. Prison construction

   Tough on crime: stories covering the planning or building of a new prison(s).

   Smart on crime: stories covering a decision not to build a new prison(s) or a delay in new prison construction.

8. Corrections budget

   Tough on crime: stories covering the appropriation of money for prisons and corrections; budget increases for prisons and corrections.

   Smart on crime: stories covering the increasing/high financial costs of incarceration; budget increases for prisoner rehabilitation, community corrections programs, or drug courts.

9. Institutional issues

   Tough on crime: stories covering prison rules on lock down; stories depicting correctional officials appointed or elected to correctional positions using tough on crime rhetoric; new prison rules that restrict the substantive benefits or freedoms offered to prisoners such as the use of tobacco, exercise equipment, expanded yard time or meal-related privileges.

   Smart on crime: stories covering scandals affecting prison officials.

10. Privatized prisons

    Tough on crime: stories on the opening of a new private prison; expansion of private prison contracts; reports about any financial savings that result from private prison operations.

Smart on crime: stories covering the inefficiencies/high cost of private prisons; lack of oversight within private prisons; poor treatment of prisoners in private facilities; administrative scandals within private prisons.

11. Drugs and prison

Tough on crime: stories covering the nexus between drug use and criminal behavior/violence in prison; in-prison drug busts.

Smart on crime: stories covering the rehabilitation of prisoners with special emphasis placed on prisoners who overcame drug addictions.

12. Immigration

Tough on crime: stories covering immigrants sentenced to prison; immigration causing the need for more prisons; transferring immigrants from one prison to another.

Smart on crime: stories of immigrants being released from detention or stories of immigrants being wrongly imprisoned.

13. Prisoner treatment/rights

Tough on crime: stories covering claims about prisoner mistreatment being false or overblown.

Smart on crime: stories covering prisoner beatings; poor prisoner health care; filthy prison conditions; poor legal representation; legal challenges to false imprisonment; wrongly accused prisoners; prisoner disease caused by squalid conditions or inadequate health care.

14. Prisoner release/parole

Tough on crime: stories covering prison escapees; parolees returned to prison because of a technical violation or commitment for a new crime.

Smart on crime: stories covering prisoners released to community corrections, prisoners' early release; good time credits.

15. Death penalty

Tough on crime: stories covering death sentences or executions.

Smart on crime: stories on DNA evidence leading to a death row inmate's exoneration; stays of execution; the innocence of death row inmates.

16. Community issues

    Tough on crime: stories covering community members' support for new prisons because of the job opportunities prisons provide; community fear of prisoners; crimes committed by prison escapees.

    Smart on crime: community support for rehabilitation; community reintegration of prisoners or family members.

17. Prison legislation

    Tough on crime: stories covering specific legislative bills or bureaucratic rules that increased criminal penalties, expanded correctional budgets, or the type of behaviors considered to violate criminal law.

    Smart on crime: stories covering specific legislative bills or bureaucratic rules that expanded prison alternatives, community corrections programs, or prisoner rehabilitation opportunities.

7

Ohio

Texas was not the first state to adopt smart on crime reforms; however, for both substantive and symbolic reasons, it is one of the most important states. Reform in Texas, given the state's size and historically high rate of incarceration, holds the promise of sending thousands fewer people to prison each year. Symbolically, what came out of the Texas story was the notion that if even Texas could reform its prison system, what could possibly stop the same thing from happening anywhere? We know that the smart on crime movement reform did not stop at the Texas border. Prison reform has continued to spread to other states in every part of country.

This chapter examines reform processes in one of these states: Ohio. Investigating reform in Ohio provides another window into how and why the smart on crime coalition formed and how state context shaped reform efforts. It also allows us to consider another important question if we are to fully grasp how prison reform spread, and continues to spread, at the subnational level: In criminal justice policy making, how do prison reform ideas travel from place to place? Can a state like Ohio learn from what transpired in Texas or some other state?

DIFFUSION OF SMART ON CRIME POLICY IDEAS

When Supreme Court Justice Louis Brandeis referred to the American states as "laboratories of democracy," it was an apt description of the role state governments play in the U.S. federalism system. States have the freedom to innovate and find unique solutions to problems. Collectively, through trial and error, state policy makers can learn about which policies work and which do not. Political scientists recognize this idea as policy diffusion.

What distinguishes policy diffusion from a mere increase in the incidence of a policy is that in the former case, state policy makers are aware of existing policies elsewhere (Karch 2007b). Lawmakers in one state might adopt a new policy; that policy appears to be effective or perhaps its approach matches the ideological beliefs of lawmakers elsewhere (who might want to adopt it despite knowing whether it works) and the policy idea quickly spreads. Such a process can be seen in the diffusion of state lotteries, medical marijuana laws, three-strikes laws, and environmental sustainability initiatives.

Given the fluid nature of information in a policy subsystem, no singular source has a monopoly on information or innovative policy ideas. Researchers, however, have come to recognize the outsized role interest groups play as evangelizers of strong position taking and suppliers of information (Walker 1969). Tighter linkages between national offices and state and local affiliates facilitate the spread of policies from place to place. Think tanks, policy research institutes, and professional associations publish books, issue research reports, and host conferences to transmit ideas and build professional networks across state lines (Clark and Little 2002; Karch 2007b; Rich 2004). We can see this type of process in the aftermath of Texas's reform efforts when the Council of State Governments (CSG) and other newly emerging organizations with the resources and organizational capacity to operate across state lines spread the justice reinvestment model.

The Public Safety Performance Project (PSPP), launched in 2006, by the Pew Charitable Trusts, was another of these organizations. The Pew Charitable Trusts is a nonpartisan and nonprofit organization funded by the heirs of Joseph Pew and his wife Mary Anderson Pew, founders of the Sun Oil Company. The PSPP is housed within Pew's Center on the States, a domestic policy shop designed to improve states' fiscal health and governing performance. Initiatives on health care, the environment, early childhood intervention and investments, pensions, and state economic competitiveness are just a handful of the issues it has addressed over time. As corrections and public safety spending ate up an ever-larger slice of states' budgets, the issue became a ripe target for Pew's dollars and research energy.

The PSPP's Washington, DC office, complete with the modern amenities and open floor plan similar to that of a Silicon Valley tech company, does not fit the image of a financially strapped nonprofit. Nor should it; estimates in 2009 placed the value of Pew's endowment at over 5 billion. Similar to the Justice Center, PSPP's mission is described as helping states "advance fiscally sound, data-driven policies and practices in sentencing that protect public safety, hold offenders accountable, and control corrections costs." PSPP's work falls into two primary categories. It provides technical analysis to state policy makers by identifying sources of growth in corrections costs and different policy options for reform. It also disseminates information—sharing knowledge with policy makers and practitioners about best practices and innovative ideas through research, public opinion surveys, and policy forums.

PSPP's information dissemination work is emblematic of a two-pronged approach advocates of reform have used it to alter the dimensions of crime policy debate. On one hand, the PSPP educates policy makers and practitioners about size, scope, and economic costs of the contemporary penal system in America. On the other hand, it quantifies economic and public safety benefits of evidence-based alternatives. What have states gained, if anything, by lengthening the average prison term? What prison alternatives offer better public safety benefits per dollar spent? PSPP's "One in 100" report published in 2008, which presented data showing 1 out of every 100 adults in the United States were behind bars, best characterizes this two-pronged strategy (Pew Center on the States 2008). The report received extensive news media coverage, including prominent stories in the *Washington Post, New York Times*, and the Associated Press (Aizenman 2008; Liptak 2008). For close observers of the criminal justice system, of course, the largess of the U.S. prison system was old news. The One in 100 report received the attention it did because of the way PSPP communicated its findings. The report was designed to resonate from more than one frame. Jake Horowitz, a senior researcher at the PSPP who played a major role in shaping the report, explained it this way:

> Part of it was the number. It's a sobering threshold … It was a way people could conceive of the scale. Academia has different levels of gauging success. It's more about publications and less about press coverage. People used to focus on the 750 per 100,000 number. Well people can't perceive 750 per 100,000. It doesn't mean anything to people. But 1 in 100 means something. So part of it was figuring out how to make the statistics comprehensible. (Horowitz 2010)

Horowitz continued,

> Everyone cares about people. Seeing the systems through individuals generally appeals to some segment of the public. Seeing issues through dollars appeals to another part of the public. So the first few pages of the report were all about populations, but the next few pages were about cost … that grabbed people. Putting those together was a good recipe. (Horowitz 2010)

The report documented the growth in state corrections spending from $10 billion in 1982 to over $50 billion by 2007. In fact the report noted that $1 in $15 of the state general fund in 2007 were spent on corrections. Correctional costs were placed in comparative policy perspective, documenting, for example, how growth in states' corrections costs outpaced growth in higher education spending. "All of that means something to people and they get a sense of priorities," Horowitz noted. "You have to write for a different audience. You have to tell your story … You have to reach out; to the media, to opinion leaders and folks on both sides of the aisle … We've done that" (Horowitz 2010).

Over a fairly short period, the PSPP and CSG's Justice Center were part of a growing network of organizations and groups disseminating smart on crime policy ideas. They joined forces with other criminal justice reform advocacy organizations, including the Vera Institute of Justice, the Prison Fellowship, and the Center for Effective Justice within the Texas Public Policy Foundation. They also partnered with organizations with a more general but state-focused mission such as the National Center for State Courts, the National Conference of State Legislatures, and the National Governors Association. Collectively they make up a crucial part of the smart on crime coalition. "We want to echo messages in the states," Horowitz said. "We want to be able to take what happens in Kansas or Texas and help New Hampshire learn from it. Or we want to take what we know from many states and help the feds support it" (Horowitz 2010).

This type of "echoing" effort can be found in the diffusion of "performance incentive funding." As part of its reform package, Texas adopted an incentive funding program that allowed selected counties to financially benefit when fewer probationers were sent to state prison for new crimes. The idea was not born in Texas. It had been tried earlier in Maricopa County, Arizona. If Maricopa County (which includes Phoenix) sent fewer probationers to prison for new crimes, the state would kick back some of the savings. Maricopa would share in some of the "profits" that accrued from averting the need for prison beds.

It was a fairly simple idea. As Horowitz explained, "We took that idea (which had also played out in Kansas but in a slightly different form) and put it in our policy framework to strengthen community corrections. It was sort of 'model legislation light' … we essentially said here is a great idea … we provided some examples of legislative language … and the rationale behind it." The PSPP then disseminated the policy with their partner organizations. "We have biweekly calls with all the partner teams. We have Internet project space where all documents are shared. We pull each other in to speak at different conferences and meetings. And then we do a big e-blast over our Listserv. When a new publication comes out we'll blast it out" (Horowitz 2010).

Similar strategies were used with Hawaii's HOPE program. After outside researchers completed an evaluation of the program, PSPP worked with the National Institute of Justice to draft a summary of its strengths. PSPP then took the idea to the National Center for State Courts (NCSC) (which also houses the Council of State Court Administrators) and asked if they would consider endorsing it. After the PSPP supplied NCSC with further counsel on the program, it offered a resolution in support. Now, Horowitz noted, "you have state court administrators who are aware of the idea and you have the Conference of Chief Justices who are aware. And then in few days you start getting phone calls—people saying they want to start pilots ... ideas disseminate" (Horowitz 2010).

In the early going, advocacy organizations like the Justice Center and the PSPP were forced to drum up their own business. They identified states where they thought opportunities for reform existed—naturally looking first to states with large or growing prison populations. But they thought carefully about a state's potential interest in and capacity to reform. What did a state's political landscape look like? Would they have access to the necessary data?

Over time with a record of success in Texas, and as ideas diffused more rapidly, the process morphed into one where states themselves sought out help from the Justice Center and its partner organizations. As routines became familiar, the Justice Center and the growing network around it used a general formula to decide how (or whether) to assist states requesting help. First, lawmakers from both sides of the aisle and across the different branches of a state's government needed to express a desire for change. CSG and Pew officials would then sit down with important stakeholders—prosecutors, public defenders, judges, sheriffs, probation and parole officials, gubernatorial staff, community corrections agencies, and Republican and Democratic legislators—to identify goals. A more intensive collaboration could only begin if there was general agreement among the stakeholders.

OHIO SEEKS TECHNICAL ASSISTANCE

Ohio would be one of the more than a dozen states to ask for the Justice Center and its partners for assistance. In December of 2008, Ohio

Democratic Governor Ted Strickland, leaders in the General Assembly, and Ohio's Supreme Court Chief Justice Thomas Moyer made a request to the CSG's Justice Center for technical assistance. The state's slow-burning corrections crisis took on greater urgency after the financial crisis caused the state's economy to crumble. By the end of the year Ohio's unemployment rate had jumped nearly 3 percentage points to over 8 percent. With fewer people working, less tax revenue came into the state's coffers. By the middle of 2009 Ohio faced a budget deficit that had reached $1.1 billion (National Conference of State Legislatures 2009).

Ohio's request for technical assistance was undoubtedly influenced by its declining economy; however, it would be misplaced to suggest that request for assistance happened in Ohio *only* because of the economy. Concerns conducive to reform had been simmering in political debate for a prolonged period.

To examine this argument further, I present Figure 7.1 which tracks trends in Ohio newspaper coverage of prison overcrowding, prisoners' health concerns, and prison costs between 1993 and 2011.* Prison overcrowding was a major topic of debate (as measured by the number of stories mentioning prison overcrowding in any one year) in the 1990s when prisons filled up faster than existing capacity could handle. Ohio rectified the problem by tripling its number of prisons between 1979 and 2000, with many constructed in the 1990s (Lawrence and Travis 2004). When attention to overcrowding waned, coverage of prisoners' health (including challenges dealing with mental illness) spiked in the 2001–2003 period, which coincided with the Ohio Department of Rehabilitation and Correction's (ODRC's) newfound focus on

---

* The goal of the analysis in Figure 7.1 is to present a general picture of the trends in news coverage along dimensions favorable to reform. The newspapers in the analysis, the *Cleveland Plain Dealer*, *Columbus Dispatch*, and the *Dayton Daily News*, were chosen for both substantive and pragmatic reasons. The *Columbus Dispatch*, located in the state capitol, should be expected to provide extensive coverage of issues capturing the attention of lawmakers in the General Assembly. Each of the three papers is considered one of Ohio's ten most read papers. The *Cleveland Plain Dealer* ranks first in the state with a circulation of 246,500; the *Columbus Dispatch* is third with approximately 136,000; and the *Dayton Daily News* ranks seventh with 93,000 readers—see http://www.mondo times.com/newspapers/usa/ohio-newspaper-circulation.html (accessed July 12, 2014). The papers are also located in different regions of the state. Combined, these characteristics should increase the likelihood that trends in media coverage are generalizable to the state as a whole. All three papers were searchable in LexisNexis or ProQuest newspaper archives in each year of the time period studied. The *Cincinnati Enquirer*, the state's second largest newspaper, was unavailable for analysis in the LexisNexis and ProQuest newspaper databases. The total number of stories in Figure 7.1 should not be interpreted as representing the total sum (or population) of stories in Ohio in any one year since not all papers were sampled. Search terms included (prison* near/3 overcrowd*); (prison* near/3 costs OR prison* near/3 expenditures OR prison* near/3 budget); (prison* near/3 health OR inmate* n/3 health).

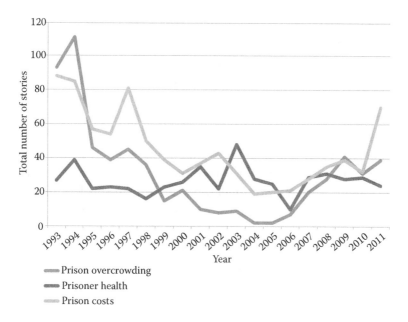

FIGURE 7.1
Newspaper coverage of the Ohio penal system, 1993–2011.

prisoner reentry during this time. Prisoner health-related concerns remained a significant part of the public conversation through much of the 2000s. Notably the financial cost of prison was hardly a new issue in Ohio as the economy collapsed in 2008. Media coverage of prison costs was more prominent in the 1990s when crime carried greater saliency in American politics.

The 2008–2011 period, more so than any other time, saw both an upward trend and a convergence of problems in political debate favorable to reform. Longer running debates over prison costs and prisoner health issues, when mixed with renewed but growing concern about prison overcrowding, all lent to a crisis atmosphere. What the economic crisis did, then, was to quicken the pace of policy learning. This was most notable among conservatives who began reinterpreting (and placing new meaning on) problem signals that had long filtered into the political system but were too often ignored.

POLICY LEARNING AMONG CONSERVATIVES IN OHIO

One of these lawmakers was Bill Seitz. Seitz entered the Ohio Senate in 2007 after serving seven years in the state House where he climbed the ranks of the chamber's leadership. Representing one of the more conservative areas of the state near Cincinnati, Seitz, an attorney by training, was one of the House's most active lawmakers on criminal sentencing, championing legislation that stiffened penalties for violent offenders and sex offenders. In the Senate, he quickly gained a reputation for his keen sense of humor, memorable floor speeches, and his strong advocacy for smaller and more efficient government.

As the Tea Party movement took hold in the wake of Barack Obama's election, Seitz quickly identified with the movement's putative push for smaller, more efficient government. It was through this lens that prison reform began to resonate. And from his post on the Senate's Criminal Justice Committee, he was in a good position to advance change. "Most states today do three things: educate, medicate, and incarcerate," Seitz said (Seitz 2010). While obviously an oversimplification, the fact that Seitz understood incarceration to be one of state's leading functions also meant, in tough economic times, prisons, not unlike education or health care, would be a major part of the conversation in the struggle to solve the state's budget crisis.

Seitz saw prison reform as serving two goals: saving the state money and improving public safety. But these were views he only came to over time. Part of his transformation is traced to what he witnessed at the local level. In his own Hamilton County, commissioners and the local sheriff had twice in five years asked voters to pay for a local tax levy to build a new local jail to alleviate overcrowding. Both levies were soundly defeated. For Seitz this served as a wake-up call. "If these law and order people are not willing to put their money where their mouth is, in terms of providing the resources to incarcerate more people, then it was perhaps time to explore some smart on crime common sense sentencing reforms" (Seitz 2010).

But it also became apparent to Seitz that the sheer size of Ohio's correction system was a growing problem. "We have roughly 52,000 people in the state prison system. And it was only built to house 36,000. As my mother always said, you cannot put 10 pounds in a 5 pound bag. It was quite impossible for us in the current circumstances to build additional prisons because of the high capital costs associated with construction and the additional costs associated with operation" (Seitz 2010). Seitz continued,

> Therefore, doesn't it make sense to relieve the prison overcrowding system in a responsible way before some court orders us to do a mass release which is a blunt instrument approach to a problem that, frankly, is less promotive

of public safety than is a more nuanced approach. Our focus is, for the most part, on lower level offenders and to make changes that will help triage them out of the system to make sure we reserve our prison space for more … serious offenders. (Seitz 2010)

This "nuanced" approach, as Seitz called it, is one of the fundamental differences within Republican ranks in the smart on crime era. Violent offenders and nonviolent criminal offenders are now clearly demarcated in criminal justice politics. Seitz, for example, thought of saving space in an overcrowded prison environment as one might think of an overcrowded hospital. "If one has limited space, people with less serious illnesses are not going to get housed there—they are going to go somewhere else. And so the people who are seriously ill can get one of the scarce beds in a hospital that is overcrowded. With prisons it's the same principle" (Seitz 2010).

Like John Whitmire in Texas, Seitz realized the political import of a Republican taking the lead. A year earlier, Democratic Governor Ted Strickland had offered a number of reform proposals in his budget plan. Strickland, though, was an imperfect messenger. He was up for reelection but electorally vulnerable given the shaky economic times. "It was a bit of a Nixon to China moment," Seitz said. "I told the Governor, if you propose [a reform package], being a Democratic governor, it would be tough for you to sell it. For the same reason that if Lyndon Johnson had tried to normalize relations with Mao Zedong it would have been more difficult than Richard Nixon doing so" (Seitz 2010). Seitz decided to introduce his own stand-alone bill, SB 22, to "get the issue up on people's radar's screen and to bring some bipartisan support for the idea that in tough times we have to be to be smarter with the taxpayers' money" (Seitz 2010).

Among the major reforms, SB 22 expanded "earned credits" for inmates from one day to five. It raised monetary thresholds for felony property crimes from $500 to $1,000. The bill allowed the ODRC to petition the court for the release of offenders who had served at least 85 percent of their term.* People charged with less serious crimes would be supervised in community corrections rather than mandated to serve prison time. In a provision pushed by the Ohio chapter of the American Civil Liberties Union (ACLU) and members of the Ohio Black Caucus, the bill eliminated the crack/powder cocaine disparity (Fields 2009).

---

* The proposal excluded inmates serving a life term and those serving time for a variety of other violent offenses.

The bill was not without opposition. Early on some rank-and-file Republicans and, indeed, some Democrats, confounded "earned credits" with "good time" credits, the latter of which did not require much at all from inmates. The director of the ODRC, Terry Collins, who openly supported the bill, said "there was a misperception by some people, maybe premeditated on their part, to try to make it sound like we were going to open the prison doors and let all these people out" (Fields 2009). In truth, good time credits were largely disbanded when the state went to a determinate sentencing model. Under Seitz's bill, earned credit was exactly that: *earned*. It would be only given to inmates who participated in ODRC-approved job training, education, and substance abuse programs. To help sell the idea, Seitz pointed lawmakers to the research. "These programs have been shown to reduce the rate of recidivism. It only makes sense. Folks that have no education, no job skills, and people with substance abuse problems, when they are released from prison are much more likely to revert back to their old ways ... they lack the attributes for success" (Seitz 2010).

When some of his colleagues expressed concern about the possibility of a Willie Horton–type crime, Seitz was careful not to oversell. "I never ever guarantee a zero chance of recidivism." Lawmakers, Seitz thought, needed to face the reality that prisoners return to their communities. "They will all get out sometime" Seitz said, channeling Jeremy Travis's "iron law of incarceration" (see Chapter 4). "Doesn't it make sense to better equip them with tools and skills that make them less likely to reoffend?" (Seitz 2010).

Indeed much of the misinformation surrounding the bill could be sourced to prosecutors. The Ohio Prosecuting Attorneys Association believed that by expanding earned time credit, SB 22 violated the principle of determinate sentencing adopted in SB 2 in the mid-1990s. But prosecutors who for years had found a sympathetic ear within Republican ranks were now finding themselves on the defensive as the dimensions of debate shifted. "Prosecutors have a role to play in the system. Public safety is their number one goal. They believe people should be locked up. That's fine." Seitz said. "Yet, prosecutors aren't funding the state prison system. They don't have to provide the money."

In many ways Seitz is the embodiment of how the many years of passing stiffer sentencing sentences and the consequences thereof have reshaped conservatives' thinking. "You can't stand on the Holy Grail of SB 2 bill unless you are also willing to take the criminal code back to where it was *in* SB 2," Seitz said. "If determinant sentencing is so sacrosanct then prosecutors have forgotten about the fact that in the ensuing 15 years scores of bills have passed the Ohio General Assembly that increased the length of stay ... *we need to reconsider our policy in light of the intervening 15 years of sentencing enhancement bills*" (emphasis added) (Seitz 2010).

Seitz was making headway although the process was a grind. The bill narrowly passed the Senate Criminal Justice Committee that spring. In an attempt to bring prosecutors along, SB 22 was amended to cap at 8 percent the amount of earned credit prisoners could receive off their sentence. But with years of distrust around the crime issue serving as a backdrop, the process effectively turned into a game of legislative chicken. Democrats controlled the House of Representatives but Democratic leaders did not want to vote on the bill until after that 2010 election out of fear Republican opponents (as they had done numerous times before) would use it against them in the fall campaign. In response, House Republican leaders reaffirmed their support of the bill. But with little trust of Republicans' motives, Democrats stalled by calling for more study. Without a vote in the House, state Senate leaders said they would not move on the bill either—why take a tough vote if the House had no intention of moving at all? With neither chamber wanting to move first, the bill stalled.

In a process that paralleled Seitz's efforts, the CSG's Justice Center and its partners were working to capture a deeper understanding of the state's correctional system. The Justice Center examined Ohio's crime rate; it analyzed the state's data on arrests, court dispositions and sentencing, prison admissions and releases, and probation and community corrections programs. The Justice Center revealed its findings in an all-day Justice Reinvestment Conference in late July 2010.

One of the principal contributors to the overcrowding problem, the Justice Center found, was a change in Ohio prisoners' average length of stay. Between 2003 and 2008 the average length of stay (across all offenders) had grown from twenty-six to twenty-eight months. This seems inconsequential until we consider that a two-month average increase in length of stay, when applied to the 2008 admission cohort, equated to needing an additional 4,400 beds than if the cohort served the same average sentence of those admitted in 2003. It was also determined that a large share of low-level offenders were going to prison. Offenders charged with fourth-degree (F4) or fifth-degree (F5) felony offenses comprised 56 percent of admissions in 2008. Of these, almost 70 percent were charged with drug or property crimes. Sentencing judges in the prison "feeder" counties were sending F4 and F5 drug and property offenders to prison at a particularly high rate. In Cuyahoga County (which includes the city of Cleveland), which contributed to 20 percent of Ohio's prison admissions, just under half (49 percent) of its F4-classified offenders were sent to prison. Among its F5 caseload, 34 percent were admitted. The Justice Center estimated that in 2008, the people sentenced to prison on low-level drug and property crime charges (whose length of stay averaged just nine months) were filling over 4,700 prison beds at a cost of $121 million. Many of the offenders could be safely sentenced to probation or placed in prison diversion or community-based correctional programs and facilities.*

Part of the difficulty lay with Ohio's challenges with its community corrections treatment programming and service delivery. Although Ohio had recently increased investment in community corrections and weeded out poor-performing programs and behavioral health treatment services, the supply of services was still too small to meet demand. Probationers, especially, expressed a high demand for mental health and substance abuse services. Yet due to low treatment capacities in the community, judges reported placing offenders in more expensive residential treatment programs even if risk assessment instruments suggested nonresidential settings would elicit better outcomes.

The probation system was also troubled. Ohio's probation system epitomized the institutional fragmentation of American federalism. The state's 260,000 probationers were supervised by a combination of state, county, and municipal agencies. The ODRC provided probation supervision to forty-seven of the state's eighty-eight counties, but supervised only 20 percent of the state's felony probationers. The remaining 80 percent of felony probationers were supervised by forty-one different county probation agencies. Adding to the complexity, probationers with misdemeanors were supervised by municipal agencies. Some were even assigned to both misdemeanor and felony probation, forcing them to report to two different officers in two separate departments.

As a general rule decentralized systems invite variation in both processes and policy outcomes. The quality of data collected by Ohio's county probation departments varied significantly; some agencies, in fact, collected no data at all. The minimum qualifications to be hired as a probation officer differed across agencies, as did the training requirements. A number of probation departments failed to use evidence-based practices such as risk-base

---

* Community correction facilities (or what Ohio calls CBCFs) are secure residential facilities with a maximum length of stay of 180 days. Prison diversion programs in the state are typically nonresidential programs administered by county and city officials. Programs might include electronic monitoring, work release, day reporting, or more intensive probation supervision.

probation caseloads and progressive sanctions to improve offender compliance. Agencies used a hodgepodge set of risk-assessment instruments that mostly failed to connect probationers to the right mental health or drug treatment services. Not surprisingly, the number of probationers sent to prison on technical violations or new crimes had steadily increased over the previous five years (The Council of State Governments 2010).

The parole system was still a work in progress despite efforts connected to the Ohio Plan (see Chapter 4). By law, most violent offenders and all sex offenders received postrelease control (PRC). For nonviolent offenders and all F4 and F5 offenders, however, PRC was discretionary. With discretionary cases the Parole Board was too often failing to assess parolees' risk of recidivism, helping better allocate postrelease supervision resources. Almost the same proportion (56 percent) of "high-risk" offenders were supervised as "low-risk" (53 percent) offenders despite statistics showing high-risk offenders were twice as likely to recidivate.

Overall, the Justice Center's analysis of Ohio's correctional system painted a sobering picture. But over the next months the smart on crime coalition continued to advocate and to strengthen. Marc Levin of the Texas Policy Foundation, who had begun spreading TPPF's resources and expertise, penned an article published by the Buckeye Institute, an Ohio-based conservative think tank, advancing many of the same justice reinvestment themes offered by the CSG while also drawing on his experiences in Texas (Levin 2010). The Chamber of Commerce, which had earlier supported Seitz's legislation, continued to express support for reform. The ACLU of Ohio and members of the Ohio Black Caucus continued their fight to eliminate the crack/powder cocaine disparity and to push for an end to felony-based discrimination in hiring.

By January 2011 Ohio had a new governor in John Kasich, a conservative Republican and former member of Congress who defeated Ted Strickland in one of the most bruising gubernatorial contests in the 2010 election cycle. Like Scott Walker, his newly elected counterpart in Wisconsin, one of Kasich's first moves as governor was to weaken the bargaining rights of public sector labor unions. So while progressives were rightfully dismayed over the attack on labor rights, their hopes of seeing a major prison reform bill pass actually grew. Kasich made prison reform a central part of his first term agenda. "We've got to do this together, folks. Republicans and Democrats have long favored sentencing reform … we didn't do this because we were afraid," Kasich said in his first State of the State speech. He then alluded to the churn of prisoners through the system. "Forty-seven percent of our inmates sit in prisons for less than a year and they sit next to hardened criminals. It raises the recidivism rates, costs taxpayers a fortune. We need to restrain them in a setting that makes sense. We've got to keep the public safe. But think about if we can keep them somewhere where we can save money, reduce the recidivism rate, and they can be rehabbed and go out and get a job" (Malcolm 2011).

Kasich struck a moral tone when he spoke directly to the Black Caucus about the troubling story of an African American man who worked at the Cleveland Clinic for years until it was found that he had a felony conviction and was then promptly fired. "I must tell you, I am deeply, deeply troubled by the issue of some of these felony convictions. Members of the legislature, we don't want to ruin people's lives if there is a chance to give them a second chance if it is appropriate, and we have to work through it together. We don't want to wreck somebody forever when it makes no sense" (Malcolm 2011).

With the Republican governor's endorsement, Ohio legislators pieced together a reform package, HB 86, that combined elements from the Justice Center's analysis and Seitz's SB 22. The bill expanded community-based treatment and increased prison diversion programs for low-level offenders. It developed statewide criteria to prioritize placement for offenders who would benefit from intensive community supervision and treatment. It allowed for risk reduction sentencing by introducing earned credit for inmates who participated in drug treatment and education programming. It strengthened probation by codifying statewide standards on probation supervision. It eliminated the crack/powder cocaine disparity. To spur justice reinvestment, the bill included an incentive-based funding formula that allowed probation departments to share in cost savings when fewer offenders were sent to prison. All told the legislation was predicted to save the state $500 million in averted prison construction costs and $78 million in forgone operating costs.

By late June 2011, the final votes in the General Assembly belied the years of struggle. Despite the continued opposition of the Ohio Prosecuting Attorneys Association, the House passed HB 86 on a 95 to 2 vote. In the Senate the vote was no less lopsided, 30 to 3. "I believe this is the most sweeping criminal justice reform bill that we have passed," Seitz said after the Senate vote (Bischoff et al. 2011). "I get emotional about this issue because I think the passage of this bill and the changing of this law is going to result in the saving of many, many lives, maybe even thousands," Governor Kasich added (Johnson 2011). Indeed, a sense of hope and justice, too long absent from Ohio's criminal justice politics, had made a welcome comeback.

8

California

In California there would be no starring roles from policy analysts in the Justice Center, no warmly received policy presentations to a receptive bipartisan audience in the state legislature, or all-day conferences pointing a clear path forward. More important, Republican lawmakers in the legislature would show no support for prison reform. California Republicans' intransigence, as we will see, severely weakened the smart on crime coalition and helps explain the very different path reform took in the Golden State.

The tragic state of California's penal system ranks as perhaps the biggest public policy abomination in the state's history. Over time, more than a dozen reports from expert panels and independent commissions studied what ailed the California penal system and what could be done to fix it. Eventually a general diagnosis emerged. Tougher sentences and countless "add-ons" for robbery, rape, and aggravated assault increased the likelihood that an arrest would lead to a prison sentence in California. Once in prison, inmates stayed longer. Contrary to popular belief, drug convictions played only a minor part in the prisoner buildup, accounting for only 10 percent of the overall increase in the state's prisoner population (Petersilia 2006). Convictions for violent crime were a bigger driver, explaining two-thirds of the increase since the 1990s (Petersilia 2006).

One of the biggest problems was found in the state's parole system. A 2003 report by the independent Little Hoover Commission called California's parole system a "billion dollar failure." Two-thirds of California's parolees returned to prison within eighteen months of their release, a figure more than double the national average (Little Hoover Commission 2003). California had a two-tiered parole system. One set of rules guided parole release decisions for offenders serving indeterminate life sentences (this is usually reserved for people convicted of violent and serious crimes). A second set of rules applied to individuals serving a determinate sentence.

Inmates falling in the former category were parole eligible after completing the minimum stated term of imprisonment (for example, someone serving a third strike, twenty-five years to life sentence, would be eligible for parole after serving twenty-five years minus any good time credits). Then they had to persuade the Board of Parole Hearings (BPH) that they were suitable for release. This was the general practice for indeterminate lifers until 1988 when California voters passed Proposition 89, giving the governor authority to review all parole cases and, if desired, overturn or modify a BPH's release decision. As one might imagine in the get-tough era, very few people eligible for parole actually got released.

The system, then, made it almost impossible for a lifer with the possibility of parole to ever leave prison. For individuals serving a determinate sentence, the issue was not whether they would be released but rather how the parole system's design almost guaranteed released inmates would get returned to prison. When the California legislature adopted a determinate sentencing model for most crimes in 1976, it also mandated postprison parole supervision for *all* offenders (most received a parole term of three years) on a fixed sentence. A state like Texas, in contrast, released far fewer inmates using a nondiscretionary (or determinate) process and kept more risky individuals incarcerated.* Under California's old (pre-1976) indeterminate sentencing system, the state would have been able to do the same. It could use parole for what it was originally designed to do: reward inmates who showed signs of rehabilitation or posed a minimal threat to the community. California's unique hybrid approach (California was just one of two states to use it) that mixed determinate sentences with mandatory parole for everyone created the worst of both worlds. The system did almost nothing to successfully transition inmates back into the community. Under fixed sentences, rehabilitation programming had little impact on an inmate's length of term, which gave them little (except for altruistic reasons) incentive to participate. A 2007 report found that fewer than 10 percent of California's inmates participated in treatment programs, yet 80 percent had substance abuse histories ("California Expert Panel" 2007). When a prisoner served his legislatively mandated time, he was released on parole even if parole officials determined the inmate was likely to reoffend. And with everyone on parole, the California Department of Corrections was forced to manage huge caseloads—120,000 parolees were released every year—by far the

---

* Although as noted in the analysis of reform in Texas, even low-risk offenders were not paroled at sufficient rates.

largest number in the nation. Scarce resources spent supervising so many low-risk offenders took away resources for high-risk offenders. The system suffered from a severe mismatch of needs and resources.

As if blanket imposition of parole, large caseloads, and poorly designed surveillance strategies were not bad enough, the entire culture within the parole system shifted. The system's original emphasis on rehabilitation and community reintegration turned instead to surveillance. This is most clearly seen in how parole officials dealt with technical violations. In California, technical violations were divided into two broad categories: "administrative criminal returns" and "administrative noncriminal returns" (Petersilia 2006, p. 75). By the mid-2000s, 80 percent of the parolees returned to prison following allegations of new criminal activity (Petersilia 2006, p. 75). Despite their relatively benign-sounding name, administrative violations were not always so. Offenses could include robbery, rape, and even murder (Travis 2003). Returning a parolee on a technical violation allowed authorities to act quickly, but it created other problems.* With administrative sentences capped at one year, the system created an administrative headache of monumental proportions as thousands of returned parolees came into one of the state's (only) dozen reception centers that quickly became severely overcrowded. Parole officials played a never-ending game of catch and release. One study found that nearly 10 percent of California prisoners cycled between home and prison six or more times over a seven-year period (Blumstein and Beck 2005).

Fewer lifers released on parole, longer prisoner terms, and California's high rate of recidivism combined to create a prison system overstuffed with bodies. Aside from raising the threat of prison violence, the effects of prison overcrowding were most acutely felt in the delivery of medical services (Koehler 2013). Nowhere was this truer than in California. The newest prisons in California were almost all built in lower-income rural areas, which has impeded the delivery of swift medical care to a population that is already more sickly to begin with. Officials in overcrowded prisons double and triple bunked prison cells *and* prison gyms to make room; however, with clinical beds, there was no such luxury. Staff needs per inmate are much higher in medical wings than in other parts of the

---

* Sentencing a parolee to prison through administrative parole violations instead of a new conviction benefited the state in the sense that it lowered the standard of proof required. Under the rules of administrative returns, alleged crimes would be heard before the Hearing and Operations Division of the Bureau of Prison Terms where the standard of proof followed civil, not criminal, standards.

institution, yet California medical units were often dangerously under-staffed, as comparatively low salaries (relative to similar professional positions in the private sector) made recruiting difficult (Koehler 2013).

The California Department of Corrections was failing in its crime-fighting duties as much as it was failing the taxpayers. By the mid-2000s the correctional system burned through money as never before, both on a per-inmate basis and as a share of the state's total spending. An adult inmate in California cost an average of nearly $31,000 a year to incarcerate in 2004—32 percent above the national average (American Correctional Association 2005). By 2009, the cost grew to nearly $50,000 (California Legislative Analysts Office 2009). As a share of the state's total spending, corrections expenditures grew from 2 percent in 1981 to a number more than five times that (11.0 percent) by 2009 (California Legislative Analysts Office 2009; Petersilia 2006).

SHIFTING POLITICAL ENVIRONMENT

Figure 8.1 presents data from a content analysis of news coverage of prisons in three major California newspapers: the *Los Angeles Times*, the *Sacramento Bee*, and the *San Francisco Chronicle* between 1995 and 2011. Similar to the analysis of Ohio's media coverage in Chapter 7, the goal is to assess the degree to which coverage of prison overcrowding, prison costs, and prisoner health concerns made their way into political debate over time.[*] As shown, news

---

[*] The goal of the analysis in Figure 8.1 is to present a general picture of the trends in news coverage along dimensions favorable to reform. The newspapers in the analysis, the *Los Angeles Times*, *San Francisco Chronicle*, and *Sacramento Bee* were chosen for both substantive and pragmatic reasons. The *Sacramento Bee*, located in the state capital, should be expected to provide extensive coverage of issues capturing the attention of lawmakers in the state legislature. All three papers are considered among California's ten most read papers. The *Los Angeles Times* ranks first in the state with a circulation of 645,575; the *Sacramento Bee* ranks eighth with approximately 196,667; and the *San Francisco Chronicle* ranks sixth with 229,176 copies—see http://www.mondotimes.com/newspapers/usa/california-newspaper-circulation.html (accessed September 14, 2014). The papers are also located and distributed in southern, central, and northern (Bay Area) parts of the state. Combined, these characteristics should increase the likelihood that trends in media coverage are generalizable to the state as a whole. The total number of stories in Figure 8.1 should not be interpreted as representing the total sum (or population) of stories in California in any one year, given that not all papers were sampled. All three papers were searchable in LexisNexis or ProQuest newspaper archives in each year of the time period studied. Search terms included (prison* near/3 overcrowd*); (prison* near/3 costs OR prison* near/3 expenditures OR prison* near/3 budget); (prison* near/3 health OR inmate* n/3 health).

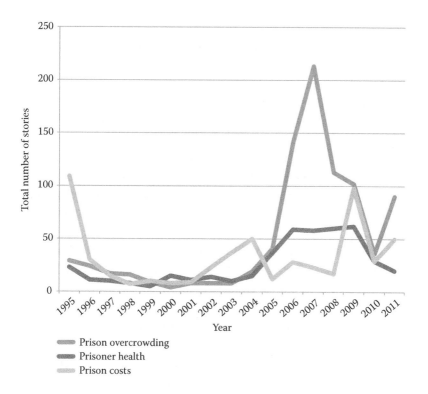

FIGURE 8.1
Newspaper coverage of the California penal system, 1995–2011.

stories on prison overcrowding were almost nonexistent in the 1990s, only to spike dramatically between 2006 and 2009.

In 2007 alone, more than 200 stories across the three papers mentioned prison overcrowding. Stories on prisoner health care grew beginning in 2004 and reached their peak in 2009. Stories covering prison costs received considerable coverage as far back as 1995 when the state was in the midst of a prison construction boom before ebbing in the late 1990s. Coverage increased again in 2003–2004 when prison costs became enwrapped in a debate about how California could close its budget deficit, which had ballooned after the 9/11 attacks. Coverage reached a peak in 2009 as the Great Recession unfolded and piggybacked on stories on overcrowding and prisoner health care.

By the mid-to-late 2000s, issues that signaled major problems in the California penal system had prominently made their way into the political system. During this time blue ribbon panels and expert commissions called on state leaders to expand community-based treatment and diversion programs for nonviolent offenders, reform parole supervision, and create a sentencing commission that could bring badly needed rationality to the state's convoluted sentencing rules (Rappaport and Dansky 2010*). Unlike conservative lawmakers in Ohio and Texas, however, Republicans in the legislature did not take the signs of trouble as an opportunity for reform. Instead, calls for reform were met with outright hostility. There was only one prominent Republican, Governor Arnold Schwarzenegger, who pledged to reform the system.

Schwarzenegger was elected in 2003 after Democratic Governor Gray Davis became only the second U.S. governor in history to be recalled from office. Schwarzenegger ran as an outsider, promising to "clean house" by challenging special interests (Gerston and Christensen 2004). One of Schwarzenegger's vociferous targets was the California prison guards union, an organization formally known as the California Correctional Peace Officers Association (CCPOA). "This is an agency in which there has been too much political influence, too much union control, and too little management courage and accountability ... California was once the national leader, a pioneer, in corrections integrity, innovation, and efficiency. We can make it so again" (Petersilia 2006, p. 20).

To understand Schwarzenegger's excoriation of the prison guards requires knowing more about what made the CCPOA unique. Twenty-eight other states have unionized correctional guards. But in terms of supplying benefits to its members and the union's influence on policy, the CCPOA is without doubt the strongest, most effective guards union in the nation (Page 2011). The prison guards were not always a potent political presence in Sacramento. Until 1980 the guards were split between two unions, which limited their capacity to mobilize (Page 2011). It was not until Don Novey consolidated prison guards and parole officers under one roof that the CCPOA turned into a political juggernaut. Between 1980 and 2005, the CCPOA saw its ranks increase from 5,000 to more than 33,000 members (Petersilia 2006, p. 21). Salaries improved dramatically. With an average yearly salary of $73,000 (in 2005), California prison guards earned nearly 60 percent above the national average. Their retirement and pension benefits were also the best in the country (Petersilia 2006, p. 21).

The CCPOA followed a simple political strategy: advocate for politicians and policies that produced more prisoners. More prisoners meant

---

* Ten different bills calling for an independent sentencing commission have been introduced in the California legislature since 1984. Three passed the legislature but were vetoed by Republican governors Duekmejian (1984) and Pete Wilson (1992 and 1994).

a greater need for guards. More guards brought more membership dues, fundraising capability, and political influence. Yet the guards risked looking overly self-interested if they painted their mission in exactly these terms. Led by Novey, the CCPOA crafted their image as public servants who walked "the toughest beat in the state," protecting the public from dangerous predators along the way (Page 2011). They also joined with victims' rights organizations, such as Crime Victims United of California, to lobby for tougher sentencing. It was a perfect pairing. With deep pockets, the CCPOA bankrolled victims groups' entire lobbying operations. Crime victims supplied sympathetic figures that bestowed a sense that the movement was something much larger and far more important than guards' parochial self-interests; the fight was really about supporting victims of crime and bolstering public safety (Simon 2007).

As an independent union (CCPOA is not affiliated with national labor organizations like the American Federation of Labor and Congress of Industrial Organizations) the CCPOA had greater control over how it spent its membership dues—$23 million worth by 2005 (Petersilia 2006, p. x). The guards spent lavishly on politics; thirty-five percent of their revenue was spent on lobbying each year. In one high-profile instance, the guards contributed over $400,000 to Pete Wilson's 1994 gubernatorial reelection campaign just as Wilson vigorously campaigned for California's draconian three-strikes law. Four years later the guards spent $2 million in direct and indirect contributions to help tough on crime Democrat Gray Davis win election and then contributed another million-plus dollars to Davis during his first term (Petersilia 2006, p. x). Contributions such as these paid off handsomely. Wilson awarded the guards an 11 percent pay increase as he left office in 1998. Their 2001–2006 contract negotiated during Davis's administration increased their general salaries (not counting overtime and merit pay) by a whopping 34 percent (Page 2011). The prison guards also accumulated a long track record of legislative success. In the CCPOA's first six years of existence, twenty-four of the twenty-seven bills it supported were signed into law. Through the 1990s it achieved legislative success rates of over 80 percent. Most notable was the popular three-strikes legislation, which between 1994 and 2005 funneled 80,000 second strikers, and more than 7,500 third strikers to state prison (Brown and Jolivette 2005).

Schwarzenegger began his reform effort by renaming the California Department of Corrections, the California Department of Corrections and Rehabilitation (CDCR). The governor promised the name change was more than a symbolic gesture. "It is a new day for Corrections in

California ... After 30 years of stressing punishment, rehabilitation is back" (Petersilia 2010). Schwarzenegger promised to reduce the inmate population by 15,000 by 2005 after he introduced parole reforms making greater use of community-based treatment and prison diversion programs (Page 2011). If successful it would have marked the biggest reduction in the prisoner population in two decades (Petersilia 2010). Schwarzenegger, though, soon found that achieving substantive policy and cultural changes was a lot harder than renaming the agency or offering attention-grabbing rhetoric on the campaign trail. The CCPOA once again mobilized and joined with victims' rights groups to lobby against reform. Their strategy, well tested over many years, equated reform with threats to community safety. At a public hearing of the Board of Prison Terms, Christy Ward, a member of the Board of Crime Victims United said, "Simply stated, the governor's new parole policy is placing citizens of the state of California in greater danger. This is a very bad plan and it is very clear that the governor is not interested in public safety" (Page 2011, Chapter 4, see Petersilia et al. 2013). Crime Victims United of California took to television to run fear-inducing advertisements bankrolled by the CCPOA. Schwarzenegger's parole policies "kept murderers, rapists, and child molesters on our streets," the advertisements said (D'Elia 2010). Schwarzenegger scrapped the plan shortly thereafter.

After his defeat on parole reform, Schwarzenegger only added to the crisis. Proposition 66, the first serious effort to soften California's three-strikes law, lost by just a few percentage points after Schwarzenegger led a CCPOA-funded campaign against it. And while the governor worked with the legislature to increase drug treatment and rehabilitation programming in 2007, it came only as part of a massive $7 billion prison construction bill (AB 900) designed to relieve overcrowding.*

By 2009 the prison population had actually grown by 10,000 since Schwarzenegger took office. When the federal three-judge panel ruled in early August 2009 that California needed to submit a plan to reduce the inmate population by 40,000 (or face a court ordered release), a palpable sense of urgency swept over Sacramento. In less than two weeks after the court's ruling, the governor put forward a $1.2 billion cost-cutting plan that would reduce the inmate population by 37,000 over two years. The

---

* The Great Recession forced huge cuts in all types of social services in California. The new rehabilitation programming installed as part of AB 900 largely disappeared when the legislation cut rehabilitation and education services funding by $250 million in the 2009–2010 fiscal year—see Petersilia (2010).

plan called for enhanced good time credit for inmates who participated in rehabilitation programming, parole reform, a reduction of some property crimes to misdemeanors, and last but not least, a much-needed sentencing commission. The parole-related elements of the plan were strong. The plan required the CDCR to use a risk assessment instrument for *all* individuals released on parole, with the risk score determining a parolee's level of supervision. Individuals with nonviolent, nonserious, and non-sex offense backgrounds would no longer face parole supervision. More important, the plan ended the practice of sending these parolees back to state prison on technical violations (Petersilia 2010). Saving resources on lower-risk parolees, the CDCR could assign higher-risk offenders to lower caseloads allowing the agency to supervise them more strictly.

All of these policies were designed around evidence-based practices and research findings flowing through the policy subsystem. Matthew Cate, then secretary of the CDCR, noted that there was a growing sense in the legislature that evidence-based policies worked.

> Policymakers in general now agree that there are programs that will reduce recidivism. This wasn't always true … after efforts to reduce recidivism in the 1970s were debunked as ineffective there was a sense to lock them up because nothing was going to help … I hardly hear anyone say it doesn't work anymore. Now I can go to them [the legislature] and say listen if you take … these basic principles and you run the programs the way they are designed to run you're going to get about this result. It could be better if you run a good program or a little worse if you don't, but almost everyone I talk to [in the legislature] says you should be doing rehabilitation in the prisons. (Cate 2009)

Cate had started to witness the change as far back as 2004 when he was inspector general of the CDCR.

> When I arrived in 2004 I was already seeing the shift start to take place. The good research had just started to come out. It was becoming known. We've also had key researchers who have become prominent in California—Dr. Petersilia at Irvine—and a couple others who have gone out and made the rounds … to talk about what works. Slowly but surely … people are getting the fact that there is something to this rehabilitation issue. It resonates with folks when you talk about a living wage job, stable housing and support to be clean and sober as being core components to this. You don't have to get into whether we're talking about a therapeutic community or whether it's [a program] cognitive behavioral based, but just that there is stuff out there that works and we should be investing in it. (Cate 2009)

Although "smart" prison alternatives proved to be crucial political building blocks in Texas and Ohio, what happened next in California suggests the political effect of evidence-based practices goes only so far. Once Schwarzenegger's prison reform (what became Senate Bill 18) entered the legislature, Senate Republicans quickly attacked it. A governor's executive power, similar to that of the president, is constrained by institutions. Given the legislature's status as a coequal branch of government, Schwarzenegger could not force his Republican colleagues in the legislature to do anything.

The main controversy surrounded the proposed sentencing commission. For advocates of the plan, a sentencing commission seemed like a rational solution. What was once a fairly straightforward system, the state's criminal code had turned into an administrative nightmare. As Little Hoover Commission member Carole D'Elia notes, the state's criminal law had been incrementally and radically rewritten with no consistent or informed evaluation of the laws for their effect on public safety or the state treasury (D'Elia 2010, p. 145). California had more than 1,000 felony sentencing laws spread across 21 separate sections of California law; even sentencing judges and lawyers needed complex software to make sense of it. Among many Republicans a sentencing commission raised questions about democratic accountability, and they expressed concern that an unelected commission would hold too much power. Others objected on the belief that the bill offered "early release" or a "get out of jail free card." State Senator Sharon Runner even went as far to suggest (or warn) Californians "get a gun, buy a dog, and put an alarm system in" (Yi 2009). Without any Republican support, the Senate adopted the bill but only by a slim 21 to 19 margin.

In the Democratic-controlled Assembly, Speaker Karen Bass had plenty of votes to work with, at least in theory. Democrats held forty-nine of the Assembly's eighty seats. Yet when debate began on SB 18, Bass could not even reach a simple majority (forty-one votes) in her chamber. Like Schwarzenegger, Bass had problems whipping votes in her own party. Nearly 40 percent of the Democratic Assembly members were running for another office; three were competing in the race for state attorney general (Skelton 2009). Democratic Assembly members expressed deep reservations about looking soft on crime in an election year.

While the media naturally focused on Democrats infighting, this particular juncture is more important because of what it teaches us about the effect of Republican positioning on Democrats' vote choices in the smart on crime era. Because conservative Republicans often led reform efforts in Ohio and Texas, Democrats could follow with little fear. But in California, Republicans went to the old playbook. No Republican Assembly member voted for SB 18. As Republican assemblyman Jeff Miller said during debate, "We might as well set off a nuclear bomb in California with what we are doing with this bill" (Rothfeld 2009b). Republican Joel Anderson of San Diego warned Democrats that he "did not want your state-sanctioned jail break in my backyard" (Rothfeld 2009b). Republican Jim Nielsen warned of "blood in the streets" (Yi 2009). Martin Garrick, another Republican assemblyman asked, "What's this about prisoners getting good time credit? You're in jail. You've already proven you're bad. We don't reward someone for not breaking the law" (Yi 2009).

Republicans' hard-line stance and Democrats' subsequent nervousness had a substantial effect on policy. Speaker Bass stripped provisions that reduced penalties for some crimes and allowed some inmates to complete their terms in home detention (Rothfeld 2009a). The proposal for a sentencing commission was also removed. The CDCR estimated the weakened assembly bill would reduce the prison population by only 11,000—far short of the three-judge court order (Spector 2010). After the vote Schwarzenegger lambasted Assembly members, telling them they were more concerned about "safe seats" than "safe streets" (D'Elia 2010, p. 146). In the end the legislature settled on something much closer to the Assembly's more conservative version of the bill.

The storyline thus far appears emblematic of patterns that played out repeatedly in the get-tough era. Some lawmakers like Senate Pro-Tem Darrell Steinberg took a more sanguine view when he described the final bill as "not a complete package" but "a good first step" (Rothfeld 2009b). An important question is what did California lawmakers accomplish if anything? By reforming key aspects of the parole system, especially ending the practice of sending low-risk parolees to prison for technical violations, California took a step it had repeatedly failed to take in the past. Yet the state came up short in other ways, most notably its failure to solve the immediate crisis. The three-judge court required a reduction of 40,000 prisoners, but the state's plan achieved only 30 percent of that number. Two things seemed to dim hope for future reductions. First, when the Assembly removed the sentencing commission, it also removed the state's most politically viable tool to reduce criminal sentences. Second, and perhaps more important, conservatives were acting and sounding as if they were stuck in some 1980s time machine.

RETURN OF THE STRUCTURAL INJUNCTION

Examining the role of the federal courts on state prison administration matters more generally, and the *Plata* decision specifically, is helpful to understanding what happened next. In the 1970s state prison systems were among a number of public institutions that found themselves under federal oversight for constitutional violations. As Linda Greenhouse notes, this was the era of the "structural injunction"—an order by which a court takes control of public institutions—to remedy severe constitutional harms (Greenhouse 2011*). Litigation proved to be an important tool for prison reformers. The door of opportunity quickly closed during the 1980s. When get-tough politics attained hegemony and later as Congress made it more difficult for courts to intervene with legislation like Prison Litigation Reform Act, federal intervention in state prison administration ended. Prisoners' rights lawyers in the Prison Law Office, the Berkeley-based nonprofit who brought the *Coleman* and *Plata* cases, surely knew this history. They also surely knew that pursuing reform through the legal system was far from ideal. Court rulings are unpredictable, and if change comes at all, it can take years. But when the politics within elected institutions are seemingly immovable, fighting for change through legal institutions often becomes the only viable path (Schattschneider 1960).

The *Plata* decision represented the first federal injunction of a state prison system in a generation (Greenhouse 2011). That the three-judge panel issued a prisoner reduction order is a testament to the deplorable conditions in California prisons. But as legal scholar Jonathan Simon argues, *Plata* went "beyond individual instances of cruelty to instead put the whole political system on trial that facilitates inhumane and degrading punishment and which cannot be trusted to reform itself" (Simon 2011a). Indeed, perhaps the most innovative part of the three-judge court's ruling is when it referenced California's get-tough politics and its progeny to help it meet federal rules that said a reduction order could only be issued as a "remedy of last resort." After years of trying smaller interventions (including imposing a federal receiver to oversee the state's prison mental health and medical care services) with no appreciable improvement in prison conditions, the panel concluded California's political system was incapable of reform. "Tough on crime politics have increased the population

---

* Schools, mental hospitals, child welfare agencies were other institutions that received intervention.

of California's prisons dramatically while making necessary reforms impossible," the three-judge court noted as it quoted findings from a Little Hoover Commission study.* "As a result, the state's prisons have become places of extreme peril to the safety of persons they house" (see footnote *). "The problem of highly dysfunctional, largely decrepit, over bureaucratic, and politically driven prison system ... is too far gone to be corrected by individual measures."†

Federal courts can alter the strategic positions and relative political leverage of groups or parties engaged in a prolonged policy fight (McCann 1999). Court decisions can shape whether parties choose "to continue, to escalate, to settle, or even withdraw from the dispute or relationship at stake" (McCann 1999, p. 73). By either altering or reaffirming the pre-existing status of relevant parties, courts provide a bargaining chip that determines the outcome of the conflict itself (McCann 1999, p. 73). After the three-judge court's ruling, Schwarzenegger could hardly escalate his fight with the legislature. Dubbed a Republican In Name Only (RINO) by many conservative activists, Schwarzenegger had burned out far too many matches with Republican legislators; his political capital was spent. With only a diluted legislative solution achieved thus far and seemingly out of other options, Schwarzenegger appealed the three-judge court's reduction order to the U.S. Supreme Court on technical grounds. He alleged the panel failed to sufficiently account for the order's effect on public safety—a consideration required by the Prison Litigation Reform Act.

PRISON REALIGNMENT IN CALIFORNIA

The Supreme Court accepted the state's appeal in June 2010 and heard oral arguments that November. That same month, Democrat Jerry Brown, the sitting attorney general, was elected governor. It was an ironic twist of history that Jerry Brown was tapped to find a solution to the crisis. It was Brown, after all, who signed the state's determinate sentencing law in 1976 during his first stint as governor. With pressure brought by the federal court reduction order combined with the political capital of a newly

---

* United States District Court for the Eastern District of California, Three-Judge Court, No. 2:90-cv-0520 LKK JFM P; N0. C01-1351 THE, 2009: 6.
† United States District Court for the Eastern District of California, Three-Judge Court, No. 2:90-cv-0520 LKK JFM P; N0. C01-1351 THE, 2009: 16.

elected governor, the state's $26 billion budget deficit adding a sense of urgency, and an unparalleled political acumen developed over years serving in California elected offices, Brown likely knew he had political leverage that Schwarzenegger did not. He wasted no time in brokering a larger deal.

By April 2011 an ambitious piece of legislation called the Public Safety Realignment Act (AB 109)—better known as "Prison Realignment"—was in place. Prison Realignment would completely upend the way incarceration was practiced in the state. The plan had two major components. First, it changed where people served time, under county jurisdiction or the state. Low-risk offenders whose current and prior convictions were nonviolent, nonserious, and non–sex related—or what California calls N3 offenders—would now serve their sentence under county jurisdiction. The law amended hundreds of punishments available for felonies in the state and then removed the one-year cap on county jail terms. This made county jail or county felony probation available to a whole new crop of felonious offenders. Under Realignment virtually all drug and property crimes would be punished at the county level. Commercial burglary, forgery, possession of marijuana for sale, vehicular manslaughter, and child custody abductions were no longer eligible for state prison (Petersilia et al. 2013). Hundreds of criminal offenses fell within the jail-only category (Petersilia et al. 2013, p. 27*).

Second, Realignment would continue to reshape the state's broken parole system. Offenders sentenced to county jail under Realignment would face no postrelease supervision after completing their terms.[†] For inmates released from state prison but whose current offense qualified as nonviolent, nonserious, or non–sex related, Realignment kept in place the three-year mandatory postrelease supervision.[‡] The key difference was that supervision responsibilities moved from the BPH (a state-level agency) to county probation departments, under what was called

---

* One area that created a lot of confusion was how Realignment would affect N3s currently serving a state prison term. Opponents of the law claimed Realignment would force "early release." Realignment did not allow early release. Inmates serving their sentence when Realignment was adopted were required to complete their terms in state facilities.

† An exception to this rule is if a county court chooses to impose a post jail period of supervision such as in the case of a split sentence.

‡ The three-year term of supervision represented the maximum time an offender could be placed under probation supervision. Offenders on PRCS could be discharged from probation as early as six months after release. Those who remained violation free for one year were required to be discharged.

"postrelease community supervision," or PRCS.* As Jonathan Simon notes, this presented a larger shift in policy than it first appeared. Relative to parole, county probation departments maintained a cultural orientation toward rehabilitation and prisoner reentry. Released prisoners who committed technical (noncrime) violations of their supervision (including those offenders on PRCS and those supervised by the state on parole) would serve their revocation term in county jail or county jail alternatives (such as house arrest, drug treatment, or "flash" incarceration).† Offenders would be closer to their community and family support systems that (at least potentially) were better equipped than state facilities to handle the needs of returning offenders. To help in this process, Realignment funding encouraged all aspects of community supervision to be consistent with evidence-based practices.

This dramatic plan to shift many responsibilities from state prisons down to the counties was designed to relieve state prison overcrowding through two primary mechanisms. The first involved a natural attrition process. N3 offenders who would have previously served their sentence in state prison would instead do so at the county level. As offenders sentenced before AB 109 completed their term and returned home, a new cohort would no longer replace them, causing the overall state prison population to decline. Second, by reforming parole and preventing almost all offenders who violated their terms of community supervision to avoid a return to state prison, Realignment sought to reduce down to a trickle California's horrendous problem of prisoner "churn."

This latest reform effort, by far the most ambitious in the state's history, was once again a Democrat-only-backed plan. Republican lawmakers did voice some legitimate concerns: Would the state supply sufficient funding to the counties for their added responsibilities? Would counties with full or overcrowded jails before Realignment be forced to release jailed inmates early to make room for the onslaught of offenders coming in under Realignment? County jails normally held offenders waiting for trial or those held on relatively minor crimes. Would counties be properly equipped to supervise more serious offenders under Realignment?

---

* State parole now supervises only those offenders released from prison with a *current conviction* categorized as a serious or violent felony as defined by California penal code 1192.7(c) or 667.5(c). See Petersilia et al. (2013, p. 39).
† For offenders on PRCS, the maximum jail revocation term is six months, although offenders can earn half-time conduct credits to shorten the term; see Simon (2011b).

When a state devolves major policy responsibilities down to county or municipal governments, it raises questions about localities' capacity or willingness to implement change. Indeed, Realignment called on all Californians to be willing participants in a grand corrections policy experiment with high stakes. It did not have to be this way. If Republican lawmakers had at any time in the previous decade dropped their worn-out fear campaign and been serious participants in reforming the state's broken system, then many of Republicans' greatest concerns would have been addressed. Instead, Democrats were forced to find a suitable but certainly more haphazard plan in the eleventh hour.

Despite Republicans' carnival barking, Brown successfully mobilized Democratic legislators around the Realignment package that in its capacity to address California's overcrowding crisis went far beyond the weakened SB 18 bill. What was different this time? First, with the Supreme Court's *Plata* decision just days or weeks away, Democrats were by then fully aware that if the state could not devise a suitable prisoner reduction plan, the federal courts (pending the Supreme Court's final decision) would force the release of tens of thousands of prisoners—some of whom posed a real threat to public safety. Second, law enforcement organizations were either supportive of the Realignment plan or did not openly lobby against it. Many law enforcement agencies, particularly police and sheriffs, expressed deep reservations. But with no viable alternatives in light of the three-judge court's order, they chose to work within the confines of the plan rather than oppose it altogether.

Of greatest import was the CCPOA's support for Prison Realignment. To grasp the CCPOA's position on Realignment requires recognizing that by 2011 the CCPOA was an organization undergoing a quiet but no less remarkable apostasy. The guards strongly endorsed Brown for governor over former eBay CEO Meg Whitman, in large part because they saw Brown as the better of two candidates to negotiate a new contract. This does not by itself illustrate a renunciation of their hardline strategy; after all, the CCPOA had supported Democratic governors previously. The real change started a couple years earlier when the guards issued a report they shared with the legislature titled, "From Sentencing to Incarceration Release: A Blueprint for Reforming California's Prison System." Given the source, it was a remarkable policy document. Among a laundry list of reforms, the CCPOA called for "behavioral-based risk assessment instruments," specialized rehabilitation centers, the expansion of good behavior credits, and, miraculously (considering the CCPOA had lobbied against it numerous times), a sentencing commission (California Peace Officers Association 2007).

What explains the CCPOA's prodigious change in direction? Joshua Page emphasizes a turnover in CCPOA leadership (Page 2011). Mike Jimenez, who succeeded Don Novey as president of CCPOA in 2002, came to the job with a different set of experiences and a more collaborative style. While style certainly matters, it is also true that the union's leadership team could only pursue reform to the extent that it aided union members. CCPOA's newfound collaborative style is best explained by the fact that the guards' self-interests increasingly aligned with reform. CCPOA may have defeated changes to three strikes and Schwarzenegger's parole reforms, but it became clearer over time that those victories came at the expense of their public standing. The CCPOA became known as the "800-pound gorilla in prisons" (Page 2011, Chapter 8). In a series of editorials in 2004, the *Los Angeles Times* said the CCPOA was "among the largest political contributors in the state" but had "defeated all major reform efforts for well over a decade" (Page 2011, Chapter 1; see Rappaport and Dansky 2010). The paper accused the union of threatening "political retribution on politicians who suggest reform" and said "today, they run the system" (Page 2011, Chapter 1; see Rappaport and Dansky 2010). Beyond their public relations problems, correctional officers were facing an increasingly hostile and dangerous work environment. That same CCPOA blueprint for reform, for example, cited an alarming statistic that an average of nine guards a day were assaulted in California's prisons due to staff shortages and overcrowded conditions. In 2009 the guards filed an amicus brief with the Supreme Court contending that prison overcrowding had become a danger to guards (Cavanaugh 2011). Perhaps Mike Jimenez described the situation best when he told a legislative committee, "We are sitting on the edge what NASA calls catastrophic failure" (Abramsky 2008).

The next month a closely divided Supreme Court brought an end to more than 20 years of prison litigation in the state when it upheld (in what was by then *Brown v. Plata*) the three-judge panel's prison reduction order in a close five-to-four ruling. The immediate effect of the ruling was that California would be forced to continue to reduce its prison population. What is remarkable about the Supreme Court's opinion, as Jonathan Simon argues, was that it once again returned dignity as an important value underlying protections against "cruel and unusual punishment" under the U.S. Constitution's Eighth Amendment (Simon 2011a).

"Prisoners retain the essence of human dignity inherent in all persons," Justice Anthony Kennedy wrote in the majority opinion.* "Respect for that dignity animates the Eighth Amendment prohibition against cruel and unusual punishment." The court's dignity-laden ruling was anathema to the long-standing imagery surrounding incapacitation—the image of prisoners "as predators, a constant risk to others, but not themselves subject to change, or illness or death" (Simon 2011a, p. 251). The court even took the unusual step to attach photos to its decision; photos of "bad beds"—prisoners stacked on bunks in gyms—and so-called dry cells—the vertical chained cages used to hold suicidal or psychotic prisoners, sometimes for weeks on end, while they awaited transfer to another facility (Simon 2011a, p. 251).

As did the three-judge panel, the Supreme Court repudiated California's entire penal system. "In addition to overcrowding the failure of California's prisons to provide adequate medical and mental health care may be ascribed to chronic and worsening budget shortfalls, a lack of political will in favor of reform, inadequate facilities, and systemic administrative failures," Kennedy wrote (see footnote *). In another notable passage, Justice Kennedy signaled the days of federal absence (at least in extreme cases like California's) in matters of state prison administration systems were over. "Courts may not allow constitutional violations to continue simply because a remedy would involve intrusion into the realm of prison administration" (see footnote *). For Justice Antonin Scalia, one of the four dissenters in the case, this all went too far. Scalia wanted to see the court act in its more traditional role as a neutral arbiter of the law in a litigant-driven adversary system (Bosworth 2001). From Scalia's vantage point, constitutional challenges of prison conditions and any subsequent remedy should be dealt with on an individual basis only. In an angry dissent, Scalia called the ruling a "judicial travesty," "absurd," and "perhaps the most radical injunction by a court in our nation's history."†

Over the years scholars have participated in a robust debate about the role of the federal courts, particularly the Supreme Court, in American policy making. Is the court an instigator of change or a follower? The general consensus is that the Supreme Court rarely exercises bold or independent

---

* *Brown v. Plata*, No. 09-1233, Kennedy, J., May 23, 2011.
† *Brown v. Plata*, No. 09-1233, Scalia, A., May 23, 2011.

policy initiatives. Research dating back to Robert Dahl indicates the court generally follows the policy agenda of legislation majorities (Dahl 1957). In this case, the court seemed to be expressing newfangled arguments about prisoner dignity. But if we examine *Brown v. Plata* in the larger context of smart on crime movement, the decision is best understood as offering credence to ideas and arguments that had already experienced a reemergence in American political debate. Supreme Court justices, as do other engaged citizens, bear witness to the shifting tides of political debate. This can be seen even as early as 2003 when Justice Kennedy spoke about incarceration at the annual meeting of the American Bar Association. Kennedy advanced themes reminiscent of the Prison Fellowship Ministries and progressive advocacy groups who saw prisoners as human beings deserving of a second chance. Regardless of the crime, "still, the prisoner is a person; still, he or she is part of the family of humankind," Kennedy remarked (Greenhouse 2011). In calling for shorter sentences and abolition of mandatory sentences, Kennedy said, "A people confident in its laws and institutions should not be ashamed of mercy" (Greenhouse 2011).

In the end, the federal courts helped deliver to California what its failed state politics could not deliver on its own. This is not to say California's route to reform was a better one than those taken by Texas or Ohio; quite the opposite. The process was more contentious, time consuming, and haphazard than it needed to be. Over time this may decrease the likelihood that Prison Realignment meets its objectives. One of the central lessons of the California story is that prison reform in the smart on crime era flows from multiple paths and venues within the decentralized system. In no case will reform follow the exact same pattern. Nonetheless, prison reform has become fixed around a core set of ideas and values that now have a pervasive presence in our democratic politics and institutions.

One last, albeit important, question remains: Why were California Republican lawmakers, unlike their counterparts in Ohio and Texas, unable or unwilling to support prison reform? What, in other words, made California Republicans different? Recall from Chapter 1 that policy learning serves an instrumental purpose. New evidence flowing into the political system is more likely to change a coalition's policy beliefs when new information matches a set of core interests. Republicans' monomaniacal opposition to reform is best understood with this in mind: despite overwhelming evidence of a failed penal system, Republicans simply did not understand prison reform to match their core beliefs and political self-interests.

One possible reason for this is that California Republicans' conservative base was uniquely adamant about maintaining the status quo. Under this scenario Republican lawmakers were simply following the traditional majoritarian model—reflecting their strongest supporters' preferences for a robust penal system. Although state-specific public opinion data is limited on this issue, comparing conservatives' attitudes toward reform in Texas with conservatives' attitudes toward reform in California (two states closest in size and demographic characteristics) offers at least some evidence of a meaningful difference. A poll conducted by Baselice and Associates in March 2011 asked a random sample of registered voters in Texas the question, "Would you favor or oppose stronger court oversight and mandatory treatment instead of prison for low-level drug possession offenders with no prior felonies on their record?" Seventy-eight percent of self-identified conservatives in Texas expressed "strong support" or "support," while only 16 percent of conservatives said they were "strongly opposed" or "opposed." A California Field Poll conducted in June 2011 asked California voters for their views on prison realignment (without naming it specifically) by asking, "Governor Brown is proposing to comply with the ruling by transferring about 30,000 of the state's lower risk prisoners to local county jails and community-based facilities. Generally speaking, do you think this is a good or bad idea?" Among voters who self-identified as "strong conservatives," 57.4 percent said the plan was a "bad idea." Only 27 percent thought it was a "good idea."

Students of public opinion probably already recognize that interpreting survey results with different samples, and similar but sufficiently different questions asked at different times, requires caution. Even putting these methodological challenges aside, however, research shows the public tends to follow elite messaging on crime rather than the opposite (Beckett 1997; Cunningham 2003; McCarty et al. 2008). Attitudinal differences among conservatives were likely only echoing the (very different) tone of elite-level debate in each state.

Little evidence pointing to public opinion as the culprit brings the need to examine more broadly how California's institutional structures and political context have shaped lawmakers' political incentives on crime over time. One of these institutional structures to consider is the presence of legislative term limits in California. Since voters passed Proposition 140 in 1990, California lawmakers have faced the strictest term limits in the nation. State Assembly members were limited to just three (two-year) terms;

service in the state Senate was capped at two (four-year) terms. No politician could serve longer than fourteen years in the legislature.*

Advocates contend term limits reduce special interest deal making and corruption by forcing lawmakers to leave office quickly. No politician gets too comfortable. Empirical research indicates, however, that term limits affect policy making in troubling ways, especially on complex or highly emotional issues like crime and prisons. One major study of term limits in California found lobbyists' influence actually grew in a term-limited environment (Cain and Kousser 2004). This should not be a surprise. Lobbyists carry a wealth of policy expertise. Expertise is required to formulate technical policy. Knowledgeable lawmakers forced to leave office because of term limits are replaced by neophytes who then turn to lobbyists for help. Term limits also shorten lawmakers' time horizons (Cain and Kousser 2004). Forcing lawmakers from office causes them to consider a policy's short-run benefits more so than its longer-term costs. In a tough on crime political environment, California lawmakers with term limits have found it far too easy to enhance criminal penalties. Mark Leno, a Democratic State Senator and Chairman of the Public Safety Committee from 2008 to 2010 said,

> Due to the severity of our term limit system, there is probably more than in other states an overlay of politics in everything that we do. On issues that are as hot button and as emotional and can be used for demagoguery as public safety, the politics rule over the policymaking almost without exception. Assembly members are running every two years and [with term limits] after two or four years their eyes are looking for the next race or next political office ... Everyone is enormously cautious and people are gone in six years ... There is no accountability. What they do is someone else's problem. (Leno 2009)

Contrast California's system with that of Texas or Ohio. Texas lawmakers are not even subject to term limits. Ohio has a term limits law but it is comparatively weak. Ohio's law imposes a "consecutive limit," meaning a lawmaker can serve eight years in the House, jump to the Senate to serve another eight years, and then return to her original position in the House ("The Term-Limited States" 2013). Comparing California's system with his own in Texas, Republican Jerry Madden said this: "No one [in California]

---

* Only Arkansas has term limits as stringent as California's. In 2012 California modified its term limits law. Ballot Proposition 28 reduced the total number of years state lawmakers could serve to twelve but allowed lawmakers to serve that time in any one chamber.

knows the issue. Everybody's new. Every four years you have to retrain everybody. They don't have time to sit back and think. They don't take the time to study. Here [in Texas] I have time to think" (Madden 2010).

The incentives shaped by term limits has magnified other punitive-oriented policy feedback effects found in the Golden State. Policy feedback is the idea that the design of a policy itself can structure ongoing political contestation (Hacker and Pierson 2011). The traditional approach in political science is one that sees policy choice as the end result of a complex political process. Scholars of policy feedback suggest this is an accurate but an incomplete description (Pierson 2004). Distinct features of a public policy can shape politics by incentivizing collective action in particular ways over time. It can alter political identities. It can shift both elite- and mass-level attitudes about what is considered normal, what is possible, or what is desired (Hacker and Pierson 2011). This idea is important because just two related issues—crime and taxes—have animated a large share of collective action efforts in post-New Deal California politics (Simon 2007). Draconian tax cuts imposed by Proposition 13 and the subsequent decline in what were once the most generous social programs in America, contributed to an electorate with growing concerns about downward social mobility and economic insecurity. Economic anxieties, coupled with a growing fear of crime, have made the prison a public good that is directly aimed at insecurity (Simon 2007). "Each prison cell built by the state," Jonathan Simon argues, "adds to the capacity of the state to provide this public good in a way that is beyond any 'program failure' of the sort that haunted the projects of the New Deal, such as public housing, school desegregation, and so on" (Simon 2007, p. 157).

In California the prison has, perhaps, more than any other state in the neoliberal era, served as the chief state-making institution. For conservatives who led the charge against an activist government in areas of social welfare, prisons proved to be politically intoxicating. Punitive crime policy developed into a routinized norm—a symbolic offering to all Californians that elicited, over time, a belief among conservative elites that prisons offered a rare chance for the party to remain politically relevant in a state where Democrats controlled the legislature for all but two years since 1971.* Conservative Republicans in Texas and Ohio, in contrast, routinely control the legislature, chair committees, and hold leadership positions. Republicans played, and continue to play, a major

---

* Republicans controlled the state assembly for a brief period between 1994 and 1996.

role in shaping the policy agenda. This offers them a variety of means to build legitimacy with voters. Republicans in California have had no such luxury. Tough on crime policy is how the game has been played in an environment where the rest of the party's platform failed to appeal, the party has had no institutional control, and when the true costs of punitive crime policies (because of term limits) are not felt until long after the individuals who produced them have left elected office.

The good news is that as long as the dimensions of the crime policy debate remain on their current course, conservatives in California are likely to align themselves with their more reform-minded conservative colleagues around the country. If succeeding generations of conservative politicians continue to serve in times of lower crime rates, tight budgets, and in a state with an electorate as diverse as California's (a block of voters conservatives cannot continue to alienate), they are likely to see monomaniacal tough on crime positions as anachronisms. Even more important, continued encouragement for prison reform from powerful and well-financed groups like the CCPOA may liberate conservatives insofar as they can support reform without the fear of losing campaign financing, or worse yet, see themselves as the subject of a CCPOA-funded attack advertisement. In the short to medium term, however, the politics of reform in California are likely to remain difficult and divided.

9

Evaluating the Smart on Crime Movement

In this final chapter we turn to evaluate the smart on crime movement. Of course, the meaning of the smart on crime movement, and with that, the best criteria used to judge it, will differ depending on who is asked. Most observers agree that we need to ask some variant of the question, is it working? To this question some people's interests will lie in gauging any monetary savings that flow from the smart on crime movement; others will want to know about changes in incarceration or recidivism; still others will concern themselves with issues of equity and justice and whether the smart on crime movement advances both. These important questions, and surely others, need to be asked both now and in the future. Unfortunately, there is much we do not know; the movement is, in many ways, still in its infancy.

At its most fundamental level, the smart on crime movement is about two things: reducing incarceration and reducing crime. Are policy changes sending fewer people to prison? If so, is crime declining as advocates promised? These seem like natural areas to begin inquiry. We can also assume that the political process will shape outcomes surrounding the smart on crime movement. Our evaluative efforts, therefore, must consider questions about the movement's political feasibility and viability, and its capacity to shape broader change over time.

DE-INCARCERATION AND CRIME

At the programming level, researchers are just beginning to evaluate reforms designed to scale (LaVigne et al. 2014). We do know, however, that the U.S. incarceration rate is falling. In 2009 the prisoner population fell for the first time in 40 years and has done so every year since (U.S. Department of Justice 2013). State-level trends offer more refined assessments. Texas, Ohio, and California—our three case study states—each saw their incarceration rates decline in the "postreform" period. When Texas adopted its justice reinvestment legislative package, the state's prison population declined by 1,257 inmates, declining 11 percent by 2012 (Pew Charitable Trusts 2013). California's incarceration rate is down 26 percent since 2007. The largest decline began in the postrealignment period; between October 2011 and June 2012, California's prison population dropped by nearly 25,000 prisoners. The decline was so steep that California contributed to about half of the overall decline in the U.S. incarceration rate that year (U.S. Department of Justice 2013). By May 2013 the decline reached 28,000 (Lofstrom and Raphael 2013a). The decline in California state prisoners led to a concomitant rise in the county jail population—increasing 11,100 from mid-2011 to mid-2013 (U.S. Department of Justice 2014a). Prison realignment is not simply a shell game moving prisoners out of state prison and into county jails, as some observers feared. A report by the Public Policy Institute of California (PPIC) found that "Realignment increased the average daily jail population by roughly one inmate for every three fewer offenders going to state prison" (Lofstrom and Raphael 2013a, p. 19). Progress in Ohio is slower than anticipated. Since the adoption of HB 86, Ohio's incarceration rate has declined just 2 percent, although the state got a later start than Texas, and its reforms were not designed to be as dramatic as California's (LaVigne et al. 2014). Ohio officials have begun a systematic assessment of its justice reinvestment policies. The process is expected to inform continuing implementation efforts in the coming years (LaVigne et al. 2014).

The de-incarceration trend has not been limited to these three states. A report by the Public Safety Performance Project (PSPP) found incarceration rates have declined in 31 states since 2007. Fourteen states saw their rates decline by 10 percent or more (Pew Charitable Trusts 2013). A drop in state prison admissions appears to have animated much of the decline. Bureau of Justice Statistics data show that in 2012, state prison admissions dropped to their lowest levels since 1999, marking the fourth year in a row that prison releases outstripped the number of admissions (U.S. Department of Justice 2013). The drop in admissions looks even more remarkable if we account for population change. Keith Humphreys computed the annual rate of admissions to state and federal prison per 1 million residents and found that under current policy, admissions are at a two-decade low. "By the end of Obama's first term," Humphreys notes, "[admissions] had dropped to a level not seen since President Clinton's first year in office" (Humphreys 2014a).

What about crime? Texas, Ohio, and California have each witnessed reductions in crime in recent years. Between 2007 and 2012, Texas's crime rate dropped 19 percent; Ohio and California each saw declines of 11 percent (Pew Charitable Trusts 2013). In California the greatest interest in the property crime question came in the midst of the debate over Realignment. With the rapid de-incarceration trend in California, have crime levels skyrocketed as many Republicans predicted? The best evidence available says no. A PPIC report analyzing crime in the postrealignment period (2011–2012) found that both violent and property crimes had increased slightly (Lofstrom and Raphael 2013b). Realignment was only linked to small increases in property crime; the PPIC estimated an additional "one to two property crimes per year on average for every offender who is not incarcerated as a result of realignment" (Lofstrom and Raphael 2013b, p. 1). There was no evidence that Realignment "had an effect on the most serious offenses, murder and rape." Considering the costs of incarceration, the report concluded that alternative strategies (e.g., Realignment) would likely "provide improved outcomes at lower costs" (Lofstrom and Raphael 2013b, pp. 1–2).

Analyzing trends in all fifty states captures a clearer picture of the nexus between de-incarceration and crime. As noted above, a report by Pew's PSPP found that incarceration rates had declined in thirty-one states between 2007 and 2012; yet the report also found that in fifteen states, the incarceration rate actually increased. This variation, when coupled with differences in states' crime rates, allows for direct comparisons. Did crime increase in states that witnessed declining imprisonment rates relative to states where imprisonment rates increased? The Pew study found no correlation. The ten states with the largest reductions in imprisonment witnessed average crime reductions of 12 percent; the ten states with the largest increases in imprisonment saw crime decline by an average of 10 percent (Pew Charitable Trusts 2013). Crime trended downward almost everywhere regardless of whether imprisonment rates went up or down.

To reiterate, these studies do not provide definitive answers and there is a lot we do not know. Implementation is ongoing; many later adopting states are just beginning to institutionalize changes (LaVigne et al. 2014). Moreover, correlation and causation are not the same. The extent to which recent declines in incarceration and crime are being driven by recent state-level reforms versus local forces, such as changes in policing, is unknown.

New York, for instance, experienced reductions in both crime and incarceration without major changes in state legislation (Subramanian et al. 2014). More research is needed to draw definitive conclusions. But at least in the early stages of the smart on crime movement, the signs are encouraging that we can have fewer people in prison *and* less crime.

IS THE GLASS HALF FULL OR HALF EMPTY?

This naturally leads to the question of whether the proverbial glass is half full or half empty. Are we making real progress, or is the smart on crime movement and the progress made a mirage? Admittedly it is difficult to have hope. The impacts of the smart on crime movement can look unremarkable in light of the entire tough on crime project built over four decades. Even when considering recent progress, the U.S. prison population has declined just 2.4% percent from its peak, as a recent report by the Sentencing Project emphasized (The Sentencing Project 2015). States such as South Dakota and West Virginia have seen their imprisonment rates increase—seemingly canceling gains elsewhere. Some observers have wryly noted that at the current pace of change, it would take *88 years* before the U.S. prison population reached its 1980 level (Mauer and Ghandnoosh 2014). Securing sufficient funding for prisoner reentry is also a constant concern. In 2011, for example, Second Chance Act money for prisoner reentry amounted to less than $120 per released prisoner (Mauer and Cole 2011).

For these reasons and others, it is imperative to place the smart on crime movement into direct dialogue with what I call "sympathetic critics" of prison reform. These scholars want to put an end to mass incarceration and return the U.S. prison rate to what is was around 1965, just before the prison boom began, but for different reasons are skeptical—pessimistic even—about the movement's capacity and where this is all leading. We might think of sympathetic critics as we might how a die-hard baseball fan feels about their favorite but perennially losing baseball team. Consider a fan of the Seattle Mariners (I would know, as a long-suffering supporter of the team) who feels only anxiety when the team starts to play well because it is, after all, the Mariners (or enter your favorite losing team here). They almost always find a way to lose in the end. Why get excited? Why have hope?

Marie Gottschalk, for example, contends that the Great Recession and its progeny may actually hamper reform efforts over the long run. "Growing economic despair, rising uncertainty about the country's economic future, and massive dislocations in the labor, real estate, and financial markets may effectively fortify the 'culture of control' that sociologist David Garland identified as the lifeblood of the prison boom launched nearly four decades ago," Gottschalk writes (Gottschalk 2010, p. 63). Drawing on lessons from the Great Depression when the construction of prisons and the expansion of law enforcement were used as public works programs, Gottschalk warns that lawmakers may once again see the prison and law enforcement as job creation mechanisms.

Another argument is that "justice reinvestment" efforts merely reflect tinkering at the margins given the scope and size of the problem. Mark Kleiman, for example, forcefully and convincingly advocates for "swift, certain, but not severe" probation and parole reforms, and showers less praise on the service delivery side of the justice reinvestment model. "The literature on recidivism reduction via service delivery—the 'reentry' literature for the most part—makes for fairly depressing reading; a program that moves the 3 year return to prison rate from 66% to 60% counts as a success" (Kleiman 2011, p. 651). With a total annual prison budget reaching only $60 billion (indeed, investment levels look far smaller when viewed within the totality of federal and state government spending), potential savings from having fewer prisoners would not be enough to offer major increases in social services even if resources (from savings) targeted affected neighborhoods. Implementing better-designed probation and parole supervision as opposed to enhancing services, Kleiman notes, can make a "big difference in reoffending and reincarceration, and can do so for small sums compared with the savings from reduced incarceration" (Kleiman 2011, p. 651).

Michelle Alexander laments that recent reforms do not do nearly enough to reduce racial inequality and the destruction that four decades of mass incarceration have reaped on minority communities and the urban poor (Alexander 2010). She calls for a new civil rights movement. "Those who believe that advocacy challenging mass incarceration can be successful without overturning the public consensus that gave rise to it are engaging in fanciful thinking, a form of denial (Alexander 2010, p. 222). For Alexander, changing the trajectory requires that Americans talk honestly about race. Alexander argues, "We must stop debating crime policy as though it were purely about crime. People must understand the racial history and origins of mass incarceration—the many ways our conscious and unconscious biases have distorted our judgments over the years about what is fair, appropriate, and constructive. ..." (Alexander 2010, p. 225).

In a similar vein, Michael Tonry takes the position that reformers need to simplify their message. Reform should be motivated by the injustice of the criminal justice system and advocates should just say so. Framing reform in terms of cost savings, inefficiencies, or recidivism reduction distract from the larger mission. Tonry writes,

> For the past 40 years, most advocates for humane criminal justice policies have made the fundamental mistake of arguing disingenuously. Instead of arguing that unduly harsh penalties are unjust, and should be repealed or modified for that reason, they much more often argued that policies— which they believed to be unjust—should be changed because they are too ineffective or too costly. Proposed alternatives—exemplified by most reentry initiatives—are generally supported by arguments about reduced cost or improved recidivism reduction. This is a mistake. (Tonry 2011b, p. 237)

For Tonry, placing moral claims at the heart of the effort protects against the likely return of stiffer penalties when the economy improves or when programs fail to perform as promised. "When the good times roll once again, as they will, changes adopted to save money or improve efficiency, rather than because they are the right thing to do, are likely to be inherently unstable" (Tonry 2011b, p. 238).

Sympathetic critics' frustrations, then, derive from the framing of the reform movement, different points of emphasis, and the limited scope of policy change. I certainly recognize the constraints and limitations of the smart on crime movement as it currently stands. The smart on crime coalition's main focus, for example, on nonviolent offenders, neglects more severe penalties for violent offenders—a major source behind the increase in the custodial population. How will officials curtail the prison population if they fail to limit violent crimes and lengthy prison sentences for such offenses?

There are a number of reasons why these arguments rest on shaky assumptions, or why the movement provides more hope than many critics contend. When Gottschalk's pessimistic position is combined with competing but more optimistic views on the effect of the economy, what is portrayed is a prison–economy nexus that is suspiciously powerful. A sour economy can explain America's continued willingness to incarcerate on a mass scale. It can explain the recent decline in incarceration as lawmakers look to cut costs and balance budgets. Quite simply there is no trend that the economy cannot explain. But as even Gottschalk herself recognizes, there is a far from a perfect correlation between the health of the macroeconomy and the rate of incarceration (Gottschalk 2010, pp. 63–64). Historically, incarceration rates have moved irrespective of macroeconomic conditions (and in the tough on crime era only increased). We must be cautious in our predilection for predicting how economic conditions will shape our future use of prisons. Moreover, if we consider one of the major lessons of this book—that the smart on crime movement and the progress achieved are about more than simply a decline in the economy— then arguing otherwise oversimplifies complex political forces.

Sympathetic critics also pay insufficient attention to how policy is made in the U.S. governing system, or how and why policy change occurs. Criminologists, for example, rarely engage with political science–generated theories of public policy making. University of Texas Criminologist William Spelman's article published in the journal *Criminology and Public Policy* offers a case in point. Using a methodologically sophisticated model of state prison population growth between 1977 and 2005, Spelman finds that traditional political factors such as Republican control of state governments, conservative public opinion, racial demographics, and income inequality played a relatively minor role in the increase in states' incarceration rates. Crime rates, state spending on prisons, and a series of policy changes—namely, increases in drug arrests and convictions, and the widespread adoption of truth-in-sentencing laws—were the primary culprits (Spelman 2009). "It is fairly easy to document *how* we got to this point," Spelman writes. "The criminal justice system is in some sense a simple machine, in which the number of prisoners is equal to crime rates, times arrest rates per crime, times incarceration rates per arrest, times sentences served" (Spelman 2009, p. 31).

What makes Spelman's research especially relevant is that he asks: given what we know caused the increase in the U.S. penal population, how might we begin to shrink it in a meaningful way? Like most reform advocates, Spelman believes that far too many people are behind bars. "Enormous cutbacks—reductions of 50% or more in the prison population—are not difficult to justify and would probably save the U.S. public billions of dollars each year," Spelman argues (Spelman 2009, p. 30). Yet perhaps because Spelman found politics mostly inconsequential, his prescriptions for reform also give little consideration to political forces. He calls for greater federal leadership in enticing states (through the budgetary process) to draw down their prison populations. He points to the spread of truth in sentencing laws (of course, the opposite of what reformers want) and the closing of state mental hospitals in the 1960s as two relevant examples of the federal government shaping policy change at the subnational level. If Spelman is correct in saying more federal leadership is needed, then we also must consider how and in what ways politics will shape that effort and its likelihood of success. Spelman leaves these questions largely unanswered.

In fairness to Spelman, it is easy to quibble over the primary objectives and scope of a single piece of research. All of this is to say, however, that scholars need to give the politics of prison reform greater consideration if we are to answer the question of how do we get *there*—that is, a more effective and morally just penal system—from *here*?* Dismantling a generation-long war on crime and drugs will not be done in short order. The social movements of the twentieth century—the civil rights and progressive movements most notably—teach us that social and political reform is a slog. Even with strong empirical evidence or favorable moral arguments, change requires reformers to participate in a sort of organized combat in multiple institutional venues across time. Reform's path is never linear, especially when powerful interests fight to maintain the status quo. Today's prisoner population is a product of decisions made over many years. Even if policy makers were to somehow reduce new admissions to a trickle, the decline in the rate of incarceration would be slower than many advocates realize, given that many inmates today are serving long sentences for crimes committed years ago (Humphreys 2014b). The prison boom was not a natural phenomenon; it was not a by-product of governments responding organically to ever-increasing crime rates (although as noted in Chapter 2, crime rates did increase in the 1960s and into the 1970s). It was built and shaped by politics. And this, in an ironic twist, is what provides optimism: politics can destroy as well as build.

Advocates must think carefully about the *political viability* of their efforts. If they do, the strengths of the smart on crime movement and, indeed, the reason for optimism, become clearer. A successful prison reform must also survive within a political system of divided power; a system where voter misinformation is real, where interracial differences exist about the perceived fairness of the criminal justice system, and historic levels of party polarization all present barriers to collective action.

---

* Indeed, there are some encouraging signs on this front. Todd Clear, for example, recently developed an outline for a justice reinvestment model using private sector incentives—see Clear (2011). Lisa Miller and Mona Lynch's work has carefully thought about how the institutional arrangements of American federalism and local context will shape future reform efforts. See Lynch (2011) and Miller (2011).

That prison reform means different things to the smart on crime coalition's diverse members speaks directly to the movement's viability. This is a point too often missed. For any movement, let alone a movement that reduces penalties or extends benefits to a target group that elicits little public support, motivations for collective action must be numerous.

Take the smart on crime movement's public safety frame as one example. It is not difficult to see why many progressives see the movement's focus on public safety, especially in a time of declining crime rates, as a secondary concern to the more important and enduring problem of racial inequality in the criminal justice system. Although crime rates have declined over the past two decades, progress remains uneven; victimization rates in poor urban communities of color are still too high. Crimes in minority neighborhoods too often go unsolved, meaning that black or Hispanic victims are less likely to see their perpetrators brought to justice. This is every part a violation of "equal protection" as the disproportionate number of racial or ethnic minorities behind bars in America today (Kleiman 2013). Middle and upper class Americans are objectively safer than they were a generation ago, but somehow they still perceive crime trending upward. Research by the Gallup organization, which has regularly tracked the public's perceptions of crime patterns since 1989, offers some enlightening findings. While the percentage of Americans who believe that crime rates are increasing has declined since Gallup first asked the question, an astonishing number of Americans today still perceive crime to be getting worse. In 2011, for example, 68 percent of Americans surveyed said (erroneously) that crime had increased from the year before.* Similar results are found throughout the 2000s. That Americans' short-run perceptions of crime poorly reflect what the statistics say may seem minor. After all, Americans are misinformed about a lot of issues. Yet perceptions matter in politics. People mobilize and vote on the basis of what they believe to be true. Advocates who ignore public safety as an important part of the equation do so at their own peril. The smart on crime movement recognizes this.

The emphasis on budgets and cost savings offers another poignant example of the movement's viability. Framing reform in terms of its cost savings or, better yet, its "return on investment," brings people into the debate that might not otherwise engage. Most middle and upper class Americans, despite the size and scope of the modern penal system, will

---

* Gallup Poll, 15064. Available at http://www.gallup.com/poll/150464/americans-believe-crime -worsening.aspx.

never be arrested; they will never be incarcerated. New prisons today are built in nowheresville, far removed from the public's consciousness. When Americans *do* think about the criminal justice system, they have very different beliefs about its fairness. Most notable are differences between blacks and whites. In a national survey, Mark Peffley and John Hurwitz tested how blacks and whites evaluated the justice system and whether they perceived the system as "unfair" or "biased against blacks." Results showed that blacks were more likely to view the system as "unfair" or "biased" by more than 30 percentage points when averaged across the two categories. This so-called race gap, Peffley and Hurwitz explain, results from differences in blacks and whites' personal or vicarious experiences with the criminal justice system (Peffley and Hurwitz 2010).

In a more perfect world, reformers could discuss the prison system's injustices and have those messages motivate elites and the mass public into collective action. These messages may find a more receptive audience in the not-too-distant future when today's young adults and succeeding generations—each more racially and ethnically diverse and seemingly tolerant than the one before—comprise a greater share of the electorate. But alas, that is not yet the world we live in. Conceptually, we still have two criminal justice systems in America. Framing prison reform as a tool to balance state budgets or to deliver costs savings may not be normatively ideal, but it is far from a distraction if it expands the coalition and mobilizes actors who would otherwise ignore the problem.

This is not to say that reformers should wait until the future to make the morally centered arguments that talented scholars like Michelle Alexander and Michael Tonry so value. Indeed, advocates need to talk about race and the moral injustices in the system, *now*, even if it seems half of the audience is not listening. This is how seeds of change are planted. Yet it is also true that we do not have to look to the future for a "moral turn." If we care to look closely, a new moral debate is unfolding, and it is unfolding as part of the smart on crime movement. Strong moral arguments coming from the Prison Fellowship Ministries and other religious organizations, the Congressional Black Caucus, and indeed scholars themselves, are making important inroads.

Race has played an important but selective role in the smart on crime movement as well. As discussed in Chapter 5, evidence of gross racial inequities in cocaine sentencing animated efforts to pass the Fair Sentencing Act in 2010. Critics are correct to say that the smart on crime movement still has not gone far enough to attack racial injustices; the Fair Sentencing

Act's "18–1 compromise" is a good example of this. At the same time critics undervalue the smart on crime movement's capacity to do less harm. As Michael Tonry notes, perhaps the justice system's greatest racialized harms are caused by its magnitude. If this is true, policies that reduce the overall size of the system, given the (historically) racialized patterns in prison admissions, afford an opportunity to shrink the minority custodial population even without explicitly targeting (in a beneficial way) minorities, or race dominating our political discourse (Tonry 2011c).

For some readers this may be too cute by half. To examine this further, consider a hypothetical example using state prison admissions data from 2011. If we consider new court commitments and parole violators, 599,190 offenders were admitted to state prisons (U.S. Department of Justice 2013). Nearly 71 percent, or 424,645 admissions, were for property, drug, or public order offenses (the most serious offense)—those offense types targeted by smart on crime policy reforms.* Among these admissions, 162,288, or 38.2 percent, were blacks. If prison diversion programs, sentencing reductions, smart probation and parole reforms, and investments in prisoner reentry programs could reduce admissions by 30 percent (in total), while holding all other factors constant including the relative percentage of blacks in the admissions cohort, 48,664 [(424,645*0.30)*0.382] fewer blacks would have been admitted in 2011 alone. In reality the exact number in any one year could rise or fall depending on the overall size of the admissions cohort, the relative proportion of minorities in it, and the success of reforms in the aggregate. The key point, however, is that even without policies specifically designed to disproportionately aid blacks or other minorities—again, the number above assumes no changes in the relative proportion of black admissions (i.e., relative to whites)—by simply reducing the number of overall admissions, the smart on crime movement is advancing justice.

Fortunately, we can turn to more than a hypothetical example. As prison admissions have declined in recent years, black incarceration rates have also gone down. Between 2000 and 2009, the incarceration rate for black men decreased by 9.8 percent. The incarceration rate of black women declined by 30.7 percent (Humphreys 2014b). Blacks continue to be overrepresented in the prison system, but contrary to popular belief, the racial gap is narrowing. Real progress is under way (Humphreys 2014b).

---

* Data is compiled from Tables 5, 8, and 9 in the U.S. Department of Justice (2014b).

Perhaps most important over the long run, critics overlook how the structure and success of policy itself can reshape the ongoing politics of crime by bringing opportunities to expand the nature of the conflict in future years through policy feedback. Policy feedback, recall, is the idea that policy itself can shift ongoing politics surrounding an issue. Seemingly small changes in policy can, over time, produce big changes in politics that, in turn, lead to even larger policy changes in the future. Distinct features of a public policy's design shapes politics by incentivizing collective action of groups in particular ways. Policy can alter political identities and political coalitions; it can shift both elite and mass-level attitudes about what is considered normal, what is possible, or what is desired. Eric Patashnik argues sustainability of reform depends to a large degree on which reforms "upset inherited coalitional patterns and stimulate the emergence of new vested interests and political alliances" (Patashnik 2008, p. 4). In the long run, public policies are not simply outputs of a given polity. They can have a strong impact on the composition and nature of the polity itself.

When viewed in its full arc, the smart on crime movement fits this argument well. At the national level, what began as a battle over prisoner reentry melded into a historic debate over our draconian crack racial disparities and the first rollback of federal drug laws in a generation. The Justice Reinvestment Initiative, a joint federal/state partnership, serves as yet another example of the fluidity in which further change is unfolding in the criminal justice subsystem. Justice reinvestment efforts in Texas and other "early adopting" states captured the attention of Congress. In 2010, Congress appropriated funds to the Bureau of Justice Assistance, which, in collaboration the Pew Charitable Trusts, the Council of State Governments, and a host of additional partners, carried the justice reinvestment model to seventeen states (LaVigne et al. 2014). Hawaii's HOPE program has spread to forty jurisdictions in eighteen different states (Pearsall 2014). The largest of these can be found in Washington where more than 15,000 offenders under community corrections supervision participate in the state's swift and certain program (Pearsall 2014). Since 2000, more than twenty-nine states have modified or reduced mandatory sentencing laws (Subramanian et al. 2014). Of greatest symbolic import, if not substantively as well, was the decision by California voters in 2012 to rollback the most draconian aspects of the state's three-strikes law. In 2013 alone, more than two dozen states expanded prison reentry programs and problem-solving courts, strengthened community corrections, and removed or mitigated collateral consequences for people with criminal convictions (Subramanian et al. 2014). All of these signal a gathering momentum for prison reform in the United States.

As legislative victories accumulate, the smart on crime coalition that made it possible continues to grow and strengthen. Of greatest import, perhaps, has been the continued mobilization on the political right. In late 2010, Marc Levin, the director of Texas Public Policy Foundation, nationalized the foundation's efforts by forming a campaign called "Right on Crime." When Pat Nolan of the Prison Fellowship heard about the campaign, he called it an "answered prayer" and quickly offered Levin his support (Dagan and Teles 2012; Nolan 2011). Soon after, dozens of conservative luminaries signed on to Right on Crime's Statement of Principles. Ed Meese, President Reagan's tough on crime attorney general; Newt Gingrich, the former Speaker of the House whose Contract with America once called for tougher sentencing and more prisons; William Bennett, the former drug czar under President George H.W. Bush; and David Keene, the longtime chairman of the American Conservative Union (and former NRA President), climbed aboard, as did conservative think tank representatives from the Manhattan Institute, the Heritage Foundation, and the Cato Institute.

As discussed in Chapter 5, Grover Norquist entered the debate when he supported the Fair Sentencing Act in 2010. Since then his efforts have focused on imploring further change in the states. Norquist signals as much, albeit in his own maddening partisan way. "We've traditionally taken our lead by looking at what the liberals want and do the opposite. That's often the good way to go, but not always. We don't always have to be reflexively against what the idiots are for" (Conant 2011). More than that, Norquist believes conservatives must lead if prison reform is to succeed. "Conservatives approach criminal justice reform with a history of being serious about punishing criminals. Conservative criminal justice reformers are not weepy eyed apologists for bad behavior ... Some of our friends on the left lack the credibility, the moral authority to face victims and their families and asked to be trusted to reduce prison sentences ... Conservative state leaders start with greater trust on the issue" (Norquist 2014).

Texas often serves as Norquist's example to get his message across. In an interview with National Review Online, Norquist recalled his testimony to Florida lawmakers. "When I would say, 'You know, in Texas they did this,' all of a sudden the Republicans on the committee would look up and go, 'Oh, you mean this is real. This isn't something from Vermont'" (Woodruff 2014). Conservative power brokers of the Right on

Crime campaign are raising awareness and distributing policy ideas. "If our prisons are failing half the time, and we know there are more humane, effective alternatives, it is time to fundamentally rethink how we treat and rehabilitate our prisoners," wrote Newt Gingrich, along with Pat Nolan, in a 2011 *Washington Post* op-ed (Gingrich and Nolan 2011). The American Legislative Exchange Council—a network of conservative state lawmakers who pushed for privatized prisons and mandatory sentencing in the 1990s, is now working closely with states on sentencing reform (Dagan and Teles 2012). Collectively, these efforts are resonating with conservative lawmakers, particularly in the deep southern states of Georgia, South Carolina, and Mississippi, who each passed major reform legislation in recent years.

As a first (or even second) choice of a dancing partner, this cast of characters is surely not what most progressive reformers had in mind. And indeed, the conservative movement, with its inexorable run to the right on immigration, the environment, taxes, finance, and their scorched-earth use of the Senate filibuster, has caused the country immeasurable damage. But politics, as the aphorism says, makes strange bedfellows. Progressive reformers need to seize the opportunity.

It is not a coincidence that as figures like Norquist endorse prison reform, candidates positioning themselves for a 2016 Republican presidential run have made the issue a part of their domestic policy platform. Senator Rand Paul of Kentucky, for example, often thought to represent the libertarian wing of the Republican Party, has notably infused his speeches on criminal justice reform to race and poverty. "Our federal mandatory minimum sentences are simply heavy handed and arbitrary," Paul said in a speech at Howard University in 2013. "They can affect any one at any time, but they disproportionately affect those without the means to fight them. … We should not have drug laws or a court system that disproportionately punishes the black community" (Carrol 2013). Along with longtime Democratic Senator Patrick Leahy, Paul introduced the Justice Safety Valve Act in March 2013. A "safety valve" keeps mandatory minimums in place but gives judges more discretion to divert from the statutory defined sentence if it is deemed inappropriate (Subramanian et al. 2014, p. 8). Under current federal law, only one safety valve exists; first-time nonviolent drug offenders whose cases do not involve a weapon are eligible for reduced sentences. The Leahy/Paul bill creates a broader safety valve that applies to all federal crimes with a mandatory minimum (Wing 2014).

The Smarter Sentencing Act, introduced by Republican (and Tea Party member) Senator Mike Lee of Utah, and Democrat Richard Durbin of Illinois, would go even further by halving mandatory minimums for certain nonviolent drug offenses. Moreover, their bill would give judges more discretion to sentence below some mandatory minimums by modifying the federal safety valve. It would also offer a chance of early release for thousands of offenders sentenced for crack cocaine crimes who were not eligible for sentence reductions under the Fair Sentencing Act because the law was not applied retroactively (*New York Times* Editorial Board 2014).

The outcome of these bills, at the time of this writing, is yet to be determined. Fortunately many are not waiting around for one of the least productive congresses in American history. Attorney General Eric Holder issued a memorandum in August 2013 instructing prosecutors to alter how they charge some nonviolent drug offenders to avoid triggering mandatory minimums. Mandatory minimums for drug offenses, as detailed in Chapter 5, are tied to drug quantities. To get around this, Holder's memo instructs prosecutors not to specify the volume of drugs when a charge is filed. "Too many Americans go to too many prisons for far too long and for no good law enforcement reason," Holder said in a speech to the American Bar Association's House of Delegates, shortly before he issued the memorandum (Williams 2013). Incarceration should be used "to punish, deter, and rehabilitate, not merely to convict, warehouse, and forget" (Williams 2013).

The U.S. Sentencing Commission followed Holder's lead in April 2014 when it declared federal drug penalties remained overly punitive. As it did just before the passage of the Fair Sentencing Act, the Sentencing Commission voted yet again to change federal sentencing guidelines, reducing the seriousness for quantities of all drugs by two base offense levels (Lind 2014a). Once implemented, federal drug sentences are expected to decrease by an average of eleven months (Lind 2014b). The April vote applied only prospectively to new drug offenders entering the federal system. In July 2014 the Sentencing Commission took a bolder step when it made the changes retroactive. Unless Congress takes proactive steps to block the sentencing reduction, the Sentencing Commission estimates that as many as 46,000 federal drug offenders, or nearly half of all federal drug offenders, will be eligible to apply for shorter sentences beginning in November 2015 (Lind 2014b).

The extent to which policy fosters positive feedback effects will inevitably be tied to the success of implementation efforts. The implementation process is fraught with challenges. Problems of greater complexity, inadequate funding, or the presence of implementing actors whose interests collide with a law's creators, all raise the potential of failure. Losing actors in the legislative arena have another bite at the apple in the implementation part of the process. Opponents can take deliberate action to undermine its success. It is a cynical game, but this kind of strategy can reclaim advantage lost in previous fights.

The implementation of smart on crime reforms poses a number of challenges. Take, for example, programs in the mold of Hawaii's HOPE program, which require collaboration among probation officers, prosecutors, judges, police, and social service providers—groups with different backgrounds, training, and world views. Traditionally, they have not seen eye to eye. Law enforcement officials see drug rehabilitation specialists and social workers as naive; drug rehabilitation specialists, in turn, often view law enforcement officials as thugs in a fancy blue uniform. Can all of these actors work toward a common purpose?

They have in Hawaii; however, as reforms begin to scale around the country, the answer is likely to be both yes and no. This qualified answer results directly from the decentralized nature of criminal justice institutions and the recognition that political context matters. "Smart" probation reforms, for example, may be designed by the most well-intentioned state lawmakers, but because probation is mostly under the jurisdiction of county governments, local actors may not implement them effectively because of self-interested conflicts or administrative capacity shortfalls. Progress will be uneven over time and space. This does not make criminal justice policy making unique. In environmental policy, California and Minnesota (as just two examples) have adopted "renewable portfolio standards" and tightened energy efficiency regulations to reduce greenhouse gas emissions; other states like West Virginia retain a reliance on dirty coal. California and Washington State have implemented the Affordable Care Act (ACA) with a seriousness not found in West Virginia, Florida, or Texas. Just as West Virginia's love of coal or its failure to expand Medicaid under the ACA do not spell defeat on the environment or in lowering the rate of the uninsured, the same must be said to critics who point to the increasing incarceration rate of a state like West Virginia as a sign of the smart on crime movement's deficiencies. With the seventh largest economy in the world, and a population of nearly 40 million, California's policy choices have, quite simply, a greater effect on U.S. environmental or health care goals than does West Virginia. Likewise, in the smart on crime movement, progress (or reversion) in California, Texas, Florida, New York, Ohio, Michigan, or any other large state that has practiced tough on crime politics to the fullest, will have outsized political and policy effects over the short-to-medium term.

Continuing to disseminate information on best practices, and continuing to provide technical expertise to improve implementation efforts, will be crucial. The good news is that, slowly, a coalition is now in place, more so than at any time in the past generation, with the capacity to challenge the traditional way of doing things and maximize this window of opportunity. New activist organizations on the left, right, and center of the political spectrum are disseminating evidence-based practices and encouraging their use. At the same time, generational changes are under way in the corrections profession. Younger prison staffs are replacing the old (Siggins 2009). People new to the profession are entering in a time when "smart on crime" is a clarion call; resistance decreases as front-line officers trained in the get-tough culture retire.

Any future failure, if it occurs, cannot be blamed on public opinion or lack of public support for smarter penal policies. A 2012 national survey conducted for the Pew Center on the States found a plurality (45 percent) of Americans believe that "too many prisoners" are behind bars. Only 13 percent of people surveyed said the United States has "too few" prisoners (Pew Center on the States 2012b). The same survey found broad support for strengthening community corrections programs with money saved from diverting nonviolent offenders from prison. This result held regardless of respondents' partisan views. The public supports reducing prison time of lower-risk offenders for a variety of reasons, including "re-investing in alternatives," "good behavior," and "age and illness." Alas, there is much to celebrate, but hard work remains. A generation's worth of destructive policy remains waiting to be wiped away.

References

Sasha Abramsky, "When Prison Guards Go Soft," *Mother Jones*, July/August 2008. Available at http://www.motherjones.com/politics/2008/07/when-prison-guards-go-soft.

Stuart Adams, "Evaluation: A Way Out of Rhetoric," *Rehabilitation, Recidivism, and Research*, eds. Robert Martinson, Ted Palmer and Stuart Adams (Hackensack, NJ: National Council on Crime and Delinquency, 1976).

Nurith C. Aizenman, "New High in U.S. Prison Numbers: Growth Attributed to More Stringent Sentencing Laws," *The Washington Post*, February 29, 2008.

Michelle Alexander, *The New Jim Crow: Mass Incarceration in the Age of Colorblindness* (New York: The New Press, 2010).

Francis Allen, *The Decline of the Rehabilitative Ideal: Penal Policy and Social Purpose* (New Haven, CT: Yale University Press, 1981).

American Correctional Association, *Directory* (Lanham, MD: American Correctional Association, 2005).

Donald A. Andrews, "The Psychology of Criminal Conduct and Effective Treatment," in *What Works: Reducing Reoffending—Guidelines from Research and Practice*, ed. James McGuire (New York: John Wiley and Sons, 1995).

Donald A. Andrews and James Bonta, *The Psychology of Criminal Conduct* (Cincinnati, OH: Anderson, 2003).

B. Jaye Anno, Camelia Graham, James E. Lawrence and Ronald Shansky, "Addressing the Needs of the Elderly, Chronically Ill, and Terminally Ill Inmates" (Middleton, CT: U.S. Department of Justice, National Institute of Corrections, Criminal Justice Institute, 2004). Available at http://static.nicic.gov/Library/018735.pdf.

Walter C. Bailey, "Correctional Outcome: An Evaluation of 100 Reports," *The Journal of Criminal Law, Criminology, and Police Science* 57 (1966): 153–160.

Peter Baker, "Obama Signs Law Narrowing Cocaine Sentencing Disparities," *The New York Times*, August 3, 2010.

Vanessa Barker, *The Politics of Punishment: How the Democratic Process Shapes the Way America Punishes Offenders* (New York: Oxford University Press, 2009).

Frank R. Baumgartner and Bryan D. Jones, *Agendas and Instability in American Politics* (Chicago: University of Chicago Press, 1993).

Frank R. Baumgartner, Suzanna L. DeBoef and Amber E. Boydstun, *The Decline of the Death Penalty and the Discovery of Innocence* (Cambridge, MA: Cambridge University Press, 2008).

Alyssa L. Beaver, "Getting the Fix on Cocaine Sentencing Policy: Reforming the Sentencing Scheme of the Anti-Drug Abuse Act of 1986," *Fordham Law Review* 78 (2010): 2531–2575.

Gary Becker, "Crime and Punishment: An Economic Approach," *The Journal of Political Economy* 76 (1968): 169–217.

Katherine Beckett, *Making Crime Pay: Law and Order in Contemporary American Politics* (New York: Oxford University Press, 1997).

Katherine Beckett and Theodore Sasson, *The Politics of Injustice: Crime and Punishment in America* (Thousand Oaks, CA: Pine Forge, 2000).

William Bennett, John J. DiIulio and John P. Walters, *Body Count: Moral Poverty and How to Win America's War Against Crime and Drugs* (New York: Simon and Schuster, 1996).

William C. Berleman and Thomas W. Steinburn, "The Value and Validity of Delinquency Prevention Experiments," *Crime and Delinquency* 15 (1969): 471–478.

Laura A. Bischoff, Lynn Hulsey and Joanne Huist Smith, "Sentence Reductions May Save $1 Billion; Bill with Sweeping Criminal Justice Reform Likely To Be Enacted," *Dayton Daily News*, June 23, 2011. Available at http://www.highbeam.com/doc/1P2-28979785.html.

Alfred Blumstein and Allen J. Beck, "Reentry as a Transient State between Liberty and Recommitment," in *Prisoner Reentry and Crime in America*, eds. Jeremy Travis and Christy Visher (Cambridge, MA: Cambridge University Press, 2005).

Matthew Bosworth, *Courts as Catalysts: State Supreme Courts and Public School Finance Equity* (Albany, NY: SUNY Press, 2001).

Brian Brown and Greg Jolivette, "A Primer: Three Strikes—The Impact After More than a Decade" (Sacramento, CA: California Legislative Analyst's Office, 2005).

Bureau of Labor Statistics, "The Recession of 2007–2009," *BLS Spotlight on Statistics*, February 2012. Available at http://www.bls.gov/spotlight/2012/recession/pdf/recession_bls _spotlight.pdf.

Paul Burka, "No Justice," 2007. Available at http://www.texasmonthly.com/burka-blog /no-justice.

Bruce E. Cain and Thad Kousser, "Adapting to Term Limits in California: Recent Experiences and New Directions" (Denver, CO: National Conference of State Legislatures, 2004). Available at http://www.ncsl.org/Portals/1/documents/jptl/casestudies/Californiav2 .pdf.

James D. Calder, *The Origins and Development of Federal Crime Control Policy* (Westport, CT: Praeger, 1993).

"California Expert Panel on Adult Offender Recidivism Reduction Programming: A Roadmap to the California Legislature" (Sacramento, CA: California Department of Corrections and Rehabilitation, 2007).

California Legislative Analysts Office, "A Primer: Three Strikes after More Than a Decade," October 2005. Available at http://www.lao.ca.gov/2005/3_strikes/3_strikes_102005.htm.

California Legislative Analysts Office, "California Department of Corrections and Rehabilitation." Presented to Senate Budget Subcommittee No. 4, 2009. Available at http://www.lao.ca.gov/handouts/crimjust/2009/CDCR_03_19_09.pdf.

California Peace Officers Association, "From Sentencing to Incarceration Release: A Blueprint for Reforming California's Prison System," 2007.

Conn Carrol, "Text: Sen. Rand Paul's Speech at Howard University," *Washington Examiner*, April 10, 2013. Available at http://washingtonexaminer.com/text-sen.-rand-pauls -speech-at-howard-university/article/2526772.

Matthew Cate, personal communication with the author, November 14, 2009.

Tim Cavanaugh, "The Golden State's Iron Bars: How California's Prison Guards Became the Country's Most Powerful," *Reason Magazine*, July Issue, 2011. Available at http:// reason.com/archives/2011/06/23/the-golden-states-iron-bars.

Jill Clark and Thomas H. Little, "National Organizations as Sources of Information for State Legislative Leaders," *State and Local Government Review* 34 (2002): 38–44.

Todd R. Clear, *Imprisoning Communities: How Mass Incarceration Makes Disadvantaged Neighborhoods Worse* (New York: Oxford University Press, 2010).

Todd R. Clear, "A Private-Sector Incentives-Based Model of Justice Reinvestment," *Criminology and Public Policy* 10 no. 3 (2011): 585–606.

Todd R. Clear, Dina R. Rose and Judith R. Ryder, "Incarceration and the Community: The Problem of Removing and Returning Offenders," *Crime and Delinquency* 47 (2001): 335–351.

Eve Conant, "The GOP's Born Again Prison Reformers," *The Daily Beast*, 2011. Available at http://www.thedailybeast.com/articles/2011/07/03/gop-leaders-warm-up-to-prison-reform.html.

Libby Copeland, "Faith Based Initiative," *The Washington Post*, June 7, 2006.

Ellis Cose, "Closing the Gap: Obama Could Fix Cocaine Sentencing," *Newsweek*, July 20, 2009. Available at http://www.november.org/stayinfo/breaking09/Closing_Crack_Gap.html.

Council of State Governments, Justice Center, *Justice Reinvestment State Brief: Texas* (New York: Council of State Governments, 2007). Available at http://www.pewstates.org/uploadedFiles/TX%20State%20Brief.pdf.

Council of State Governments, Justice Center, "Justice Reinvestment in Texas: Assessing the Impact of the 2007 Justice Reinvestment Initiative," 2009a. Available at http://www.ncsl.org/portals/1/Documents/cj/texas.pdf.

Council of State Governments, "Justice Reinvestment in Ohio Reducing Spending on Corrections and Reinvesting in Strategies to Increase Public Safety," 2009b. Available at http://csgjusticecenter.org/wp-content/uploads/2012/12/JR_Ohio_Overview_Final.pdf.

Council of State Governments, Justice Center "Justice Reinvestment in Ohio: Summary Report of Analysis," 2010. Available at http://csgjusticecenter.org/wp-content/uploads/2012/12/ohio_conference_report.pdf.

David Courtwright, "The Controlled Substances Act: How a Big Tent Reform Became a Punitive Drug Law," *Drug and Alcohol Dependence* 76 no. 1 (2004): 9–15.

Douglas F. Cousineau and Darryl B. Plecas, "Justifying Criminal Justice Policy with Methodologically Inadequate Research," *Canadian Journal of Criminology* 24 (1982): 307–321.

Donald R. Cressey, "The Nature and Effectiveness of Correctional Techniques," *Law and Contemporary Problems* 23 (1958): 754–771.

Brian Crowell, "Amendment 706 to the U.S. Sentencing Guidelines: Not All It Was Cracked Up To Be," *Villanova Law Review* 55 no. 5 (2010): 959–984.

Francis T. Cullen, "The Twelve People Who Saved Rehabilitation: How the Science of Criminology Made a Difference," *Criminology* 43 no. 1 (2005): 1–42.

Francis T. Cullen and Paul Gendreau, "The Effectiveness of Correctional Rehabilitation," in *The American Prison: Issues in Research and Policy*, eds. Lynne Goodstein and Doris Layton MacKenzie (New York: Plenum Press, 1989).

Francis T. Cullen and Karen E. Gilbert, *Reaffirming Rehabilitation* (Cincinnati, OH: Anderson, 1982).

Francis T. Cullen, Gregory A. Clark and John F. Wozniak, "Explaining the Get Tough Movement: Can the Public Be Blamed?," *Federal Probation* 49 (1985): 16–24.

Francis T. Cullen, Bonnie S. Fisher and Brandon K. Applegate, "Public Opinion about Punishment and Corrections," *Crime and Justice* 27 (2000): 1–79.

Francis T. Cullen, Kristie R. Blevins, Jennifer S. Trager and Paul Gendreau, "The Rise and Fall of Boot Camps: A Case Study in Common-Sense Corrections," *Journal of Offender Rehabilitation* 40 no. 3/4 (2004): 53–70.

Brent Cunningham, "Re-thinking Objectivity," *Columbia Journalism Review* 42 no. 2 (2003): 24–32.

Elliot Currie, *Confronting Crime: An American Challenge* (New York: Pantheon, 1985).

Theodore Curry, "Conservative Protestantism and the Perceived Wrongfulness of Crimes: A Research Note," *Criminology* 34 no. 3 (1996): 454–464.

Rebecca Cusey, "Look Down! Look Down! An Interview with Justice Fellowship's Pat Nolan on the Released Prisoners Walking in Jean Valjean's Footsteps," *Patheos*, December

20, 2012. Available at http://www.patheos.com/blogs/tinseltalk/2012/12/look-down-look-down-an-interview-with-justice-fellowships-pat-nolan-on-the-released-prisoners-walking-in-jean-valjeans-footsteps/.

Maxine Cutler, "Letter to the Editor," *The New York Times*, August 13, 1976.

David Dagan and Steven M. Teles, "The Conservative War on Prisons," *Washington Monthly*, November/December 2012. Available at http://www.washingtonmonthly.com/magazine/novemberdecember_2012/features/the_conservative_war_on_prison041104.php?page=all.

Robert Dahl, "Decision-Making in Democracy: The Supreme Court as National Policy Maker," *Journal of Public Law* 6 (1957): 279–295.

Joseph Dillon Davey, *The Politics of Prison Expansion: Winning Elections by Waging on Crime* (Westport, CT: Greenwood Publishing Group, 1999).

Roger H. Davidson, Walter J. Oleszek and Francis E. Lee, *Congress and Its Members*, 13th ed. (Washington, DC: CQ Press, 2011).

James M. Day and William S. Laufer, *Crime, Values, and Religion* (Westport, CT: Ablex Publishing Corporation, 1987).

Carole D'Elia, "The Politics of Public Safety Reform in California," *Federal Sentencing Reporter* 22 no. 3 (2010): 144–147.

Democratic Party Platform of 1968, *The American Presidency Project*, 1968. Available at http://www.presidency.ucsb.edu/ws/?pid=29604#axzz2i1IPVJth.

Democratic Party Platform of 1972, *The American Presidency Project*, 1972. Available at http://www.presidency.ucsb.edu/ws/?pid=29605#axzz2i1IPVJth.

John DiIulio, "Two Million Prisoners are Enough," *Wall Street Journal*, March 12, 1999.

Eugene J. Dionne, "Bush Beats Back Robertson Challenge in Florida," *The New York Times*, November 15, 1987.

David J. Diroll, A Decade of Sentencing Reform: A Sentencing Commission Staff Report, 2007. Available at http://www.supremecourt.ohio.gov/Boards/Sentencing/resources/Publications/sentencingReform.pdf.

Todd Donovan, Christopher Z. Mooney and Daniel A. Smith, *State and Local Politics: Institutions and Reform* (Stamford, CT: Cengage Press, 2010).

Terry Eastland, "Mr. Compassionate Conservative," *The Weekly Standard* 11 no. 44 (2006): 23–28. Available at http://www.weeklystandard.com/Content/Public/Articles/000/000/012/511umjoo.asp.

Eric Eckholm, "Congress Moves to Narrow Cocaine Sentencing Disparities," *The New York Times*, July 28, 2010.

Thomas Byrne Edsall and Mary D. Edsall, *Chain Reaction: The Impact of Race, Rights, and Taxes on American Politics* (New York: Norton, 1992).

Sean Emery and Salvador Hernandez, "Probation Department Works to Keep Offenders from Returning to Jail," *Orange County Register*, November 15, 2012.

Robert S. Erikson, Gerald C. Wright and John P. McIver, *Statehouse Democracy: Public Opinion and Policy in the American States* (Cambridge, UK: Cambridge University Press, 1993).

Kevin Esterling, *The Political Economy of Expertise: Information and Efficiency in American National Politics* (Ann Arbor, MI: University of Michigan Press, 2004).

Tony Fabelo, personal communication with the author, April 17, 2010a.

Tony Fabelo, "Texas Justice Reinvestment: Be More Like Texas," *Justice Research and Policy* 12 no. 1 (2010b): 1–18.

Federal Crack Cocaine Sentencing, *The Sentencing Project*, 2010. Available at http://sentencing-project.org/doc/publications/dp_CrackBriefingSheet.pdf.

Reginald Fields, "Prison Reform Bill Allowing Early Release of Inmates Clears Ohio Senate Panel," *The Cleveland Plain Dealer*, June 17, 2009. Available at http://blog.cleveland .com/metro/2009/06/prison_reform_bill_allowing_ea.html.

Reginald Fields, "Ohio Gov. John Kasich Signs Sentencing Reform Bill That Favors Rehab over Prison for Nonviolent Felons," *The Plain Dealer*, June 29, 2011. Available at http:// www.cleveland.com/open/index.ssf/2011/06/ohio_gov_john_kasich_signs_sen.html.

Fifteen Years of Guidelines Sentencing (Washington, DC: U.S. Sentencing Commission, 2004).

"First Time in 40 Years Mandatory Drug Sentence Repealed," 2010. Available at http://open societypolicycenter.org/issues/criminal-justice-reform-racial-equality/first-time-in -40-years-mandatory-drug-sentence-repealed/ (accessed November 17, 2013).

Marvin Frankel, *Criminal Sentences: Law without Order* (New York: Hill and Wange, 1972).

David Garland, *The Culture of Control: Crime and Social Order in Contemporary Society* (Chicago: University of Chicago Press, 2001).

Amanda Geller, Irwin Garfinkel and Bruce Western, *The Effects of Incarceration on Employment and Wages: An Analysis of the Fragile Families Survey* (Princeton, NJ: Center for Research on Child Wellbeing, 2006).

Paul Gendreau, "Rational Policies for Reforming Offenders," *ICCA Journal on Community Corrections* 9 (1999): 16–20.

Paul Gendreau and Robert R. Ross, "Effective Correctional Treatment: Bibliotherapy for Cynics," *Crime and Delinquency* 25 (1979): 463–489.

Paul Gendreau and Robert R. Ross, "Revivification and Rehabilitation: Evidence from the 1980s," *Justice Quarterly* 4 no. 3 (1987): 349–407.

Larry N. Gerston and Terry Christensen, *Recall! California's Political Earthquake* (New York: M.E. Sharpe, 2004).

Newt Gingrich and Pat Nolan, "Prison Reform: A Smart Way for States to Save Money and Lives," *Washington Post*, January 7, 2011.

Frances Gipson and Elizabeth Pierce, "Current Trends in State Inmate User Fee Programs for Health Services," *Journal of Correctional Health Care* 3 (1996): 159–178.

Mark Gladstone, "Ex Assemblyman, Jailed in a Federal Probe, to Run Prison Reform Group," *Los Angeles Times*, August 27, 1996.

Jennifer Gonnerman, "Million-Dollar Blocks: The Neighborhood Costs of America's Prison Boom," *Village Voice*, November 16, 2004.

Kara Gotsch, personal communication with the author, May 19, 2009.

Kara Gotsch, "After the War on Drugs: The Fair Sentencing Act and Unfinished Drug Policy Reform," *American Constitution Society for Law and Policy*, 2011. Available at http:// www.acslaw.org/Gotsch%20-%20'After'%20the%20War%20on%20Drugs.pdf.

Marie Gottschalk, *The Prison and the Gallows: The Politics of Mass Incarceration in America* (Cambridge, MA: Cambridge University Press, 2006).

Marie Gottschalk, "Cell Blocks and Red Ink: Mass Incarceration, the Great Recession, and Penal Reform," *Daedalus* 139 no. 3 (2010): 62–73.

John C. Green, *The Faith Factor: How Religion Influences American Elections* (Westport, CT: Praeger, 2007).

Linda Greenhouse, "A Voice from the Past," *The New York Times*, June 1, 2011.

Lawrence A. Grossback, Sean Nicholson-Crotty and Daniel A. M. Peterson, "Ideology and Learning in Policy Diffusion," *American Politics Research* 32 no. 5 (2004): 521–545.

Vanita Gupta, Inamai Chettiar, Rachel Bloom, Zoë Bunnell, Elana Fogel, and Jon Martin, "Smart Reform Is Possible: States Reducing Incarceration Rates and Costs While Protecting Communities," *American Civil Liberties Union*, 2011. Available at https://www.aclu.org/criminal -law-reform/smart-reform-possible-states-reducing-incarceration-rates-and-costs-while.

Jacob S. Hacker and Paul Pierson, *Winner-Take-All Politics: How Washington Made the Rich Richer and Turned Its Back on the Middle Class* (New York: Simon and Schuster, 2010).

Jacob Hacker and Paul Pierson, "A Case for Policy-Focused Political Analysis." *Working Paper* (2011).

Kamala D. Harris and Joan O'C. Hamilton, *Smart on Crime: A Career Prosecutor's Plan to Make Us Safer* (San Francisco: Chronicle Books LLC, 2009).

Patricia Kilday Hart, "Texas Lawmakers in Lockstep on Juvenile-Justice Reform Efforts," *Houston Chronicle*, May 22, 2011.

Jake Horowitz, personal communication with the author, March 12, 2010.

"How Federal Sentencing Law Works: Mandatory Minimums, Statutory Maximums, and Sentencing Guidelines," *Families Against Mandatory Minimums*, 2013. Available at http://famm.org/wp-content/uploads/2013/08/Chart-How-Fed-Sentencing-Works-9.5.pdf.

Keith Humphreys, "Will the Obama Administration Implement a More Health-Oriented Approach to Drug Policy?" *Journal of Drug Policy Analysis* 5 no. 1 (2012a): 3.

Keith Humphreys, "Federal Policy on Criminal Offenders with Substance Abuse Disorders: How Can We Maximize Public Health and Safety?," *Substance Abuse* 33 no. 1 (2012b): 5–8.

Keith Humphreys, "U.S. Prison Admissions Are at a Two-Decade Low," 2014a. Available at http://www.samefacts.com/2014/01/drug-policy/u-s-prison-admissions-are-at-a-two-decade-low/.

Keith Humphreys, "The Five Myths of American Incarceration," *Politix*, February 14, 2014b. Available at http://politix.topix.com/story/10426-the-five-myths-of-american-incarceration.

Nathan James, "The Federal Prison Population Buildup: Overview, Policy Changes, Issues and Options" (Washington, DC: Congressional Research Service, 2013).

Alan Johnson, "Sentencing Overhaul Law to Reduce Ohio's Prison Population," *The Columbus Dispatch*, June 30, 2011. Available at http://www.dispatch.com/content/stories/local/2011/06/30/sentencing-overhaul-to-reduce-prison-population.hml.

Byron R. Johnson and David B. Larson, "The InnerChange Freedom Initiative: A Preliminary Announcement of a Faith-Based Prison Program" (Waco, TX: Baylor Institute for Studies of Religion, 2008).

Donald B. Johnson, *National Party Platforms, Volume II, 1960–1976* (Urbana, IL: University of Illinois Press, 1978).

Bryan D. Jones and Frank R. Baumgartner, *The Politics of Attention: How Government Prioritizes Problems* (Chicago: University of Chicago Press, 2005).

Andrew Karch, "National Intervention and the Diffusion of Policy Innovations," *American Politics Research* 34 (2006): 403–426.

Andrew Karch, *Democratic Laboratories: Policy Diffusion among the American States* (Ann Arbor, MI: University of Michigan Press, 2007a).

Andrew Karch, "Emerging Issues and Future Directions in State Policy Diffusion Research," *State Politics and Policy Quarterly* 7 no. 1 (2007b): 54–80.

Mark A. Kellner, "A Jailhouse Conversion," *Liberty Magazine*, September/October 2003.

David M. Kennedy, *Don't Shoot: One Man, a Street Fellowship, and the End of Violence in Inner-City America* (New York: Bloomsbury Press, 2011).

Neil King Jr., "As Prisons Squeeze Budgets, GOP Rethinks Crime Focus," *Wall Street Journal*, June 21, 2013.

Ryan S. King, "Disparity by Geography: The War on Drugs in America's Cities" (Washington, DC: The Sentencing Project, 2008). Available at http://www.sentencingproject.org/doc/publications/dp_drugarrestreport.pdf.

John W. Kingdon, *Agendas, Alternatives, and Public Policies*, 2nd ed. (New York: Harper Collins, 1995).

Bernard C. Kirby, "Measuring Effects of Treatment of Criminals and Delinquents," *Sociology and Social Research* 38 (1954): 368–374.

Mark A. R. Kleiman, "Faith Based Fudging," *Slate*, August 5, 2003. Available at http://www.slate.com/articles/news_and_politics/hey_wait_a_minute/2003/08/faithbased_fudging.single.html#pagebreak_anchor_2.

Mark Kleiman, *When Brute Force Fails: How to Have Less Crime and Less Punishment* (Princeton, NJ: Princeton University Press, 2009).

Mark Kleiman, "Justice Reinvestment in Community Supervision," *Criminology and Public Policy* 10 no. 3 (2011): 651–659.

Mark A. R. Kleiman, "A New Role for Parole," *Washington Monthly*, January/February 2013. Available at http://www.washingtonmonthly.com/magazine/january_february_2013/features/a_new_role_for_parole042045.php?page=all.

Johann Koehler, "Why Problems in Prison Concentrate in Medical Units," 2013. Available at http://www.samefacts.com/2013/02/ everything-else/ why-problems-in-prisons-concentrate-in-medical-units/.

Patrick A. Langan and David J. Levin, "Recidivism of Prisoners Released in 1994." Bureau of Justice Statistics, NCJ 19427, 2002.

Nancy LaVigne, Samuel Bieler, Lindsey Cramer, Helen Ho, Cybele Kotonias, Deborah Mayer, David McClure, Laura Pacifici, Erika Parks, Bryce Peterson and Julie Samuels, "Justice Reinvestment Initiative State Assessment Report" (Washington, DC: The Urban Institute and the Bureau of Justice Assistance, 2014). Available at http://www.urban.org/UploadedPDF/412994-Justice-Reinvestment-Initiative-State-Assessment-Report.pdf.

Alison Lawrence, "Trends in Sentencing and Corrections: State Legislation," *National Conference of State Legislatures*, July 2013. Available at http://www.ncsl.org/Documents/CJ/TrendsInSentencingAndCorrections.pdf.

Sarah Lawrence and Jeremy Travis, "The New Landscape of Imprisonment: Mapping America's Prison Expansion." *Urban Institute Justice Policy Center*, 2004. Available at http://www.urban.org/UploadedPDF/410994_mapping_prisons.pdf.

Legislative Reference Library of Texas. Available at http://www.lrl.state.tx.us/legis/billSearch/index.cfm.

Jennifer Lehner, "Breaking the Chains," *The Washington Times*, August 11, 2004. Available at http://www.highbeam.com/doc/1G1-120469336.html.

Mark Leno, personal communication with the author, November 12, 2009.

Mark A. Levin, "Smart on Crime: With Prison Costs on the Rise Ohio Needs Better Policies for Protecting the Public," *The Buckeye Institute for Public Policy Solutions*, November 2010. Available at http://buckeyeinstitute.org/uploads/files/buckeye-smart-on-crime(1).pdf.

Dara Lind, "Almost Half of All Federal Drug Prisoners Could Get Out of Prison Sooner. Here's How," 2014a. Available at http://www.vox.com/2014/7/18/5915611/sentencing-retroactivity-drugs-war-reform-prison-criminal-justice.

Dara Lind, "Congress Can Make Drug Sentences Shorter in Zero Easy Steps," 2014b. Available at http://www.vox.com/2014/5/2/5672196/congress-reduce-drug-sentences-inaction-sentencing-commission-guidelines-reform.

Adam Liptak, "1 in 100 U.S. Adults Behind Bars, New Study Says," *The New York Times*, February 28, 2008.

Douglas S. Lipton, "The Effectiveness of Correctional Treatment Revisited Thirty Years Later: Preliminary Meta-Analytic Findings from the CDATE Study." Unpublished paper presented to the 12th International Congress on Criminology, Seoul Korea, August 1998.

Douglas Lipton, Robert Martinson and Judith Wilks, *The Effectiveness of Correctional Treatment: A Survey of Treatment Evaluation Studies* (New York: Praeger, 1975).

Little Hoover Commission, "Back to the Community: Safe and Sound Parole Policies" (Sacramento, CA: Little Hoover Commission on California State Organization and the Economy, 2003). Available at http://www.lhc.ca.gov/lhcdir/172/execsum172.pdf

Magnus Lofstrom and Steven Raphael, *Impact of Realignment on County Jail Populations* (San Francisco: Public Policy Institute of California, 2013a). Available at http://www.ppic.org/content/pubs/report/R_613MLR.pdf.

Magnus Lofstrom and Steven Raphael, "Public Safety Realignment and Crime Rates in California" (San Francisco: Public Policy Institute of California, 2013b). Available at http://www.ppic.org/content/pubs/report/R_1213MLR.pdf.

Arthur Lupia, "Shortcuts Versus Encyclopedias: Information and Voting Behavior in California Insurance Initiatives," *American Political Science Review* 88 no. 1 (1994): 63–76.

Mona Lynch, *Sunbelt Justice: Arizona and the Transformation of American Punishment* (Stanford, CA: Stanford University Press, 2009).

Mona Lynch, "Mass Incarceration, Legal Change, and Locale: Understanding and Remediating American Penal Overindulgence," *Criminology and Public Policy* 10 no. 3 (2011): 673–698.

Mona Lynch, "Theorizing the Role of the 'War on Drugs' in U.S. Punishment," *Theoretical Criminology* 16 no. 2 (2012): 175–199.

Doras Layton MacKenzie, "Boot Camp Prisons: Components, Evaluations, and Empirical Issues," *Federal Probation* 54 (1993): 44–52.

Doras Layton MacKenzie and Claire Souryal, "Multisite Study of Correctional Boot Camps," in *Correctional Boot Camps: A Tough Intermediate Sanction*, eds. Doris Layton MacKenzie and Eugene E. Hebert (Washington, DC: National Institute of Justice, 1996).

Jerry Madden, personal communication with the author, April 16, 2010.

Andrew Malcolm, "Ohio Gov. John Kasich: We Will Not Be Raising Taxes in This State," *Los Angeles Times*, March 9, 2011. Available at http://latimesblogs.latimes.com/washington/2011/03/john-kasich-ohio-governor-state-of-the-state-text.html.

Kamala Mallik-Kane, Barbara Parthasarathy and William Adams, *Examining Growth in the Federal Prison Population 1998–2010* (Washington, DC: The Urban Institute, September 2012). Available at http://www.urban.org/UploadedPDF/412720-Examining-Growth-in-the-Federal-Prison-Population.pdf.

Jeff Manza and Christopher Uggen, *Locked Out: Felon Disenfranchisement and American Democracy* (New York: Oxford University Press, 2006).

James M. Markham, "President Calls for 'Total War' on U.S. Addiction," *The New York Times*, March 21, 1972.

Robert Martinson, "What Works? Questions and Answers about Prison Reform," *Public Interest* 35 (1974): 22–54.

Robert Martinson, "New Findings, New Views: A Note of Caution Regarding Sentencing Reform," *Hofstra Law Review* 7 (1979): 242–258, 274.

Robert Martinson and Judith Wilks, "Save Parole Supervision," *Federal Probation* 41 (1977): 23–27.

Marc Mauer, *The Race to Incarcerate Race* (New York: The New Press, 1996).

Mark Mauer and David Cole, "Five Myths about Prisons in America," *The Washington Post*, June 17, 2011.

Marc Mauer and Nazgol Ghandnoosh, 2014. "Can We Wait 88 Years before We End Mass Incarceration?" Available at http://www.huffingtonpost.com/marc-mauer/88-years-mass-incarceration_b_4474132.html.

Marc Mauer and Ryan S. King, "A 25 Year Quagmire: The War on Drugs and Its Impact on American Society" (New York: The Sentencing Project, 2007).

Michael McCann, "How the Supreme Court Matters in American Politics," in *The Supreme Court in American Politics: New Institutional Perspectives*, eds. Howard Gillman and Cornell Clayton (Lawrence, KS: University of Kansas Press, 1999).

Nolan McCarty, Keith T. Poole and Howard Rosenthal, *Polarized America: The Dance of Political Ideology and Unequal Riches* (Cambridge, MA: MIT Press, 2008).

Aman McCloud, Ismail K. White and Amelia R. Gavin, "The Locked Ballot Box: The Impact of State Criminal Disenfranchisement Laws on African American Voting Behavior and Implications for Reform," *Virginia Journal of Social Policy and Law* 11 (2003): 66–88.

Gerald T. McLaughlin, "Cocaine: The History and Regulation of a Dangerous Drug," *Cornell Law Review* 58 (1973): 538–573.

Arnold Meltsner, *Policy Analysis in the Bureaucracy* (Berkeley, CA: University of California Press, 1976).

Lisa L. Miller, *The Perils of Federalism: Race, Poverty, and the Politics of Crime Control* (Oxford: Oxford University Press, 2008).

Lisa Miller, "The Local and the Legal: American Federalism and the Carceral State," *Criminology and Public Policy* 10 no. 3 (2011): 725–732.

Naomi Murakawa, "The Racial Antecedents to Federal Sentencing Guidelines: How Congress Judged the Judges from Brown to Booker," *Roger Williams University Law Review* 11 (Winter 2006): 473–494.

Naomi Murakawa, "The Origins of the Carceral Crisis: Racial Order as 'Law and Order' in Postwar American Politics," in *Race and American Political Development*, eds. Joseph Lowndes, Julie Novkov and Dorian Warren (New York: Routledge, 2008).

Salim Muwakkil, "Black Men: Missing," (2005). Available at http://inthesetimes.com/article/2162.

Judith Nagata, "Beyond Theology: Toward and Anthropology of 'Fundamentalism,'" *American Anthropologist* 103 no. 2 (2001): 481–498.

National Conference of State Legislatures, "State Budget Update," July, 2009. Available at http://www.ncsl.org/documents/fiscal/statebudgetupdatejulyfinal.pdf.

Ashley Nellis and Ryan S. King, "No Exit: The Expanding Use of Life Sentences in America" (New York: The Sentencing Project, 2009). Available at http://www.sentencingproject.org/doc/publications/publications/inc_NoExitSept2009.pdf.

New York Times Editorial Board, "A Rare Opportunity on Criminal Justice," *The New York Times*, March 15, 2014.

Sean Nicholson-Crotty, "The Impact of Sentencing Guidelines on State Level Sanctions: An Analysis over Time," *Crime and Delinquency* 50 (2004): 395–411.

Sean Nicholson-Crotty and Kenneth Meier, "From Perception to Public Policy: Translating Social Constructions into Policy Designs," in *Deserving and Entitled: Social Construction and Public Policy*, eds. Anne L. Schneider and Helen M. Ingram (Albany, NY: SUNY Press, 2005).

UPI, "Nixon Assails Rate of Crime in the Capital," *The New York Times*, June 23, 1968.

"Nixon Links Court to Rise in Crime," *The New York Times*, May 31, 1968.

"Nixon and Reagan Ask War on Crime," *The New York Times*, August 1, 1968.

Pat Nolan, "Right on Crime: A Call to Arms," 2011. Available at http://www.prisonfellowship.org/2011/01/right-on-crime-a-call-to-arms/.

Grover Norquist, "Republicans and Democrats Agree We Need to Fix the Prison Problem," *Huffington Post*, June 6, 2014. Available at http://www.huffingtonpost.com/grover-norquist/republicans-and-democrats_5_b_5460367.html.

Barbara Norrander, "The Multi-Layered Impact of Public Opinion on Capital Punishment Implementation in the American States," *Political Research Quarterly* 53 (2000): 771–794.

Office of the Governor, Rick Perry, "2007 State of the State Speech," February 6, 2007. Available at http://governor.state.tx.us/news/speech/5567/.

Office of National Drug Control Policy, "Alternatives to the 'War on Drugs': Obama Drug Policy and Reforming the Criminal Justice System," November, 21, 2011. Available at http://www.whitehouse.gov/blog/2011/11/21/ alternatives-war-drugs-obama-drug -policy-and-reforming-criminal-justice-system.

Office of National Drug Control Policy, "Statement of the Government of the United States of America World Federation Against Drugs 3rd World Forum," May 21, 2012. Available at http://www.likemotion.com/show/19639/obama-keeps-promise-to-send -first-time-nonviolent-drug-offenders-to-rehab-over-jail.

Office of the Press Secretary, "White House Issues Statement on Second Chance Act of 2004," *U.S. Fed News*, June 23, 2004.

Michael O'Hear, "The Second Chance Act and the Future of Reentry Reform," *Federal Sentencing Reporter* 20 no. 2 (2007): 75–83.

Joshua Page, *The Toughest Beat: Politics, Punishment, and the Prison Officers Union in California*, Kindle ed. (New York: Oxford University Press, 2011).

Ted Palmer, *Correctional Intervention and Research: Current Issues and Future Prospects* (Lexington, MA: Lexington Books, 1978).

Ted Palmer, *The Re-Emergence of Correctional Intervention* (Newbury Park, CA: Sage Publications, 1992).

Eric M. Patashnik, *Reform and Risk: What Happens after Major Policy Changes Are Enacted?* (Princeton, NJ: Princeton University Press, 2008).

Beth Pearsall, "Replicating HOPE: Can Others Successfully Implement Hawaii's Innovative Program?," *National Institute of Justice Journal* no. 273 (2014): 36–41. Available at http://www.nij.gov/journals/273/pages/welcome.aspx.

Mark Peffley and Jon Hurwitz, *Justice in America: The Separate Realities of Blacks and Whites* (Cambridge, MA: Cambridge University Press, 2010).

Robert Perkinson, *Texas Tough: The Rise of America's Prison Empire* (New York: Metropolitan Books, 2010).

Joan Petersilia, *When Prisoners Come Home: Parole and Prisoner Reentry* (New York: Oxford University Press, 2003).

Joan Petersilia, "Understanding California Corrections" (Berkeley, CA: California Policy Research Center, 2006). Available at http://ucicorrections.seweb.uci.edu/files/2013 /06/rpt_Petersilia_CPRC_blulin.pdf.

Joan Petersilia, "A Retrospective View of Corrections Reform in the Schwarzenegger Administration," *Federal Sentencing Reporter* 22 no. 3 (2010): 148–153.

Joan Petersilia, "Remembering James Q. Wilson," *The Crime Report*, 2012. Available at http://www.thecrimereport.org/news/inside-criminal-justice/2012-03-remembering -james-q-wilson.

Joan Petersilia and Susan Turner, "Intensive Probation and Parole," in *Crime and Justice: A Review of Research*, Vol. 17, ed. Michael Tonry (Chicago: University of Chicago Press, 1993).

Joan Petersilia, Sarah Arbarbanel, John Butler, Mark Feldman, Mariam Hinds, Kevin Jason, Corinne Keel, Matt Owens and Camden Vilkin, "Voices from the Field: How California Stakeholders View Public Safety Realignment." (Stanford, CA: Stanford

Criminal Justice Center, 2013). Available at http://www.law.stanford.edu/sites /default/files/child-page/183091/doc/slspublic/Petersilia%20VOICES%20no%20es %20Final%20022814.pdf.

Becky Pettit and Bruce Western, "Mass Imprisonment and the Life Course: Race and Class Inequality in U.S. Incarceration," *American Sociological Review* 69 (2004): 151–169.

Pew Center on the States, "One in 31: The Long Reach of American Corrections," (Washington, DC: Pew Charitable Trusts, March 2009).

Pew Center on the States, "One in 100: Behind Bars in America" (Washington, DC: Pew Charitable Trusts, 2008).

Pew Center on the States, "Time Served: The High Cost, Low Return of Longer Prison Terms," 2012a. Available at http://www.pewstates.org/uploadedFiles/PCS_Assets /2012/Pew_Time_Served_report.pdf.

Pew Center on the States, "Public Opinion on Sentencing and Corrections Policy in America," 2012b. Available at http://static.prisonpolicy.org/scans/PEW_National SurveyResearchPaper_FINAL.pdf.

Pew Center on the States, "Time Served: The High Cost, Low Return of Longer Prison Terms," *Public Safety Performance Project*, June 6, 2012c. Available at http://www .pewtrusts.org/en/research-and-analysis/reports/0001/01/01/time-served.

Pew Charitable Trusts, "States Cut Both Crime and Imprisonment," December 2013. Available at http://www.pewtrusts.org/en/multimedia/data-visualizations/2013 /states-cut-both-crime-and-imprisonment.

Paul Pierson, *Politics in Time: History, Institutions, and Social Analysis* (Princeton, NJ: Princeton University Press, 2004).

David Plotz, "Charles Colson: How a Watergate Crook Became America's Greatest Christian Conservative," *Slate*, March 10, 2000. Available at http://www.slate.com/articles / news_and_politics/assessment/2000/03/charles_colson.html.

Nicole D. Porter, "The State of Sentencing in 2012: Developments in Policy and Practice," *The Sentencing Project*, January 2013. Available at http://sentencingproject.org/doc /publications/sen_State of Sentencing 2012.pdf.

"President Bush Signs H.R. 1593, The Second Chance Act of 2007," 2008. Available at http:// georgewbush-whitehouse.archives.gov/news/releases/2008/04/20080409-2.html.

Prison Fellowship Ministries, "Open Letter to Congress," May 19, 2010. Available at http:// www.famm.org/Repository/Files/0510%20Prison%20Fellowship%20Crack%20 Cocaine%20letter%5B1%5D.pdf (accessed July 2, 2013).

Aaron Rappaport and Kara Dansky, "State of Emergency: California's Correctional Crisis," *Federal Sentencing Reporter* 22 no. 3 (2010): 133–143.

Report to Congress: Cocaine and Federal Sentencing Policy (Washington, DC: U.S. Sentencing Commission, 1995). Available at http://www.ussc.gov/sites/default/files/pdf/news /congressional-testimony-and-reports/drug-topics/199502-rtc-cocaine-sentencing -policy/EXECSUM.pdf.

Report to Congress: Cocaine and Federal Sentencing Policy (Washington, DC: U.S. Sentencing Commission, 2002). Available at http://www.ussc.gov/sites/default/files/pdf/news /congressional-testimony-and-reports/drug-topics/200205-rtc-cocaine-sentencing -policy/ch1.pdf.

Andrew Rich, *Think Tanks, Public Policy, and the Politics of Expertise* (Cambridge, UK: Cambridge University Press, 2004).

William H. Riker, "Some Ambiguities in the Notion of Power," *American Political Science Review* 58 no. 2 (1964): 341–349.

Julian V. Roberts and Loretta J. Stalans, *Public Opinion, Crime, and Criminal Justice* (Boulder, CO: Westview, 1997).

Dina R. Rose and Todd R. Clear, "Incarceration, Social Capital, and Crime: Implications for Social Disorganization Theory," *Criminology* 36 (1998): 441–480.

Michael Rothfeld, "Prison Plan Loses Sentencing Panel: The Assembly Speaker Takes Proposal Out of Spending Cuts Package," *Los Angeles Times*, August 25, 2009a.

Michael Rothfeld, "After delay, Assembly to take up prison measure," *Los Angeles Times*, September 1, 2009b. Available at http://articles.latimes.com/2009/sep/01/local/me -prisons1.

Gwen Rubinstein and Debbie Mukamal, "Welfare and Housing—Denial of Benefits to Drug Offenders," in *Invisible Punishment: The Collateral Consequences of Mass Imprisonment*, eds. Marc Mauer and Meda Chesney-Lind (New York: The New Press, 2002).

Paul A. Sabatier and Hank Jenkins-Smith, *Policy Change and Learning: An Advocacy Coalition Approach* (Boulder, CO: Westview Press, 1988).

Rick Sarre, "Beyond 'What Works'? A 25 Year Jubilee Retrospective of Robert Martinson's Famous Article," *Australian and New Zealand Journal of Criminology* 34 no. 1 (2001): 38–46.

Elmer E. Schattschneider, *The Semi-Sovereign People* (New York: Holt, Rinehart and Winston, 1960).

Stuart Scheingold, *The Politics of Law and Order: Street Crime and Public Policy* (New York: Longman, 1984).

Stuart Scheingold, "Constructing the New Political Criminology: Power, Authority, and the Post-Liberal State," *Law and Social Inquiry* 23 no. 4 (1998): 857–895.

Margo Schlanger, "Plata v. Brown and Realignment: Jails, Prisons, Courts, and Politics," *Harvard Civil Rights-Civil Liberties Law Review* 48 no. 1 (2013): 165–215.

Dana Adams Schmidt, "President Orders Wider Drug Fight; Asks for $155 Million," *The New York Times*, June 18, 1971.

Jennifer Schuessler, "Drug Policy as Race Policy Best Seller Galvanizes the Debate," *The New York Times*, March 6, 2012.

Bill Seitz, personal communication with the author, March 7, 2010.

"Senate Letter to House of Representatives Urging Passage of Fair Sentencing Act," 2010. Available at http://www.famm.org/Repository/Files/Fair%20Sentencing%20Act%20 House%20Dear%20Colleague%5B1%5D.pdf.

Samantha M. Shapiro, "Jails for Jesus," in *Prison Profiteers: Who Makes Money from Mass Incarceration*? eds. Tara Herivel and Paul Wright (New York: The New Press, 2007).

Heidi Shierholz, "Six Years from Its Beginning, the Great Recession's Shadow Looms over the Labor Market," *Economic Policy Institute*, January 9, 2014. Available at http://www .epi.org/publication/years-beginning-great-recessions-shadow/.

Elizabeth Siggins, California Department of Corrections and Rehabilitation, personal communication with the author, November 5, 2009.

Jonathan Simon, *Governing through Crime: How the War on Crime Transformed American Democracy and Created a Culture of Fear* (New York: Oxford University Press, 2007).

Jonathan Simon, "Mass Incarceration on Trial," *Punishment and Society* 13 no. 3 (2011a): 251–255.

Jonathan Simon, "California Penal Policy: Realignment and Beyond," October 11, 2011b. Available at http://blogs.berkeley.edu/2011/10/11/california-penal-policy-realignment -and-beyond/comment-page-1/.

Jonathan Simon, *Mass Incarceration on Trial: A Remarkable Court Decision and the Future of Prisons in America* (New York: The New Press, 2014).

Barbara Sinclair, "The New World of U.S. Senators," in *Congress Reconsidered*, 10th ed., eds. Lawrence Dodd and Bruce Oppenheimer (Washington, DC: CQ Press, 2013).

George Skelton, "Unshackling Prison Reform," *Los Angeles Times*, August 24, 2009.

Tom W. Smith, Peter V. Marsden, Michael Hout and Jibum Kim, *General Social Surveys*, 1972–2012. [machine-readable data file]. Principal investigator, Tom W. Smith; Co-principal investigators, Peter V. Marsden and Michael Hout, NORC ed. Chicago: National Opinion Research Center, producer, 2005; Storrs, CT: The Roper Center for Public Opinion Research, University of Connecticut.

Joe Soss, Richard C. Fording and Sanford S. Schram, "Governing the Poor: The Rise of the Neoliberal Paternalist State." Paper presented at the 2009 Conference of the American Political Science Association (2009).

Donald Spector, "Everything Revolves around Overcrowding: The State of California's Prisons," *Federal Sentencing Reporter* 22 no. 3 (2010): 194–199.

William Spelman, "Crime, Crash, and Limited Options: Explaining the Prison Boom," *Criminology and Public Policy* 8 no. 1 (2009): 29–77.

"States Cut Both Crime and Imprisonment," *The Pew Charitable Trusts*, December 2013. Available at http://www.pewtrusts.org/en/multimedia/data-visualizations/2013/states-cut-both-crime-and-imprisonment.

Jennifer Steinhauer, "To Cut Costs, States Relax Prison Policies," *The New York Times*, March 24, 2009.

William J. Stuntz, *The Collapse of American Criminal Justice* (Cambridge, MA: Harvard University Press, 2011).

Ram Subramanian, Rebecka Moreno and Sharyn Broomhead, "Recalibrating Justice: A Review of State Sentencing and Corrections Trends" (Vera Institute of Justice, 2014). Available at http://www.vera.org/sites/default/files/resources/downloads/state-sentencing-and-corrections-trends-2013-v2.pdf.

Chris Suellentrop, "The Right Has a Jailhouse Conversion: How Conservatives Came to Embrace Prison Reform," *The New York Times Magazine*, December 24, 2006.

The Sentencing Project, 2015. "U.S. Prison Population Trends." Available at http://sentencingproject.org/doc/publications/inc_Prison_Population_Trends_fs.pdf.

"The Term-Limited States" (National Conference of State Legislatures, 2013). Available at http://www.ncsl.org/research/about-state-legislatures/chart-of-term-limits-states.aspx.

Texas Criminal Justice Coalition, "2007 Texas' Criminal Justice Solutions: A Policy Guide," 2007. Available at http://www.texascjc.org/sites/default/files/uploads/2007%20Texas%20Criminal%20Justice%20Solutions%2C%20A%20Policy%20Guide%20%28Jan%202007%29.pdf.

"Text of President Bush's 2004 State of the Union Address," *The Washington Post*, January 20, 2004. Available at http://www.washingtonpost.com/wp-srv/politics/transcripts/bushtext_012004.html.

John Tierney, "For Lesser Crimes, Rethinking Life behind Bars," *The New York Times*, December 11, 2012.

Michael Tonry, *Malign Neglect: Race, Crime, and Punishment in America* (New York: Oxford University Press, 1995).

Michael Tonry, *Sentencing Matters* (New York: Oxford University Press, 1996).

Michael Tonry, "Explanations of American Punishment Policies: A National History," *Punishment and Society* 11 no. 3 (1999): 377–394.

Michael Tonry, *Thinking about Crime: Sense and Sensibility in American Culture* (New York: Oxford University Press, 2004).

Michael Tonry, "Explanation of American Punishment Policies: A National History," *Punishment and Society* 11 no. 3 (2011a): 377–394.

Michael Tonry, "Making Peace, Not a Desert: Penal Reform Should Be about Values Not Justice Reinvestment," *Criminology and Public Policy* 10 no. 3 (2011b): 637–649.

Michael Tonry, *Punishing Race: A Continuing American Dilemma* (New York: Oxford University Press, 2011c).

Jeremy Travis, "But They All Come Back: Rethinking Prisoner Reentry" (U.S. Department of Justice, Office of Justice Programs, National Institute of Justice, May 2000). Available at https://www.ncjrs.gov/pdffiles1/nij/181413.pdf.

Jeremy Travis, "Invisible Punishment: An Instrument of Social Exclusion," in *Invisible Punishment: The Collateral Consequences of Mass Imprisonment*, eds. Marc Mauer and Meda Chesney-Lind (New York: The New Press, 2002).

Jeremy Travis, "Parole in California 1980–2000, Public Hearing on Parole Reform, Little Hoover Commission," (Sacramento, CA, February 27, 2003). Available at http://www.urban.org/publications/900598.html.

Jeremy Travis, *But They All Come Back: Facing the Challenges of Prisoner Reentry* (Washington, DC: The Urban Institute Press, 2005).

Jeremy Travis, "Reflections on the Reentry Movement," *Federal Sentencing Reporter* 20 no. 3 (2007): 84–87.

Jeremy Travis, personal communication with the author, May 9, 2011.

David B. Truman, *The Governmental Process: Political Interests and Public Opinion* (New York: Knopf, 1951).

Susan Tucker and Eric Cadora, "Ideas from an Open Society: Justice Reinvestment," *Open Society Institute Occasional Papers* 3 no. 3 (2003).

James D. Unnever, Francis T. Cullen and Cheryl N. Lero-Johnson, "Race, Racism, and Support for Capital Punishment," in *Crime and Justice: A Review of Research*, Vol. 37, ed. Michael Tonry (Chicago: University of Chicago Press, 2008).

U.S. Bureau of Labor Statistics, "The Recession of 2008–2009," February 2012. Available at http://www.bls.gov/spotlight/2012/recession/pdf/recession_bls_spotlight.pdf.

U.S. Department of Justice, *Correctional Populations in the United States, 2012* (Bureau of Justice Statistics, 2013). Available at http://www.bjs.gov/content/pub/pdf/cpus12.pdf.

U.S. Department of Justice, "Jail Inmates at Midyear 2013—Statistical Tables" (Bureau of Justice Statistics, 2014a). Available at http://www.bjs.gov/index.cfm?ty=pbdetail&iid=4988.

U.S. Department of Justice, "Prisoners in 2012, Trends in Admissions and Releases, 1991–2010" (Bureau of Justice Statistics, 2014b). Available at http://www.bjs.gov/content/pub/pdf/p12tar9112.pdf.

U.S. Department of Justice, Bureau of Justice Statistics, "Historical Corrections Statistics in the United States, 1850–1984," NCJ-102529, 1986.

U.S. Department of Justice, Office of Justice Programs, "Prisoners in 2008" (Washington, DC: Bureau of Justice Statistics, 2009).

U.S. Department of Justice, Office of Justice Programs, "Parents in Prison and Their Minor Children," *Bureau of Justice Statistics*, 2010. Available at http://www.bjs.gov/content/pub/pdf/pptmc.pdf.

U.S. Department of Justice, Office of Justice Programs, Bureau of Justice Statistics, "Prison and Jail Inmates at Midyear 2006," 2007. Available at http://www.bjs.gov/content/pub/pdf/pjim06.pdf.

U.S. Department of Justice, Office of Justice Programs, Bureau of Justice Statistics, "Prisoners in 2011," 2012. Available at http://www.bjs.gov/content/pub/pdf/p11.pdf.

Gennaro F. Vito and Harry E. Allen, "Shock Probation in Ohio: A Comparison of Outcomes," *International Journal of Offender Therapy and Comparative Criminology* 25 (1981): 70–76.

Loïc Wacquant, "From Slavery to Mass Incarceration," *New Left Review* 13 (2002): 41–60.

Loïc Wacquant, *Punishing the Poor: The Neoliberal Government of Social Insecurity* (Durham, NC: Duke University Press, 2009).

Kenneth D. Wald and Allison Calhoun-Brown, *Religion and Politics in the United States*, 5th ed. (Lanham, MD: Rowman and Littlefield, 2007).

Jack L. Walker, "The Diffusion of Innovations among the American States," *American Political Science Review* 63 no. 3 (1969): 880–899.

Mike Ward, "Probation Overhaul Head to Governor; If Perry Agrees, Some Felon's Time under Supervision Will Be Halved," *Austin American Statesman*, May 25, 2005a.

Mike Ward, "Tough on Crime? Not This Time; Cost Made Lawmakers Think Twice about Increasing Penalties," *Austin American Statesman*, June 10, 2005b.

Mike Ward, "Probation Reforms, 18 Other Measures Killed by Pen," *Austin American Statesman*, June 18, 2005c.

Mark Warr, "Poll Trends: Public Opinion on Crime and Punishment," *The Public Opinion Quarterly* 59 no. 2 (1995): 296–310.

Vesla Weaver, "Frontlash: Race and the Development of Punitive Crime Policy," *Studies in American Political Development* 21 (2007): 230–265.

Vesla Weaver and Amy E. Lerman, "The Political Consequences of the Carceral State," *American Political Science Review* 104 (2010): 817–834.

Roger Werholz, personal communication with the author, September 4, 2009.

Heather C. West and William J. Sabol, "Prisoners in 2007" (Washington, DC: Bureau of Justice Statistics, 2008). Available at http://www.bjs.gov/content/pub/pdf/p07.pdf.

Bruce Western, *Punishment and Inequality in America* (New York: Russell Sage Foundation, 2006).

Ken White, "The Eric Holder Memorandum on Mandatory Sentences, Explained," 2013. Available at http://www.popehat.com/2013/08/13/ the-eric-holder-memorandum -on-mandatory-minimum-sentences-explained/.

John Whitmire, personal communication with the author, April 18, 2010.

Forrest Wilder, "Revealed: The Corporations and Billionaires that Fund the Texas Public Policy Foundation," 2012. Available at http://www.texasobserver.org /revealed-the-corporations-and-billionaires-that-fund-the-texas-public-policy -foundation/?mobile=1.

Forrest Wilder, "The Money behind Texas' Most Influential Think Tank," 2014. Available at http://www.texasobserver.org/money-behind-texas-public-policy-foundation/.

Reginald Wilkinson, personal communication with the author, March 5, 2010.

Pete Williams, "Attorney General Orders New Prosecution Policies for Some Drug Crimes," *NBC News*, August 12, 2013. Available at http://usnews.nbcnews.com/_news /2013/08/12/19978405-attorney-general-orders-new-prosecution-policies-for -some-drug-crimes?lite.

James Q. Wilson, *Thinking about Crime* (New York: Basic Books, 1975a).

James Q. Wilson, "Lock 'Em Up and Other Thoughts on Crime," *The New York Times Magazine*, March 9, 1975b.

James Q. Wilson and Richard Herrnstein, *Crime and Human Nature* (New York: Simon and Schuster, 1985).

Nick Wing, "Justice Safety Valve Would Give Flexibility on Mandatory Minimum Sentences," *The Huffington Post*, 2014. Available at http://www.huffingtonpost.com/2013/03/20/justice-safety-valve-act-senate_n_2918823.html.

Betsy Woodruff, "Bipartisan Prison Reform," *National Review Online*, 2014. Available at http://m.nationalreview.com/article/368877/bipartisan-prison-reform-betsy-woodruff.

Barbara Wooton, *Social Science and Social Pathology* (London: George Allen and Unwin, 1959).

Grace Wyler, "Jailbreak: Ohio Passes Prison Reform Bill that Lets Inmates Out Early," *Business Insider*, June 27, 2011. Available at http://www.businessinsider.com/ohio-prison-reform-will-let-inmates-out-early-and-send-felons-to-rehab-instead-2011-6.

Matthew Yi, "Assembly Passes Stripped Down Bill," *San Francisco Chronicle*, September 9, 2009.

John Zaller and Stanley Feldman, "A Simple Theory of Survey Response: Answering Questions versus Revealing Preferences," *American Journal of Political Science* 36 no. 3 (1992): 579–616.

Franklin E. Zimring, *The Great Crime Decline* (New York: Oxford University Press, 2008).

Index

A

Adams, Stuart, 45
Affordable Care Act (ACA), 7–8, 224
Albert, Alphonso, 117
Alexander, Michelle, 28–29, 120, 213, 218
Alito, Sam, 110
Anderson, Joel, 195
Andrews, Don, 91
Anti-Drug Abuse Act, 62, 119–121,
      125–126, 133, 143
Apprendi v. New Jersey, 129

B

Bass, Karen, 194
Baumgartner, Frank, 14, 48, 160
Becker, Gary, 43
Beckett, Katherine, 28, 77
Bennett, Robert, 111
Bennett, William, 221
Bias, Len, 120
Biden, Joe, 108–109, 111, 117, 122
Bonta, James, 91
Brandeis, Louis, 171
Brann, Joe, 85
Brown, Jerry, 197–200, 204
Brown, Johnny St. Valentine, 121
Brown v. Board of Education, 37
Brown v. Plata, 196, 201–203
Brownback, Sam, 17, 20, 109–114, 117
Bush, George H.W., 221
Bush, George W., 17, 94–97, 110–111, 118,
      135, 138
Bushman, Bruce, 134–137

C

Cadora, Eric, 157
California
   corrections crisis in, 147–149
   crime reform in, 27, 185–207
   media coverage in, 188–189, *189*
   penal system in, 185–207, *189*
   political environment in, 185–195
   prison budgets in, 188–189, 198, 202, 207
   prison overcrowding in, 187–188, *189*,
      192, 199–202
   "Prison Realignment" in, 5, 197–207
   prison reform in, 27, 185–207
   prison treatment programs, 186–189,
      192, 199, 204
   "smart on crime" movement, 4–10,
      185–207
   structural injunction in, 196–197, 202
California Correctional Peace Officers
      Association (CCPOA), 190–192,
      200–201, 207
California Department of Corrections and
      Rehabilitation (CDCR), 186–187,
      191–193, 195
Cannon, Christopher, 17, 112–113
Capital punishment, 77–78, 167
Cate, Matthew, 193
Center for Opportunity, Reentry, and
      Education (CORE), 4
Chiles, Lawton, 122
City of Boerne v. Flores, 99–102
Civil Rights Act, 37, 39
Clinton, Bill, 55, 61, 75, 86, 108, 123, 139
Coalition politics; *see also* Politics
   in criminal justice subsystem, 13–17
   policy learning and, 22–27
   "smart on crime" movement, 17–22
Coble, Howard, 112–113
Coburn, Tom, 114, 142
Cocaine sentencing reform, 122–127,
      130–140; *see also* Fair
      Sentencing Act
Coleman v. Wilson, 147, 196
Collins, James, 139–140
Collins, Susan, 111
Collins, Terry, 180
Colson, Chuck, 19, 95–96, 99–101

Controlled Substances Act (CSA), 41
Conyers, John, 116
Cornyn, John, 139
Correctional associations, 105–107
Correctional populations, 64–67, 65; *see also* Prison statistics
Corrections policy research, 89–93
Council of State Governments (CSG), 154–155, 157, 172–176, 181–183
Crack sentencing reform, 122–127, 130–144; *see also* Fair Sentencing Act
Craddick, Tom, 150–151, 154, 159
Crime
  de-incarceration and, 209–212
  fear of, 72–74, 73
  "moral individualism" crimes, 44
  poverty and, 36, 39
  public attitudes on, 72, 76–78
  racism and, 5–15, 28–29, 37–39, 67–68, 218
  saliency of, 74–78, 75
  violent crime, 73, 73–74
  war on, 39
Crime politics; *see also* Politics
  coalition politics, 13–17
  policy learning and, 22–27
  in political system, 10–13
  "smart" on, 3–29, 79–118
Crime rates, decreases, 68, 72
Crime rates, increases, 5–6, 29, 35, 38
Crime reform; *see also* Reform
  in California, 27, 185–207
  in Ohio, 27, 171–184
  in Texas, 27, 147–166, 171
Criminal justice coalitions
  coalition politics, 13–17
  nature of, 31–32, 55–58, 57
  "tough" on, 55–58, 57
Criminal justice systems
  changes in, 60–63
  contemporary systems, 11
  policy changes and, 60–63, 126–127, 130–131
  policy subsystem, 13–17, 26
  reform in, 11–17
Criminogenic factors, 91–92
Cruz, Ted, 152
Cullen, Francis, 46–51, 90
Cutler, Maxine, 49

D

Dahl, Robert, 203
Davis, Danny, 97
Davis, Gray, 55, 190–191
Death penalty offenses, 60–61
Death penalty stances, 48, 108
De-incarceration, 209–212
D'Elia, Carole, 194
Dent, Richard, 39
Dewhurst, David, 156
DeWine, Mike, 111
DiIulio, John, 52, 69
Dole, Bob, 110
Drug sentencing reform, 122–127, 130–144; *see also* Fair Sentencing Act
Drugs, war on, 40–41, 60
Dukakis, Michael, 55
Dunn, Tim, 153
Durbin, Richard, 138, 142, 223

E

Earley, Mark, 3
Economic crisis, 19, 24–25, 69–71, 75
Eisenhower, Dwight, 38
Employment Division v. Smith, 100
Escobedo v. Illinois, 37
Evaluations
  of de-incarceration, 209–212
  of Fair Sentencing Act, 218–219, 223
  of reform progress, 212–225
  of "smart on crime" movement, 209–225

F

Fabelo, Tony, 155–156
Fair Sentencing Act (FSA)
  crack sentencing reform, 122–127, 130–144
  drug abuse and, 119–126, 130–144
  evaluation of, 218–219, 223
  legal challenges to, 127–130
  new proposals for, 126–127, 130–131
  passage of, 7, 119
  policy context of, 119–122
  Prison Fellowship Ministries and, 133–134, 139–141
  support for, 132–144, 221

Falwell, Jerry, 52
Fear of crime, 72–74, *73*; *see also* Crime
Federal sentencing process, 127–130; *see also* Fair Sentencing Act
Feinstein, Dianne, 131
Ferguson, Robert, 28
Forbes Randy, 17, 116–117
Frank, Deborah, 125
Frankel, Marvin, 50–51

G

Garland, David, 21, 28, 33–34, 213
Garrick, Martin, 195
Gendreau, Paul, 48, 90–91
Gibbs, Robert, 143
Gideon v. Wainright, 36, 37
Gilbert, Karen, 47, 90
Gingrich, Newt, 17, 110, 221, 222
Gohmert, Louie, 112, 117
Goldwater, Barry, 37–38
Gotsch, Kara, 133, 139, 144
Gottschalk, Marie, 28, 212–215
Graham, Lindsey, 139, 142
Grassley, Chuck, 139
Greenhouse, Linda, 196

H

Hatch, Orrin, 102–103, 111, 131, 139, 142
Henderson, Thelton, 147
Hickman, Roderick, 140
Holder, Eric, 223
HOPE program, 92–93, 175, 220, 224
Horowitz, Jake, 173–175
Horton, Willie, 180
Humane penal systems, 6–7; *see also* Penal system
Hurwitz, John, 218

I

Inequality, 67–68
InnerChange Freedom Initiative (IFI), 95–96

J

Jackson, Raymond Alvin, 129
Jacobson, Michael, 117

Jenkins-Smith, Henk, 13, 23, 48
Jimenez, Mike, 201
Johnson, Lyndon, 36–38, 42, 179
Jones, Bryan, 14, 48, 160
Justice Reinvestment Initiative, 157–159, 220
Justice Safety Valve Act, 222

K

Kasich, John, 4, 17, 183–184
Keene, David, 221
Kennedy, Anthony, 202–203
Kennedy, David, 120
Kennedy, John F., 38
Kennedy, Ted, 102–103, 131
Kimbrough, Derrick, 129–130
Kimbrough v. United States, 129–130
King, Martin Luther, Jr., 38
Kingdon, John, 59
Kleiman, Mark, 44, 93, 213
Kristol, Irving, 45
Krone, Ray, 107
Kyl, Jon, 111

L

Law, saliency of, 74–75, *75*
Law Enforcement Assistant Act, 38, 42
"Law-and-order" coalition, 15–17, 22, 25
Leahy, Patrick, 117, 122, 138, 222
Leavitt, Steve, 68
Lee, Mike, 223
Leininger, James, 152
Leno, Mark, 205
Levin, Marc, 153, 221
Lipton, Doug, 45
LoBuglio, Stefan, 106
Loury, Glenn, 117
Lynch, Mona, 58

M

Madden, Jerry, 17, 150–155, 158–159, 166, 205–206
Mapp v. Miranda, 36
Mapp v. Ohio, 36
Marquart, James, 140
Martinson, Robert, 45–48, 50, 90

Mass incarceration
    moral failings of, 22
    racism and, 5–6, 28–29, 67–68
    reduction of, 29
    rise of, 14–19
    statistics on, 5–6, 68–69
Mauer, Marc, 28, 38, 132, 135–136
McClellan, John, 37
Meachum, Larry, 84, 85
Media coverage
    in California, 188–189, *189*
    in Ohio, 176–177, *177*
    in Texas, 160–170, *163*, *164*, *165*
Meese, Ed, 221
Miller, Jeff, 195
Miller, Lisa, 14–18, 22, 25, 28, 53–54, 105
Miranda v. Arizona, 37
"Moral individualism" criminology, 44
Moyer, Thomas, 176
Murakawa, Naomi, 37

N

Narcotics Control Act, 41
Nation, Vincent, 140
New Deal, 32, 111, 206
Nielsen, Jim, 195
Nixon, Richard, 38–41, 179
Nolan, Pat, 98–105, 112–117, 133–134,
    140–142, 221–222
Norquist, Grover, 18, 141–142, 221–222
Norrander, Barbara, 77
Novey, Don, 190–191, 201

O

Obama, Barack, 7, 119, 138, 143, 178
Ohio
    corrections crisis in, 148–149
    crime policy ideas in, 171–175
    crime reform in, 27, 171–184
    media coverage in, 176–177, *177*
    "Ohio Plan," 86–89, 97
    penal system in, 171–184, *177*
    policy learning in, 177–184
    prison budgets in, 172, 176–179
    prison overcrowding in, 176–181
    prison reform in, 27, 171–184
    prison treatment programs, 182–184

    prisoner reentry plan, 86–89, 97
    "smart on crime" movement, 4,
        171–184
    technical assistance in, 175–177
Ohio Department of Rehabilitation and
        Correction's (ODRC), 148,
        176–182
"Ohio Plan," 86–89, 97

P

Page, Joshua, 201
Palmer, Ted, 46–47, 49, 90
Parole populations, 64, *65*
Parole systems, 63, 64, *65*
Patashnik, Eric, 220
Paul, Rand, 222
Peffley, Mark, 218
Penal system
    alternatives to, 69
    in California, 185–207, *189*
    contemporary prison system, 71
    crisis in, 59–78
    debates on, 153, 157, 160–166
    economic crisis and, 24–25, 69–71, 75
    humane penal systems, 6–7 inequality
        and, 67–68
    mass incarceration and, 5–6, 14–19, 22,
        29, 67–69
    media coverage in California, 188–189,
        189
    media coverage in Ohio, 176–177, *177*
    media coverage in Texas, 160–170, *163*,
        164, *165*
    in Ohio, 171–184, *177*
    policy changes and, 60–63, 126–127,
        130–131
    policy learning and, 22–27, 69
    Prison Fellowship Ministries and, 3,
        98–99, 133–134, 139–141
    public attitudes on, 72
    racism and, 5–15, 28–29, 37–39, 67–68,
        218
    rational penal systems, 6–7
    structural injunction in, 196–197, 202
    in Texas, 147–170, *163*, *164*, *165*
"Penal welfarism," 33–34, 58
Perry, Rick, 17, 151–152, 155, 158
Petersillia, Joan, 92, 193

Pew, Joseph, 172
Pew, Mary Anderson, 172
Plata v. Davis, 147, 196
Policy changes, 60–63, 126–127, 130–131
Policy learning
    crime politics and, 22–27
    in Ohio, 177–184
    penal system and, 22–27, 69
Policy subsystem, 13–17, 26; *see also*
        Criminal justice systems
Politics
    coalition politics, 13–22
    crime politics, 3–29, 79–118
    policy learning and, 22–27
    political debates, 153, 157, 160–166
    of Second Chance Act, 26–27, 81–83,
        97–98, 103–118
    "smart on crime" politics, 3–29, 79–118
Portman, Rob, 17, 97–98
Poverty, war on, 36, 39
Prison budgets
    in California, 188–189, 198, 202, 207
    economic crisis and, 19, 24–25
    in Ohio, 172, 176–179
    reform and, 9, 24–25, 213–218
    in Texas, 147–148, 155–159, *164*
Prison Fellowship Ministries
    Fair Sentencing Act and, 133–134,
        139–141
    penal system and, 3, 98–99, 133–134,
        139–141
    prison overcrowding and, 140–141
    for prisoner reentry, 19–20, 98–99,
        112–113
    reform and, 3, 17–20, 27, 95
Prison Litigation Reform Act (PLRA), 103,
    196, 197
Prison overcrowding
    in California, 187–188, *189*, 192, 199–202
    impact of, 66, 147, 187–188
    increase in, 19, 25
    in Ohio, 176–181
    Prison Fellowship Ministries and,
        140–141
    prison populations, 5–6, *12*, 12–13,
        64–67, *65*
    statistics on, 8, 19, 66
    in Texas, 147, 150, 155, *164*, 164–168, *165*
    violence and, 66

Prison populations
    decline in, 8
    mass incarcerations, 5–6, 14–19, 22,
        29, 67–69
    reduction of, 8
    statistics on, 5–6, *12*, 12–13, 64–67, *65*
    in Texas, 162, *163*
Prison Rape Elimination Act, 103
"Prison Realignment," 5, 197–207
Prison reform; *see also* Reform
    in California, 27, 185–207
    in Ohio, 27, 171–184
    in Texas, 27, 147–166, 171
Prison statistics
    imprisonments per state, *12*, 12–13
    overcrowded prisons, 8, 19, 66
    parolee numbers, 64, *65*
    prison populations, 5–6, *12*, 12–13,
        64–67, *65*
    probation populations, 64, *65*
    in Texas, 162, *163*
Prison system; *see also* Penal system
    contemporary prison system, 71
    crisis in, 59–78
    federal injunction of, 196–197, 202
    mass incarcerations, 5–6, 14–19, 22,
        29, 67–69
    past prison systems, 32, 35
    policy learning and, 22–27, 69
    structural injunction in, 196–197, 202
Prison treatment programs
    in California, 186–189, 192, 199, 204
    in Ohio, 182–184
    options for, 4–8, 21, 92–93, 175, 220,
        224
    rehabilitation and, 33–34, 37–41,
        45–50, *57*, 91–93
    in Texas, 151–159
Prisoner "churn," 19
Prisoner mistreatment, 161–162, 165, 169
Prisoner recidivism
    increase in, 81–82
    rates of, 85–97, 105–109, 183–187
    reduction in, 96, 111–116, 180–184
Prisoner reentry
    conceptualizing, 83–86
    correctional associations, 105–107
    corrections policy research, 89–93
    "Ohio Plan" for, 86–89, 97

Prison Fellowship Ministries and,
19–20, 98–99, 112–113
push for, 93–96, 219–220
Second Chance Act and, 81–83, 97–98,
103–118
Prisoner Reentry Initiative, 96–97
Probation populations, 64, 65
Public attitudes, 72, 76–78, 77
Public Safety Performance Project (PSPP),
172–175
Public Safety Realignment Act, 198
Punishment, 72, 76–78, 77, 167

R

Racism, 5–15, 28–29, 37–39, 67–68, 218
Rangel, Charlie, 125
Rational penal systems, 6–7; *see also* Penal
system
Reagan, Ronald, 38–39, 51, 60–61, 109,
120, 221
Reentry Policy Council, 87
Reform
in California, 27, 185–207
in criminal justice system, 11–17
in Ohio, 27, 171–184
prison budgets and, 9, 24–25, 213–218
Prison Fellowship Ministries and, 3,
17–20, 27, 95
success of, 12, 27–28
in Texas, 27, 147–166, 171
Rehabilitation in prisons, 33–34, 37–41,
45–50, 57, 91–93
Rehabilitation research, 34, 42–52
Rehabilitative model, 31, 34–42, 54–58
Reid, Harry, 102–103
Religious freedom, protecting, 99–103
Religious Freedom Restoration Act
(RFRA), 99–103
Religious Land Use and
Institutionalized Persons Act
(RLPA), 102, 103
Reno, Janet, 83–85
Richards, Ann, 162
Roberts, John, 110
Robertson, Pat, 52
Robinson, Laurie, 83
Robinson v. California, 37
Ross, Robert, 90–91

S

Sabatier, Paul, 13, 23, 48
Saliency of crime, 74–78, 75; *see also*
Crime
Santorum, Rick, 111
Scalia, Antonin, 202
Schattschneider, E. E., 14
Scheingold, Stuart, 44
Schwarzenegger, Arnold, 17, 147, 190–198,
201
Scott, Robert "Bobby," 115–116, 135–138
Sebeliuis, Kathleen, 111
Second Chance Act (SCA)
advocacy for, 108–118
evaluation of, 212
introduction of, 97–98
meaning of, 103–105
passage of, 81, 105–106, 115–119
politics of, 26–27, 81–83, 97–98,
103–118
progress of, 112–119
roadblocks to, 113–115
Seitz, Bill, 177–184
Sentencing process, 127–130; *see also* Fair
Sentencing Act
Sentencing Reform Act (SRA), 61, 123,
126–128
Sessions, Jeff, 126–127, 131, 138–139, 142
Simon, Jonathan, 28, 63, 196, 199, 201, 206
"Smart on crime" coalition
emergence of, 9–10, 22
"law-and-order" coalition, 15–17, 22, 25
policy learning and, 22–27
rise of, 17–22
"Smart on crime" movement
in California, 4–10, 185–207
in coalition politics, 17–22
de-incarceration and, 209–212
evaluation of, 209–225
in national politics, 3–29, 79–118
in Ohio, 4, 171–184
policy learning and, 22–27
progress of, 212–225
rise of, 1–29
in Texas, 147–170
Smarter Sentencing Act, 223
Smith, Lamar, 143
Soros, George, 157

Souder, Mark, 97
Specter, Arlen, 111, 114, 117, 131
Spelman, William, 215–216
Stalder, Richard, 106–107
Steinberg, Darrell, 195
Stewart, Julie, 144
Strickland, Ted, 176, 179, 183
Stuntz, William, 28

T

Taifa, Nkechi, 144
Talent, Jim, 111
Texas
    corrections crisis in, 147–152, 155–156
    crime coalition in, 159
    crime reform in, 27, 147–166, 171
    Justice Reinvestment Initiative, 157–159
    media coverage in, 160–170, *163, 164, 165*
    new groups in, 152–157
    penal system in, 147–170, *163, 164, 165*
    political debate in, 153, 157, 160–166
    prison budgets in, 147–148, 155–159, *164*
    prison overcrowding in, 147, 150, 155, *164,* 164–168, *165*
    prison populations in, 162, *163*
    prison reform in, 27, 147–166, 171
    prison treatment programs, 151–159
    "smart on crime" movement, 147–170
Texas Criminal Justice Coalition, 153–154
Texas Department of Criminal Justice (TDCJ), 147, 154–155, 158
Texas Public Policy Foundation (TPPF), 152–153
Thomas, Cal, 52
Thomas, Marvin, 4
Thurmond, Strom, 37
Tonry, Michael, 28, 29, 55, 84, 214, 218–219
"Tough on crime" coalition
    consequences of, 64–67
    nature of, 31–32, 55–58, *57*
    rise of, 17–29

Traficant, James, 122, 126
Travis, Jeremy, 63, 83–86, 180
Trop v. Dulles, 37
Truman, David, 99
"Truth-in-sentencing" laws, 60–61
Tubbs-Jones, Stephanie, 97
Tucker, Susan, 157
Turner, Susan, 92

U

United States v. Booker, 128–130

V

Violent crime, *73,* 73–74; *see also* Crime
Violent Crime Control and Law Enforcement Act, 61

W

Wacquant, Loïc, 28
Walker, Scott, 183
Wall, Ashbel, 105
Wallace, George, 39
Wallace, Mike, 46
"War on Crime," 39
"War on Drugs," 40–41, 60
"War on Poverty," 36, 39
Ward, Christy, 192
Werholz, Roger, 111
Western, Bruce, 28, 60, 117
White, Ken, 128–129
Whitman, Meg, 200
Whitmire, John, 151–152, 155–158, 166
Wilkinson, Reginald, 82–83, 87–89, 97
Wilks, Judith, 45, 47
Wilson, James Q., 42–44, 52
Wilson, Pete, 191

Z

Zedong, Mao, 179
Zeigler, Ronald, 40

Printed and bound by CPI Group (UK) Ltd, Croydon, CR0 4YY

01/05/2025

01858452-0003